GOD ENCOUNTERED

OTHER WORKS BY FRANS JOZEF VAN BEECK:

Christ Proclaimed: Christology as Rhetoric
Grounded in Love: Sacramental Theology in an Ecumenical Perspective
Catholic Identity After Vatican II: Three Types of Faith in the One Church
Loving the Torah More than God? Toward a Catholic Appreciation of Judaism

GOD ENCOUNTERED

A Contemporary Catholic Systematic Theology

Volume Two/2:
The Revelation of the Glory

Part II:
One God, Creator of All That Is

FRANS JOZEF VAN BEECK, S. J.

A Michael Glazier Book
THE LITURGICAL PRESS
Collegeville, Minnesota

Grateful acknowledgment is made for the use of the following materials. Parts of §§97-98 appeared in the context of "Israel's God, the Psalms, and the City of Jerusalem: Life Experience and the Sacrifice of Praise and Prayer," in *Horizons* 19(19-92): 219-239. Most of §§110-111 was first published in *The Toronto Journal of Theology* 9(1993): 9-26, as "'This Weakness of God's is Stronger' (1 Cor 1: 25): An Inquiry Beyond the Power of Being." The excerpt from "Choruses from 'The Rock'," in *Collected Poems 1909-1962* by T. S. Eliot (copyright ○ 1936 by Faber & Faber, Ltd.; copyright ○ 1963 by Harcourt Brace & Company; copyright ○ 1963, 1964 by T. S. Eliot), is reprinted with the permission of the publishers. Excerpts from two novels by Iris Murdoch, *The Unicorn* (copyright ○ 1963, 1991 by Iris Murdoch) and *The Message to the Planet* (copyright ○ 1989 by Iris Murdoch), are used by permission of Chatto & Windus and of Viking Penguin, a division of Penguin Books USA Inc. The illustration on the dust jacket, fol. 112r of *Codex Sanhippolytensis* N° 1 (15th cent.), is used once again by kind permission of the *Bischöfliche Alumnatsbibliothek*, Sankt Pölten, Austria.

Nihil Obstat: Rev. Charles R. Meyer, S.T.D., *Censor Deputatus.* January 23, 1994.

Imprimi potest: Very Rev. Bradley M. Schaeffer, S.J., Provincial, Chicago Province. January 31, 1994.

Imprimatur: Most Rev. John R. Gorman, Vicar General, Archdiocese of Chicago. February 1, 1994.

The *Nihil Obstat* and *Imprimatur* are official declarations that a book is free of doctrinal or moral error. No implication is contained therein that those who have granted the *Nihil Obstat* and *Imprimatur* agree with the content, opinions, or statements expressed.

Cover design by Ann Blattner.

FIRST EDITION

Library of Congress Cataloging-in-Publication Data
Beeck, Frans Jozef van.
    The Revelation of the Glory. Part II. One God, Creator of All That Is.

    (God Encountered; v. 2/2)
    Bibliography: p.
    Includes index.
    1. Theology, Doctrinal.   2. Catholic Church—Doctrines.
I. Title. II. Series: Beeck, Frans Jozef van.
God Encountered; v. 2/2
BX1747.5.B4 vol. 2/2
ISBN 0-8146-5499-1

For Walter J. Ong, S.J.

"What is written is deadly, but the Spirit is life-giving."

(2 Corinthians 3, 6)

O admirabile commercium!
Creator generis humani,
animatum corpus sumens,
de Virgine nasci dignatus est:
et procedens homo sine semine,
largitus est nobis suam deitatem.

What admirable exchange!
Humankind's Creator,
taking on body and soul,
in his kindness, is born from the Virgin:
and, coming forth as man, yet not from man's seed,
he has lavished on us his divinity.

(Antiphon at vespers, January 1,
Feast of the Holy Mother of God)

Contents

Preface

This book is the *secunda secundæ* of *God Encountered*. It also marks a change of plans. As I was working on the ambitious *secunda secundæ* promised in the preface of volume 2/1 (p. xi), I came to realize that the book would become unwieldy: it proved impossible to accommodate the theology of God and Creation, of Finitude and Fall, and of Jesus Christ and the Blessed Trinity between the covers of one usable and affordable book. So the proposed *secunda secundæ* had to be divided, like ancient Gaul, into three parts—a move to which the plan of volume 2 readily lent itself anyway. To bring volume 2 to completion, therefore, the present, comparatively slender book will be followed by a substantial *tertia secundæ* (volume 2/3: Part III, *Finitude and Fall*) and a sizable *quarta secundæ* (volume 2/4: Part IV, *The Glory of God in the Face of Christ*). This arrangement, incidentally, should also discourage any further comparisons with Aquinas.

The present book, therefore, does no more than embark upon the treatment of "the central Christian doctrines." Yet it does so by focusing on the theme that must be first and last in any theology: the One and Only True God. This God, Holy and ever Faithful, remains forever transcendent, yet is revealed, as a variety of gracious manifestations and theophanies bear out, as intimately present to as well as in the fundamental, permanently constitutive "phase" of the divine *exitus*—the reality which Jews, Christians, and Muslims know and profess as "creation."

This focus on the living God serves, first of all, to honor the doxological commitments of *God Encountered*. It is also designed to do justice to two convictions. Firstly, Christianity is and remains radically dependent, for its faith and its understanding of God, on Israel's faith and its understanding of God—a fact all too often obscured by traditional, yet (upon reflection) relatively superficial, and indeed, crypto-Marcionite assumptions and statements about allegedly fundamental differences between Israel's monotheism and Christianity's trinitarian faith.   Secondly, the common Jewish-Christian understanding of God must remain the yardstick by means of which contemporary Christianity must take the measure of modern Western civilization, both to the extent that the latter continues to profess a commitment to some form of monotheism and to the extent that it has settled for, or positively committed itself to, the various atheisms. The treatment offered in the following three chapters, therefore, not only concerns itself with the Jewish and Christian tradition understood as divine revelation; it also touches on fundamental theological issues, as catholic theology always does.

In kindly accepting the dedication of this portion of *God Encountered*, Walter J. Ong, S.J. has given me an opportunity both to acknowledge an admiration and an indebtedness that is long-standing and pervasive (and thus, hard to pin down), and to convey, once again, some of my intentions in writing *God Encountered.* These intentions concern, most of all, the central hallmarks of catholicity: integrity and openness; but they also concern the vision of God that lies at the basis of the Jesuit vocation. In its original shape, this vision is recounted in Ignatius of Loyola's autobiography (nr. 30). The date is 1522, and Ignatius is about 31 years old —the right age, we tend to think nowadays, to have a deep and lasting experience of identity.

Once, out of devotion, he was going to a church which was just over a mile distant from Manresa (I think was called St. Paul), and the road runs close to the river. Thus moving along intent on his devotions, he sat down for a moment with his face towards the river running down below. And as he sat there, the eyes of his understanding began to open. And it was not as if he beheld a vision of some kind, but he saw and understood many things, things spiritual as well as things concerning faith and learning, and this with so great an illumination that all things appeared new to him. And it is impossible to point out the particulars he then understood, although they were many; but he received a great clarity in his understanding, so much so that, it seems to him, in the whole course of his past life right up to his sixty-second year, if he should gather all the helps he has received from God, and everything he has come to understand, even if he should add them all together, he has received not as much as at that one time alone.

If Father Ong's work, in typically catholic and Jesuit fashion, has demonstrated anything, it is that the human spirit, natively (if largely unthematically) attuned to the living God, is also attuned to the countless "presences" that surround it in the cosmos—presences to which it must keep itself responsive. Inspired by this basic (and, in the last resort, mystical) intuition, Father Ong has both argued and demonstrated, implicitly and explicitly, that the human spirit has the inner resources to handle the knowledge explosion which it has unleashed in recent centuries, especially in the form of natural and social science; that it can face the vehemence and even violence it has discovered, both in the universe and in humanity; that it can face even the violence humanity has positively inflicted on itself and the cosmos; that the proliferation of information so characteristic of modernity, if dubious at times, need not daunt us; that it is indeed possible to welcome it, provided we take it as an invitation to understand its dynamics —that is, the fierce dynamics of human communication in word and gesture; that, given that understanding, we can afford to open ourselves to all that is particular, specialized, curious, strange, far-fetched, and even barbarous, because (if we persevere) we will discover that the forces of harmony, integration, and coherence run deeper, both in the universe and in ourselves, than the forces of contention, dissipation, and disintegration; that, finally, all this is within our reach because all that exists finds its unity and reconciliation in God, to whom we are more deeply attuned than we are to the universe or even to ourselves and each other, and who, therefore, is capable of enlightening honest seekers in such a way as to keep them from getting lost. The next installment of *God Encountered* will deal with humanity's moral and religious predicament in relation to the cosmos, itself, and God—promising, precarious, and downright sinful; needless to say, that book will provide ample opportunity to turn the convictions just stated into theological positions.

An important new feature of this book is the result of the replacement of the 32nd edition of the *Enchiridion Symbolorum Definitionum Declarationum de Rebus Fidei et Morum* (known as Denzinger-Schönmetzer and usually referred to as DS) by its successor: *Enchiridion Symbolorum Definitionum Declarationum de Rebus Fidei et Morum. Kompendium der Glaubensbekenntnisse und kirchlichen Lehrentscheidungen.* This 37nd edition of Denzinger, published in 1991, has been capably revised and updated by the Tübingen systematician Peter Hünermann; it has preserved the numbering of DS (with the exception of DS 3999a-e, which is now 4402-07); its most important new features are the inclusion of careful German translations of all the documents and the addition of over 800 recent magisterial texts, encompassing the principal Vatican II documents (4001-4359) as well as the most authoritative documents promulgated by both synodical and papal authority in the quarter century between July, 1963 and the end of 1988 (4400-4858). For the time being (that is, until an authoritative habit of referral establishes itself), the present work will refer to this new Denzinger by means of the siglum DH. It is, of course, to be hoped (and indeed expected) that a comparable English edition will be prepared soon. However, until such an edition becomes available, it remains necessary to refer to the Vatican II documents individually as well; *God Encountered* will continue to do so by means of the sigla used so far (with the exception of *Dignitatis Humanæ*, which from now on will have to be DHum).

Meanwhile, the English-speaking theological world *has* had the good fortune of gaining access to a collection of sources no less important than Hünermann's new Denzinger: the *Decrees of the Ecumenical Councils*, edited by Norman P. Tanner and a team of capable collaborators. This two-volume collection includes the Greek and Latin originals, with accurate and readable English translations on facing pages. The originals have been photographically reproduced from that authoritative successor of Mansi, the 1962 edition of all the conciliar decrees edited by Alberigo, Joannou, Leonardi, Prodi, and Jedin, except that the collection has been brought up to date by the inclusion of the complete texts of Vatican II. I have decided, not only to quote from this work by means of the siglum DEC, but also to refer to this collection (at least occasionally) in the body of the text—a privilege thus far reserved to references to Holy Scripture, Denzinger-Schönmetzer, the Vatican II documents, and cross-references to *God Encountered* itself, as explained in §6, 6, a.

Once again, I owe much to friends, critics, and helpers. Even though the listing of their names in this preface is an inadequate means to convey my gratitude, it is appropriate, since the reader is indebted to them as well. Four scholarly friends helped shape sizable sections of this book: Thomas H. Tobin, S.J., J. Cheryl Exum, Charles Hallisey, and Hugh Miller. Others, who helped me by their interest in, comments on, and conversation about, particular parts and specific issues are Robert DiVito, Mark Henninger, S.J., Richard Norris, Virginia M. Ryan, George Schner, S.J., David Tracy, and Robert Wilken. The flexibility and unceasing support of Father Michael

Naughton, O.S.B. and Messrs. Mark Twomey and Peter Dwyer, of
The Liturgical Press, made it possible to change plans and thus to
get the chapters contained in this book published long before I
had anticipated they would see the light. John L. Urban's hospitali-
ty, lately practiced at Saints Philip and Anthony in Highland, Wis-
consin, has provided the setting for much of the revision of the
text. The grant of a paid leave of absence by Loyola University of
Chicago in the Fall of 1993, supported by department chair Urban
C. von Wahlde and academic vice-president James L. Wiser, created
some of the freedom needed to prepare the manuscript for publica-
tion. My new graduate assistant Edward Peck prepared the indices,
and Nancy Johnson, capable as usual, once again turned the manuscript into typeset copy.

By the time this book appears, volume 2/4 is underway, while
volume 3 (to be titled *A World in Transformation*) remains to be em-
barked on. The project of writing *God Encountered* is approaching
its end. Needless to say, the realization spells relief. But it is beginning to spell regret as well: as the system is slowly nearing its completion, its limitations are becoming more glaring fast. The idea of
a full accounting of this is staggering. Still, to illustrate what I
mean, let me declare the single most serious limitation that I can
now see, and in doing so, let me also convey my most vivid regret:
the virtual absence of Karl Barth. If I were starting work on *God
Encountered* now instead of in 1985, I would hope I would have the
courage and the intelligence to do what a friend of mine did upon
being appointed, years ago, to a university chair of theology: take
a year to read the *Church Dogmatics*. For present purposes, however,
my repentance comes too late; in the imperfect world in which I
now find myself, volumes 2/4 and 3 must take precedence. Barth,
I am sure, understands.

Frans Jozef van Beeck, S.J.

Abbreviations

AF	*The Apostolic Fathers.* Edited and translated by Kirsopp Lake. *Loeb Classical Library.* 2 vols. London: William Heinemann; New York: G. P. Putnam's Sons, 1930.
ANET	*Ancient Near Eastern Texts Relating to the Old Testament.* Third Edition with Supplement. Edited by James B. Pritchard. Princeton, New Jersey: Princeton University Press, 1969.
AristBWks	*The Basic Works of Aristotle.* Edited by Richard McKeon. New York: Random House, 1941.
CC	*Corpus Christianorum.* Turnhout: Brepols, 1953-.
CF	*The Christian Faith in the Doctrinal Documents of the Catholic Church.* Edited by J. Neuner and J. Dupuis. New York: Alba House, 1982.
ConcSept	Edwin Hatch and Henry A. Redpath. *A Concordance to the Septuagint and the Other Greek Versions of the Old Testament (Including the Apocryphal Books).* Three volumes in two. Reprint. Grand Rapids, MI: Baker Book House, 1983.
CSEL	*Corpus Scriptorum Ecclesiasticorum Latinorum.* Vienna: F. Tempsky, 1866-.
DEC I, II	*Decrees of the Ecumenical Councils.* Edited by Norman P. Tanner. Two volumes. London: Sheed & Ward; Washington, DC: Georgetown University Press, 1990.
DH	*Enchiridion Symbolorum Definitionum Declarationum de Rebus Fidei et Morum. Kompendium der Glaubensbekenntnisse und kirchlichen Lehrentscheidungen.* Edited by Heinrich Denzinger; revised by Peter Hünermann, with Helmut Hoping. 37nd Edition, in Latin and German. Freiburg: Herder, 1991.
DHum	*Dignitatis Humanæ:* The Declaration on Religious Freedom (Vatican II).
DictSp	*Dictionnaire de spiritualité ascétique et mystique: Doctrine et histoire.* Edited by Marcel Villers and others. Paris: Beauchesne, 1932-.
DV	*Dei Verbum:* The Dogmatic Constitution on Divine Revelation (Vatican II).
ER	*The Encyclopedia of Religion.* Edited by Mircea Eliade. 16 vols. New York: Macmillan, 1987.
FC	*The Fathers of the Church: A New Translation.* Washington, DC: The Catholic University of America Press, 1948-.

GCS	*Die griechischen christlichen Schriftsteller der ersten drei Jahrhunderte.* Leipzig and Berlin, 1897-.
GS	*Gaudium et Spes*: The Pastoral Constitution on the Church in the Modern World (Vatican II).
LG	*Lumen Gentium*: The Dogmatic Constitution on the Church (Vatican II).
LXX	The Septuagint version of the Jewish Scriptures.
MT	The Masoretic text of the Hebrew Scriptures.
NPNCF	*A Select Library of Nicene and Post-Nicene Fathers of the Christian Church.* New York: Christian Literature Company, 1887-1892. (Reprint. Grand Rapids, MI: Wm. B. Eerdmans, 1979-83.)
PG	*Patrologia Græca.* Edited by J. P. Migne. 162 vols. Paris: 1857-66.
PGL	*A Patristic Greek Lexicon.* Edited by G. W. H. Lampe. Oxford: Clarendon Press, 1961-68.
Philok	*The Philokalia.* Edited by G. E. H. Palmer, Philip Sherrard, and Kallistos Ware. 3 vols. London and Boston: Faber and Faber, 1979-86.
PL	*Patrologia Latina.* Edited by J. P. Migne. 221 vols. Paris: 1844-64.
RW	Jan van Ruusbroec. *Werken.* 4 vols. Edited by J. van Mierlo, J. B. Poukens, L. Reypens, M. Schurmans, and D. A. Stracke. Mechelen: Het Kompas; Amsterdam: De Spiegel, 1932-34.
SC	*Sources chrétiennes.* Paris: Cerf, 1940-.
Schmitt	*S. Anselmi Cantuariensis Archiepiscopi Opera Omnia.* 6 vols. Edited by Franciscus Salesius Schmitt. Edinburgh: Thomas Nelson & Sons, 1946-61.
SchrzTh	Karl Rahner, *Schriften zur Theologie.* 16 vols. Einsiedeln, Zürich, and Köln: Benziger Verlag, 1954-84.
TheoInv	Karl Rahner, *Theological Investigations.* 21 vols. Baltimore: Helicon/New York: Herder and Herder/Seabury; London: Darton, Longman & Todd, 1966-88.
Vg	The (Latin) Vulgate text of the Scriptures.

Part II

ONE GOD, CREATOR OF ALL THAT IS

CHAPTER 9

God

THE LIVING GOD AND THE GOD OF MERE MOTION

[§96] PASCAL'S *MÉMORIAL*

[1] Blaise Pascal died at the age of 39, in Paris, at the house of Florin Périer, his brother-in-law, shortly after midnight on August 19, 1662. A few days later, a servant discovered, sewn into the seam of the dead man's cloak, a piece of parchment with a sheet of paper folded tightly inside. The parchment had inscribed on it the fair copy of a text hastily written on the paper, almost eight years before. It read:

†

THE YEAR OF GRACE 1654

Monday, November 23, feast of Saint Clement, Pope and Martyr
and others in the martyrology.
Vigil of Saint Chrysogonus, Martyr, and others.
From about half past ten at night till about half past midnight.

FIRE

God of Abraham, God of Isaac, God of Jacob, not of the philosophers
and the men of learning.
Certainty. Certainty. Feeling, Joy, Peace.
God of Jesus Christ.
My God and your God.
Your God will be my God.
Forgetfulness of the world and of everything except God.
He is found only by the ways taught in the Gospel.
Greatness of the human soul.
Just Father, the world has not known you, but I have known you.
Joy, Joy, Joy, tears of joy.
I separated myself from him. ——————————

They have forsaken me, the fountain of living water.
My God, would you forsake me? ———————
Let me not be separated from him forever.

———————————————————————

This is the everlasting life, that they know you, only true God and him whom you have sent, J. C.
Jesus Christ ———————————————
Jesus Christ ———————————————
I separated myself from him. I fled, denied, crucified him.
May I never be separated from him!
He is held on to only by the ways taught in the Gospel.
      Abandon, total and sweet.

    Total submission to Jesus Christ and to my director.
    Forever in joy in return for one day of exertion on earth.
    I will not forget your words. Amen.[1]

[2] This classical, much-quoted text, the first-hand record of Pascal's "second conversion" at the age of thirty-one, is remarkable in many ways. Most remarkable, perhaps, is the fact that we have it at all. "Intended as a private memorandum, it has become a winged word. This suggests that Pascal put into words something later generations have identified with, something that elicits enduring reflection."[2] The present discussion is an example of this; it is predicated on the conviction that the text is evidence of one person's struggle with an historic religious and theological impasse—one that is still troubling us.

[3] The catholic tradition has always insisted that there prevails a native harmony between nature and revelation—between the natural order accessible to unaided human reason and the revealed order accessible to faith as well as to reason illumined by faith (DH 3016; CF 132). That harmony is rooted in God, the author of both nature and grace. Yet here we have one of the most brilliant (if also most intractable) Catholics of modern times advocating a relationship, not of harmony, but of conflict. That conflict, however, is not of Pascal's own making; as we will see, it has been forced on to him by the culture in which he lives.

    That culture (as we now know) was the first installment of a new world indeed. The balance of power was shifting. Gone were the days when Aquinas could boldly place the embodied human soul, made in the image of God, and hence, limitlessly equipped for understanding and love, at the crossroads of reality, in a strategic position in the universe, *mediating* between God and the world of things (§2, 1):

The human soul, in a way, becomes all things, by virtue of sense and intellect; in this manner, beings that have knowledge approximate, in some way, the likeness of God, in whom all things pre-exist.[3]

By the mid-seventeenth century, there is a keen sense, in sophisticated circles in the Christian West, that humanity's position in the cosmos has changed from strategic to *precarious*. Confident Rhetoric is giving way to diffident Reason. The once-robust baroque Saints are becoming distant, and their heroic poses are turning irresolute—they are beginning to suggest the ambiguous postures and contrived mannerisms of the rococo style. Weary of the convulsions of the past century or two, the human spirit—once daring, venturesome, and ready for abandon—is yielding to an anxious preoccupation with both objective certainty and inner assurance; often, it will be torn between the two. Pascal can write, prophetically:

The human person is but a reed, the weakest part of nature, but it is a reed that thinks. To overwhelm it, there is no need for the universe as a whole to arm itself; one vapor, one drop of water are enough to kill it. Still, were the universe to overwhelm it, the human person would still be nobler than that which kills it, for it knows that it dies and it understands the advantage that the universe has over it. The universe knows nothing of that.

Our entire dignity, then, consists in this: we think. That is what we should draw on for our sense of what we are—not space and time, which we could not possibly fill up anyway.[4]

[4] The new culture is geometric and experimental (cf. §56, 12, a, [*i*]; §99, 4). Geometry, with its "objective," largely mechanical view of the universe, has become the dominant force in philosophy and learning, to the point of tyranny; it claims the ability to make everything understandable and to verify everything empirically. Pascal understands this geometrical culture from inside; a mathematical genius as well as distinguished experimenter himself, he has made decisive contributions to it. But, he warns, "the spirit of geometry" overlooks two things. First, there is no end to the knowledge we can accumulate; there is an indefinite multiplicity of things to be known; eventually, the fascination of that endless series of problems will lure human knowledge into the measureless reaches of space

and time, where it will get the knower lost [a]. Secondly, the new learning is misreading the true balance of power. The very forces of the universe it claims to understand and control—even the smallest!—are capable of overwhelming humanity. In trusting geometry and its exciting applications, is humanity, perhaps, volunteering to get itself buried under an uncontrollable avalanche of knowable *things?*

Thus, for all the promise of discovery and development, Pascal senses, something is at risk in the present situation.

> The endless cycle of idea and action,
> Endless invention, endless experiment,
> Brings knowledge of motion, but not of stillness;
> Knowledge of speech, but not of silence;
> Knowledge of words, but ignorance of the Word.
> . . .
> Where is the Life we have lost in living?
> Where is the wisdom we have lost in knowledge?
> Where is the knowledge we have lost in information?[5]

In this situation, what is in jeopardy, and hence, what is to be treasured most, is the awareness of humanity's distinctive greatness. That greatness lies in *the soul,* by virtue of which we can, in both freedom and self-awareness, cultivate true understanding, live morally, and find the living God. But in the culture we live in, what is truly great is threatened by the world of objectivity. That is, what is truly great is now vulnerable; both God and the soul demand a touch far subtler than the geometrical, cumulative mind is capable of. Hence, in order both to believe in the living God and to be truly human in the midst of the increasingly powerful world of things, and in order to shape that world aright, humanity needs, paradoxically, the spirit of delicacy—*l'esprit de finesse.*

---

[a] Pascal here shows an uncanny premonition of the fragmentation of knowledge that is so characteristic a feature of modernity (cf. §56, 11, c). However, he is also the forerunner of a *Kulturpessimismus* that will despair of the possibility of a new, unified culture, and insist on overlooking, not only the blessings of applied science, but also the liberating aspects of scientific modes of understanding. For besides causing alienation and fragmentation, our ability to know things with scientific objectivity and to handle them accordingly has also enormously stretched the range of human experience accessible to us. This has helped reveal, in palpable ways, the depth and the breadth of human nature's capacity for integration and hence, for fulfillment (cf. §28, 6, d). In the mid 'sixties, Karl Rahner devoted a set of four memorable essays to this issue: "Christian Humanism," "The Experiment with Man," "The Problem of Genetic Manipulation," and "Self-Realisation and Taking up One's Cross."

[a]   The intellectual background, both of Pascal's conversion experience and of the passage on the human person from his *Pensées*, is not far to seek.   The early seventeenth century witnessed the move to relegate the question of God's existence and nature entirely to philosophy, as (it was alleged, quite wrongly) such great Catholic thinkers as Aquinas had done.   This philosophy, however, became so captivated by the new, scientific approach to the world that it understood causality primarily (and to all intents and purposes, exclusively) in terms of *motion*—that is, in terms of chains of *efficient* causality affecting objects extrinsically (cf. §102, 4, b, [*m*]).   The move looked promising enough when it was made, but eventually Christian theology would have ample reason to regret it: by entrusting the question of God to a philosophy wholly insensitive to "immanence"—that essential precondition of religious experience—Catholic theology had signed its own death-warrant [*b*].

[b]   Pascal gives us access to the seventeenth-century shape of an impasse that is still with us, though in a far more developed form.   Before his very eyes, the book of nature, which once served both to stir and elevate the soul and to disclose God, is being closed.   It is giving way to the *system* of nature, occupied by the mighty geometers and their allies, who see nothing but things moved around by dint of efficient causality.   Surface, ratified by axiom and definition, must now reign supreme.   But if *depth*—that is, ultimately, *immanence*—is banished from the knowable system of nature, divine revelation will naturally become unthinkable.   Geometry does not know of the soul; it can only postulate it, as the hidden, unknowable animator of a knowable, manipulable body-machine [*c*].   Nor does geometry know of the living God; it can only postulate the "deity": the remote, impersonal, incorporeal power that has given regularity and design, as well as the initial impulse, to the world—this mechanical system of motionable things (cf. §28, 7, [*h*]; §103, 2 and [*u*]).

[*b*] Cf. Michael Buckley's two books, *Motion and Motion's God* and especially *At the Origins of Modern Atheism*, with its illuminating account of the thought of the Catholic thinkers Lessius and Mersenne. Cf. also his "The Rise of Modern Atheism and the Religious *Epoché*." Cf. also §68, 1, [*l*]; §84, 2, a, [*u*]; §99, 3, a.

[*c*] For a sixteenth-century example, cf. §94, 5, b, [*gg*].

[c] Cultural predicaments like this demand discernment; they also force choices. In a geometrical and experimental world, how does one regain access, both to the "greatness of the human soul" and to the living God? Encouraged by Cardinal de Bérulle to pursue his doubts to the end, René Descartes had turned inward, to the philosophy of the purely spiritual, self-conscious mind, where he had also found the idea of a wholly transcendent God (cf. §17, 1, a; §66, 4, a; §101, 9, a-b). Isaac Newton was to take a different road. In the wake of his formulation of the laws of gravity, he would turn outward, to the philosophy of nature, where he would find a (unitarian) God, as well as the assurance of human progress [d]. Blaise Pascal's choice was different from either Descartes' or Newton's. It was rather more uncomfortable as well. He insisted that there was nothing available to relieve the mutual embarrassment between faith in God (which continued to insist that it also had the key to a deeper, more humane knowledge) and geometrical-technological reason—that is, between anthropology and cosmology. That embarrassment was to prolong itself for centuries to come.

[5] *Fire.* The burning bush ablaze once again. The revelation occurs afresh. Unexpectedly and quite incomprehensibly, Pascal finds a deeper, divinely renewed self, while at the same time finding his understanding pointed away from the world of things and universal truths, to particular others—God's privileged friends: the patriarchs, Moses, and above all, Jesus Christ. With them, he recognizes the unmistakable features of the living God.

Thus Pascal's midnight experience of God's presence converts him to the great Tradition cherished by positive theology (§14, 4, a) [e]. Having long suspected the need for a wholly different mind-set—*l'esprit de finesse*—he now finds the resolve to leave mathematics and physics and natural philosophy behind, along with their

---

[d] Oddly enough, Newton ended up couching his faith in progress in a medley of millenarian motifs. Incidentally, one wonders if Iris Murdoch, in *The Message to the Planet,* was drawing upon the figure of Newton when she created the character of Marcus Vallar, the genius who moves from mathematics into a touching, if bizarre, search for the ultimate coherence of the world. Cf. §110, 4, b.

[e] Pascal was not the only one to commend that option. Some of his contemporaries in France are now counted among the most distinguished positive theologians, notably the Benedictine monks known as the Maurists (or *Maurini*), the Jesuit Denis Pétau (Petavius), and two Oratorians: Louis de Thomassin d'Eynac, and Richard Simon, the first historical-critical student of the Hebrew scriptures.

learned practitioners. Henceforth he will pledge himself, without compromise, to a wholly different authority—historic revelation and its spiritual demands. The living God is a self-revealing God, known with certainty only in the community of faith and through *other persons* (including one so awkwardly close as one's spiritual director). They, along with their predecessors and successors, form the "cloud of witnesses" (Heb 12, 1) that lead to Jesus Christ, "the reliable witness" (Rev 1, 5; cf. 1 Tim 6, 13). The patriarchs and prophets, and especially the gospel-writers, speak, not to calculating, mechanical, casuistic reason, but to the heart drawn into generous self-abandon—that is, to authentic, if feeble, humanity's native thirst for personal communication with the transcendent. Pascal decided he must join the witnesses; thank heavens he was not the last to do so.

[6] Much as he canonizes, for the foreseeable future, the uneasy standoff between faith and natural science, Pascal represents a crucial recovery of the great Tradition. The self-revealing God is encountered in authentic self-experience as well as in the faith-community—the tradition that keeps the divine self-communication to witnesses alive. Revelation is a given in the world of persons—a matter of transcendence calling to immanence and of immanence responding, as well as witnessing to the touch of transcendence in the shape of autobiographies and declarations and institutions—external (that is, *material*) testimonies symbolizing God's immemorial faithfulness.

Christianity as a positive religion has understood history in this way: it enshrines Revelation. Yet Revelation *also continues*: transcendence will yet again be appealing to immanence, and immanence will yet again bear new witness. Out of the sovereign height of the divine freedom, the Spirit of God will always surprise human persons, since their hearts are natively, deeply equipped to respond in freedom. For *Deus semper maior*: "God is forever greater."[6] The living God will always be greater than our hearts (cf. 1 Jn 3, 20) and greater than any testimony our hearts are capable of; only the eschaton will see the full revelation of the Glory.

Yet at the same time God's fresh appeals to humanity will never be entirely novel. God remains faithful to the work of the divine hands; hence, God's self-revelation will always *also* be found waiting to be discovered, at least partly, in the witness of traditions which particular persons have established, like monuments, in the world of things. So when fresh divine self-revelation breaks in and creates new witnesses, this will indeed touch the latter's hearts more deeply than any traditions can do, yet their responses will never be wholly unprecedented. For as they respond from the heart and bear fresh witness to others, they do so with hearts shaped and made attentive by the tradition; as a result they will also insert themselves once again into the existing tradition, rearranging, correcting, renewing, enhancing it.

The question of faith and reason, we may trust, will not go away. For now, then, we must follow Pascal, both in the fervor of his conversion-experience and in his appeal to the bedrock testimony of the great Tradition: "the God of Abraham, the God of Isaac, the God of Jacob" (Ex 3, 6; Mk 12, 26 parr.; Acts 3, 13; 7, 32).

GOD OF ABRAHAM, GOD OF ISAAC, GOD OF JACOB

[§97] ISRAEL'S GOD

[1] If we are to draw, in this section and the next, a vignette of the core features of Israel's experience and understanding of God, we must begin with its *particularity*—that is, its *historicity*. That historicity is radical, in more than one sense.

> [a] First of all, there is the difficult question of *historical fact.* By and large, the Bible, as it has come down to us in its post-exilic Jewish redaction and its expansions in the *diaspora,* presents the living God's self-revelation as simply constitutive of Israel's identity as a people: apart from YHWH, there is no Israel. To state that Israel's Yahwistic monotheism is a late (that is, post-exilic) development seems to fly in the face of the biblical claim that monotheistic faith in YHWH is the *articulus stantis et cadentis* of Israel's faith and self-awareness from the beginning (Deut 32, 12; cf. 6, 4). This is confirmed rather than contradicted by the fact that the Hebrew scriptures, especially the prophetic writings, are not reticent about the frequent incidence of syncretism, and even outright idolatry, throughout Israel's history [*f*], so

---

[*f*] For example, Deutero-Isaiah (Is 40-55) must be read, not simply as a profession of faith in YHWH, but specifically as a warning against temptations to idolatry in the context of the Babylonian exile. Good examples of the post-exilic awareness of Israel's history of faithlessness are communal confessions of sin like Ps 106 and Neh 9, 5-37.

much so that it can occasionally depict the exclusive worship of
YHWH as an impossible choice (Josh 24, 19-23) and as threatened by extinction (1 Kings 18, 22). In consistently depicting
syncretism and idolatry as sinful aberrations, the Hebrew Bible
implies the claim that somehow there always was a *true*, canonical
Israel—one that never compromised its original commitment to
full-fledged monotheistic worship of YHWH. And in fact, even
if it is granted that post-exilic Jewish monotheism has idealized
ancient Israel's exclusive worship of YHWH, the Hebrew Bible
contains enough passages of undisputed antiquity to bear out
the deep roots of that worship in history.

Still, in its absolute form the claim does amount to an idealized theological retrospect rather than a statement of historical
fact. It is clear that ancient Israel, given its tribalist leanings,
shared some of the henotheism found here and there in the ancient Near East. In fact, the wording of the second commandment: "There shall not be, for you, other gods before my countenance" (Ex 20, 3) precisely confirms that it is the *worship* of
other gods that is proscribed, not assumptions about their existence or even their power [g]. And the critical inquiry need
not stop here. From an historical point of view, for example,
one can legitimately wonder if Israel's faith in YHWH as God
Alone is not the fairly late result of a gradual journey out of polytheism into monotheism. Such historical questions have in fact
been increasingly asked; so far, however, the answers have re-
mained inconclusive [h].

[b] Still, what remains interesting is that such radical historical
questions can be responsibly asked at all. In fact, Israel's faith
positively invites them; entertaining them helps bring to the

---

[g] For an example of a henotheistic ambiguity overlooked by later monotheistic
editors, cf. 2 Kings 3, 27. The "wrath" that comes upon Israel, causing them to
withdraw from certain victory, was obviously understood to be, not Israel's angry
revulsion at the Moabite king's sacrifice of his eldest son, but the rage of Moab's
god, driven to an extreme endeavor on Moab's behalf by that sacrifice.

[h] Recent years have witnessed brisk discussions, on the basis of archeological
evidence, about the accuracy of both the monotheistic and the henotheistic pictures, especially in regard to the period before and immediately following the
Davidic and Solomonic kingdom. Thus Mark Smith's recent *The Early History of
God* favors the skeptical position; his book is largely written by way of a rejoinder
to J. H. Tigay's *You Shall Have No Other Gods*, which offers evidence favoring the
antiquity of monotheistic, or at least henotheistic, Yahwism.

surface the extraordinary ability of Israel's acknowledgment of YHWH as God Alone (Deut 6, 4) to both guide the changing fortunes of Israel's history and follow them. For remarkably, Israel's faith turns out to be secure enough not to compromise its distinctive identity. In the encounter with other religious cultures, Israel's absolute monotheism, by and large, turns neither aggressive nor defensive: it gets neither debased into a crude, fundamentalist, over-particularized, atavistic monotheism, nor attenuated into a rarefied philosophical deism (say, of the Platonic or Stoic variety). It is durable as well as flexible; if it changes (as it does) in accord with Israel's vicissitudes, it gains depth of identity even as it changes. Israel's understanding of the One God seems to be remarkably at home with historicity.

All of this begins to suggest that the worship of YHWH is capable of inspiring a conception of God that combines two strengths not often found to be compatible with one another in positive religions as we know them in the West: a vivid actuality of *particular, historic experience* and an enduring ability to suggest a *wider, even universal, credibility.* This in turn hints that Israel's particular conception of God might be rather well equipped to sustain the rigors of reasonable inquiry into God—which includes the inquiry into the relationship between historic, positive faith and humanity's perennial, universal knack for intellectual exploration and critical questioning.

[c] The question of the historical particularity of Israel's faith in God is connected with a different, equally fundamental issue, namely the *moral consistency* of Israel's portrayal of God. As has been pointed out, the Jewish Bible as we have it presents, by and large, a unified historical picture of Israel's faith in God; the same cannot be said in regard to its *theological* picture. Fairness commands that we recognize that not every biblical portrayal of God can be harmoniously integrated into the imposing portrayals of YHWH found, say, in Deuteronomy, Second Isaiah, and the Wisdom traditions—the portrayal accepted as theologically normative by the mainstream tradition of Jewish-Christian theology (and hence, by the treatment about to be offered in this chapter). The problem presented by this lack of theological harmony in the biblical portrayal of God is only alleviated, not resolved, if we adopt habits of appropriate respect for the literary conventions of the Bible, which require us to make generous allowances for metaphoric exaggeration and to read many anthro-

pomorphisms as theologically significant (cf. §110, 3). The persistent problem is that the picture of Israel's God drawn in many biblical passages is disturbing, not so much philosophically as *morally*: thus (to mention only three glaring examples) YHWH is frequently depicted as acting in wrath, as putting hapless Canaanite populations under a deadly curse, and as a God to whom rash vows can be legitimately made—vows that in the end turn out to involve the killing of one's own child, as in the case of Jephtha. It is tempting, of course, to solve this problem hastily by suggesting that Israel's faith developed from primitive positions and gradually found itself completely purified; the problem is that this proposition, while *prima facie* plausible, remains to be supported by detailed historical argument and analysis. And, it must be added, any credible analysis along the lines just suggested should also include a persuasive explanation of the fact that later redactions of the biblical text allowed the offensive passages to stand—readily quotable in support of all kinds of convenient misconceptions and dubious (and even murderous) causes in the course of Jewish and Christian history, right down to our day. Thus, from the point of view of theological honesty, rather than implicitly depicting our own image of God as superior to the Jewish Bible's, with its embarrassing theological crudities, it is probably wise to suggest that *all* liturgical and literary portrayals of the living God, even the most refined, will continue to bear traces of humanity's radical incompleteness: its finitude, its lack of mature faith, its sinfulness. This puts a positive theological interpretation on the presence of discordant texts about God in the Bible, while at the same time enabling us to uphold the central portrayal of God in the great Tradition as truly normative.

[2] The capacity for self-renewal of Israel's historic faith in YHWH is undoubtedly connected with the fact that the tangles of history (and hence, movement) are part of its definition [*i*]. As a matter of literary fact, post-exilic Israel positively associates YHWH with the whole course of its history (cf., for example, Ez 20). And what is more, this association is not just a matter of a fixed, hard, permanent core of monotheistic faith being somewhat reluctantly adapted

---

[*i*] Cf. Eberhard Busch, *Karl Barth*, p. 114: "The Bible does not support the view that God is God in the same way at all times."

to suit varying circumstances of time and place; rather, YHWH is positively cast in the role of Israel's shepherd and guide *in* all its peregrinations. This is consistent with the fact that vicissitudes of place and time are part of the substance of Israel's worship of YHWH from the start [*j*]: YHWH is Israel's "God from Egypt on" (Ez 20, 5; Hos 12, 9; 13, 4; cf. 11, 1).

[a]   In the consciousness of Israel, its worship of YHWH, and hence, its own identity as a theonomous nation, are unequivocally defined by the Exodus theme: YHWH, and YHWH alone, creatively orders and rearranges the world (Wisd 19, 6) and "forms" and "saves" the people [*k*], by leading it out of Egypt through the waters of the Sea of Reeds, by guiding its rovings and restings in the desert, and by directing it to the Land of Promise through the waters of the River Jordan. Accordingly, the cultic memorializing of the Exodus-experience in praise of YHWH (Is 43, 1. 21; cf. 1 Pet 2, 9), especially around Passover, helps guarantee Israel's identity, by virtue of which it will be able, in all its subsequent reversals, to give its tradition a fresh shape. This is particularly clear in that long, sustained commentary on the Name of YHWH, which is Deutero-Isaiah. It interprets the Exile as an enactment of the Exodus and the desert-journey (cf., by way of one example among many, Is 43, 8-21), and Israel's return to rebuild Jerusalem as the establishment of the new Zion viewed as the cosmic mountain, the cultic center of a world renewed (cf. Zech 8) [*l*]—a universalist vision so attractive that Jeremiah can write the people will not miss, or even remember, the Ark of the Covenant, made during the Exodus, and lost for good in the destruction of the first Temple (Jer 3, 14-17). Analogously, the visions of Jeremiah (30-33) and Ezekiel (40-47) rehearse the divine-guidance theme so prominent in the Exodus by having the Lord precede the people to a new Temple, as an encouragement for the exiles to return. Ezekiel

---

[*j*] Consequently, the memorializing of particular events in time and place that is the substance of Christian worship follows the pattern set by Israel's worship (cf. §36, 3; §45; §100, 1).

[*k*] Israel's faith combines the twin themes of creation and salvation, which the Protestant exegetical tradition has had a tendency to separate, favoring the latter over the former (cf. §20, 2; §9, 1, [*i*]). Cf. Richard J. Clifford, "The Hebrew Scriptures and the Theology of Creation."

[*l*] Cf. Richard J. Clifford, *Fair Spoken and Persuading*, pp. 59-67. Cf. also Ben C. Ollenburger, *Zion, the City of the Great King*, pp. 145-62.

20 goes even further: in the final analysis, it interprets the present, continuing *diaspora* as a new Exodus—a faith-journey in the "desert of the nations"—in the perspective of a renewed, purified worship of YHWH that will draw in the whole Gentile world (Ez 20, 33-38).

[3]   Thus, while the traditional epithet "who has led us out of Egypt," added to the Name YHWH (Jer 2, 6; cf. Ex 20, 2; Deut 8, 14), is quite conceivably rooted in historical fact, it is certainly part of the definitive profession of faith of Israel as we know it from the Bible as we have it [m]. It implies that Israel's Egypt-experience is essentially connected with the *Name* YHWH *as it is actually used.* That use involves, not only *interpretation* (to be discussed further down: §97, 5), but also, and more than anything else, *worship;* an ancient song implies that it is "from Egypt on" that Israel is "a kingdom of priests and a holy nation" (Ex 19, 6; cf. 1 Pet 2, 9):

> When Israel went forth from Egypt,
> Jacob's house from a gibbering breed,
> Judah came to be his Sanctuary,
> Israel his Dominion.
>
> (Ps 114, 1-2)

Thus it is in naming YHWH—that is, in worshipful response to God's presence from its very beginnings onward—that Israel has found its (responsive) identity established. The indwelling holiness of YHWH purifies and consecrates Israel; in response, Israel's *raison d'être* is to call upon the Name. To do that worthily, Israel is to give proof of its total worship-abandon to YHWH; it must do so by keeping the Covenant—Israel is to be "holy, as I, YHWH your God, am holy" (Lev 19, 2; cf. Josh 24, 19). Not surprisingly, the echo of God's opening words to Israel on Sinai, "I am YHWH your God" (Ex 20, 2), returns, like a refrain, in the Levitical holiness code (Lev 19, 2-37). In this world also belongs Isaiah's awesome experience, in the Jerusalem sanctuary, of the holiness of YHWH filling the universe with transcendent majesty: it both prompts his own profes-

---

[m] For much of what follows in this section, I remain indebted to my former teacher, Henri Renckens, and especially to his treatment of Israel's understanding of God, in *De Godsdienst van Israel,* pp. 82-113 (ET *The Religion of Israel,* pp. 97-139). For a review of the literature on the origin, pronunciation, and meaning of the Name, cf. G. H. Parke-Taylor, *Yahweh: The Divine Name in the Bible.*

sion of sinfulness and it becomes the mainspring of his acceptance of his prophetic vocation to call Israel to conversion and holiness (Is 6, 1-8).

[4]   The sanctification of Israel as the earthly dwelling-place of YHWH has the character of special revelation, both of God and of Israel itself. God is revealed—startlingly in the polytheistic ancient Near East—as the absolute Cosmic Sovereign. YHWH is the Sole True God—the very One who rules and overwhelms and bewilders all of humanity and the world from a position of absolute superiority, enthroned in the sanctuary above all the powers that be (Ps 89, 6-14; Pss 94-100; cf. §60, 1). This sole, sovereign God now becomes a commanding presence to a *particular* people, and hence, the overriding theme of personal and communal witness: Israel acknowledges the Sovereign God of the Universe as its very own Glory:

> Attribute power to God,
> whose majesty is over Israel,
> whose power is in the skies.
>
> (Ps 68, 34)

Accordingly, the cosmic powers must now shudder, not only before God in the heavenly sanctuary (Pss 29; 92), but also before the divine Glory as it resides *in* Israel, identifying it as God's sanctuary:

> The sea saw it and fled,
> Jordan turned backwards.
> . . . . .
> Before the countenance of the Lord, tremble, you Earth,
> Before the countenance of Jacob's God.
>
> (Ps 114, 3. 7)

Thus the Exodus marks the beginning of the mysterious call ceaselessly issued to Israel, of all peoples, to obey and to acknowledge as God Alone the God who claims the whole earth as property (Ex 19, 6), and hence, the God who will be able to be readily present to the people wherever and whenever they invoke the Name. In the theology of the priestly source ("P"), which attempts to preserve as many traditional data as possible while at the same time harmonizing them, YHWH's call had already come to the patriarchs as they prefigured both the Exile and the Exodus (cf. Gen 12, 10-13, 1; 20, 1-18; 26, 1-25). Still, it had come to them only in muted form: they had known God only as *'El Shadday*—"God Almighty"—the supreme God, regnant atop the mountain of the world. That God of

Abraham, Isaac, and Jacob had been deeply unknown, though darkly surmised, all over the earth, from time immemorial, as enthroned
above the cosmic powers. It is "from Egypt on" that this God becomes *both* worshiped as Israel's own living God, nameable—that is,
invocable—by the Name of YHWH (Ex 6, 3), *and* fully known as the
God who Alone is Lord and Creator of the whole earth as well as
of the "hosts of heaven" above it (cf. §60, 1, a) [*n*].

> [a] The explanation just given finds support in Frank Moore
> Cross' suggestion that the Name YHWH, etymologically speaking,
> is the central, verbal part of a Canaanite-Proto-Hebrew epithet to
> 'El ("God"). In Cross' proposed reconstruction, the Name
> YHWH derives from an ancient causative preterite of the verb
> *hwy* ("to be"), and the epithet that gave rise to it was *dū yahwî
> tsaba'ôt* ("the one who has caused the hosts of heaven to be").[7]

[5] Worship gives rise to thought (§35, 1, c); the awe-inspiring
connotations of the divine Name as it figures in worship warrant
the expectation of significant denotation in reflection and teaching.
No wonder, therefore, that the *Name* YHWH becomes the object of
theological interpretation. The pericope in Exodus relating the
vocation of Moses, in his dialogue with the Lord appearing to him
in the burning bush (Ex 3, 1-4, 20), is a prime instance of such an
interpretation in the Hebrew Bible. To help us interpret this classic
passage correctly, some preliminary observations are in order.

> [a] In early literate, primarily oral-acoustical societies such as
> Israel as reflected in most of the Bible, wisdom is often couched
> in quick wit and clever word-play; accordingly, biblical reflection
> tends to seek a foothold in *current idiom* and *popular etymology*. Of
> these two, the latter tends to present the modern reader with a
> special problem. Unlike scholarly etymology, which investigates
> the meaning of words and names by recourse to their *historical*
> semantic development, popular etymology is liable to attend only

---

[*n*] It is to be noted that the Yahwist, for obvious theological reasons, places the
invocation of God by the Name of YHWH at the dawn of humanity; cf. Gen 4, 26.
Incidentally, a passage in the Apocalypse (Rev 19, 11-16) contains a Christian
parallel to the Hebrew theme of the revelation of the hitherto unknown divine
Name. Jesus Christ, known by the name "Faithful and True" (cf. Rev 4, 1), has
a hidden—that is, strictly divine—Name as well, which manifests him as the One
who is above all the powers that be: "King of kings and Lord of lords."

to *present* shape and sound [*o*]; accordingly, the interpretations of the Name YHWH proposed by the biblical accounts are liable to be based on popular etymology, which helps convey Israel's *sense* of God rather than any technical philological or semantic expertise on its part.

[b] This is reinforced by the fundamental linguistic insight that names and proper names, while often etymologically meaningful, never function, *in actual use*, as bearers of ideas or concepts [*p*].   Unawareness of this may lead to misinterpretations. Medieval scholasticism affords a case in point. Using the Latin Vulgate as its authoritative Bible, it found, in Exodus 3, 14, the expression *Ego sum qui sum* ("I am who am"); understandably, it read it as a biblical expression denoting God's transcendent simplicity: "I am the One Who Is." This interpretation had long been current; it can be found in church fathers like Gregory of Nyssa, Augustine, and especially Hilary of Poitiers (cf. §75, 2; §79, 4). But scholasticism, in its excitement, proceeded to make the mistake of reading into this interpretation of the divine Name a biblical endorsement of an abstract, scholastic *conception.* That conception was the thesis *essentia Dei est ipsum suum esse:* "God's essence is God's very own being" (or "God's nature is: simply to *bé*").

[c] In the ancient Near East, *names* are connected, above all, with *real, effective existence.* Thus the Babylonian cosmogonic myth known as *Enûma Eliš* can describe the primeval chaos by saying: "When on high the heaven had not been named, firm ground below had not been called by a name, ... "[8] For persons not to have a name is tantamount to their not existing in any real sense

---

[*o*] The semantic connections suggested by Gen 2, 7. 23 between, respectively, *'ādām* ("man") and *ʷdāmāh* ("earth, soil"), and *'iššāh* ("woman") and *'iš* ("man"), are two instances of this, out of countless biblical ones that could be quoted. For an illuminating essay on the subject, cf. Yair Zakovitch, "A Study of Precise and Partial Derivations in Biblical Etymology."

[*p*] Thus, to mention one random instance, the word "handkerchief" and its German and French equivalents *Taschentuch* ("pocket cloth") and *mouchoir* ("nose-blowing device") are easily recognizable, upon inspection, as meaningful words. So are proper names like "Peter" (from Gk. *petra*—"rock"), "Rose," "Frederick" (from Old Gm. *Frithu-rîc*—"peaceful kingdom"), and "Agatha" (feminine form of the Gk. adjective *agathos*—"good"). However, *in actually using* these words and proper names, we do not advert to these etymological "meanings" at all, but only to the objects or persons we point to, handle, deal with, refer to, or address.

—to not having a father to acknowledge their legitimacy in existing. The true, ultimate fate of all, therefore, depends on whether they have their names written in the heavenly "Book of Life" or blotted out from it (cf. Ex 32, 32-33; Ps 69, 28; Is 4, 3; Mal 3, 16; Dan 7, 10; 12, 1; 2 Esd 6, 20; Rev 3, 5; 20, 12. 15). But even here on earth, names are connected with permanence and perpetuity. The writer of 2 Samuel notes the irony of the fact that David's son Absalom, turned traitor, savagely killed, and buried in shame under a pile of rocks, had in his lifetime named a stone pillar after himself, to make up for the fact that he had "no son to keep my name in remembrance" (2 Sam 18, 18; but cf. 2 Sam 14, 27, where Absalom turns out to have three sons and one daughter, Tamar).

More importantly in the present context, the *authorized use of names* establishes *relationships of commitment*; hence, names are *invoked* by way of authoritative witness. To know a name implies *the privilege of addressing the person* who bears it, and the right to use a person's name implies *a claim to mutual relatedness and commitment*. It even implies a kind of *real presence*: those whom I permit to use my name carry my name in themselves, as it were, which makes them my true emissaries, authorized to represent me and entitled to the same regard as I am [q].

[d] In Israel's understanding of God's Name, these elements of effective existence, perpetuity, and mutual commitment are very prominent. Thus the presence of God's messenger guiding the people in the Exodus is as good as God's own presence, for "My Name is in him" (Ex 23, 21). Thus, too, God has entrusted the divine Name to Israel itself, to enable it to worship him and to witness to him; thus God is present in the Temple by virtue of the Name; that Name, invoked by the people authorized to do so, also hallows the Temple in which it resounds (cf. 2 Sam 7; Jer 7, 11; Deut 12, 5. 11. 21; also, cf. 1 Kings 8, 27-30). Finally, in this context, any abusive or pointless use of the Name is bound to be a transgression that is far from merely verbal; "invoking the Name in vain" (Ex 20, 7) is a *real* offense, since it parodies the act of worship, and thwarts and offends against the relationship of devotion and commitment that inspires the Covenant.

---

[q] In the New Testament, the fourth Gospel makes abundant use of this last feature, by having Jesus act and speak as the emissary of God, his Father, authorized to make God's Name known.

[e] The Hebrew Bible as we have it traces Israel's deep sense of the divine Name's holiness back to the oldest layers of its tradition, before the Name YHWH was ever revealed (cf., for example, Gen 32, 29; Judg 13, 17-18). About a century after the return from the Exile, the restored Jewish community's keener sense of the divine transcendence (cf. §98, 5, [*ff*]), combined with the prominence of the written Torah in worship (Neh 8, 1-12), found a new focus of attention in the *written* Name YHWH. Reverence and awe of the Name came to require of the reader in the synagogue that, wherever he encountered the divine Name in the Bible text he avoid enunciating it as he found it written (*k'tîbh*); instead, he had to replace it by the verbal, spoken (*q'rê*) title *ᵃdônāy*, meaning "Lord" [*r*]. The Septuagint followed suit by rendering, by and large, the Hebrew YHWH by *Kyrios* ("Lord"), a usage taken over by the New Testament. Thus YHWH became the *tetragrammaton ineffabile*—the unpronounceable, mysterious four-lettered divine Name [*s*].

[6] In the book of Exodus, a passage in the account of Moses' vocation in the desert explains the Name YHWH by recourse to etymology and idiom. The interpretation provided constitutes an answer, not so much to the question as to what the *Name* YHWH means semantically, as to the question, What does YHWH really amount to?

[*r*] To remind the synagogal reader of this standing enunciation directive (*q'rê' perpetuum*), the Masoretic text of the Bible consistently supplies the *vowels* of *ᵃdônāy* to the consonants Y-H-W-H. In the sixteenth century, Christian unfamiliarity with synagogal practice and Hebrew learning led scholars to think that the divine Name was actually pronounced with these alien vowels, yielding the meaningless oddity YᵉHᵒWᵃH or "Jehovah." Nineteenth-century German biblical scholars with historicist leanings revived the Name YHWH as "authentic" and even encouraged the use of "Yahweh" in both writing and speaking. The fact that neither Jesus nor any in the Christian communities, from the New Testament on, had ever even pronounced the ancient Hebrew Name of God should have given them pause, not in the last place in view of its residually tribal overtones; the fact that many Jews take exception to the casual use of the Name should have positively dissuaded them. The first modern translation to encourage the use of "Jahweh" among Catholics was the *Bible de Jérusalem*, first published in 1953. Ironically, the frequent use of "Yahweh" has, in many Catholic circles, become a badge of something entirely positive: biblical literacy. It is probably unrealistic, therefore, to expect that this habit, ill-advised though it is, will be abandoned any time soon.

[*s*] Starting in the early seventeenth century, and well into the nineteenth, Christian iconography proceeded to capitalize on the mysteriousness of the *tetragrammaton*, by placing it, surrounded by shafts of light, at the center of a triangle, as a symbol of the Triune God.

For an analysis of the answer, let us turn to the text itself. God, speaking from the burning bush, first acknowledges being the God of the ancestors—of Abraham, Isaac, and Jacob. Then God goes on to promise to deliver Israel from its plight, and gives Moses the charge of leading Israel out of Egypt by confronting Pharaoh. Then the following dialogue develops (cf. Ex 3, 13-15):

Moses: So here I go to the children of Israel and I say to them:
        the God of your fathers   [*'elōhê ʾbhôthêkhèm*]
        has sent me to you.   [*śʾlāhanî ʾlêkhèm*]
        And they will say to me:
        w h a t i s h i s N a m e ?
        What shall I say to them?

        . . .

YHWH: I a m w h o I a m .   [*'èhyèh ʾšèr 'èhyèh*]
        . . .

        Thus you will speak to the children of Israel:
        I AM has sent me to you.   [*'èhyèh śʾlāhanî ʾlêkhèm*]
        . . .

        Thus you will speak to the children of Israel:
                Y H W H
        the God of your fathers   [*'elōhê ʾbhôthêkhèm*]
        —the God of Abraham, the God of Isaac, and the God
        of Jacob—
        has sent me to you.   [*śʾlāhanî ʾlêkhèm*]

        T h i s i s m y N a m e f o r e v e r ,
        this is how I am to be remembered and invoked,
        from generation to generation.

This dialogue opens and concludes with a divine assurance of continuity: Israel is to go on putting its faith in "the God of your fathers," the patriarchs. But Israel's future faith will contain an essential, definitive ("forever") element of newness: the divine Name YHWH. The revelation of the Name is, on the part of God, an act of commitment, enablement, and demand. In entrusting the Name to Moses and through him, to the people of Israel, God assures Israel of an even more intimate divine presence in the future, and this assurance both justifies and compels a deeper abandon to God on Israel's part. The introduction of the Name occupies the body of the dialogue, and the literary means by which the Name is introduced is a combination of *popular etymology* and *idiom.* From the *popular etymological* point of view, "YHWH" is still vaguely reminiscent of, and sounds like, the root *hyh*, meaning "to be," here used in the first person singular form *'èhyèh* ("I AM has sent me to you"). The word *'èhyèh* is preceded by a clarification, couched in the form of an *idiomatic* expression: *'èhyèh ⁿšèr 'èhyèh* ("I am who I am"). Thus the structure of the passage as a whole justifies the inference that this latter, longer phrase, which stands, slightly isolated, at the center of the passage, holds the key to the author's understanding of the meaning of the divine Name [*t*].

[a] Given the non-logical nature of idiom, it is wise to remember, with Th. C. Vriezen, that it is not feasible to make sense of the passage in hand without an element of "intuition."[9] That intuition is most likely to occur when the text is compared with other biblical passages where the same idiom is found. The idiom itself consists of two finite forms of one and the same verb joined together by the relative particle *ⁿšèr*—often the equivalent of "who" or "what" in English. The particle can also be modified by various prefixes, yielding compounds like *baⁿšèr*, which has the meaning of the relative adverbs "where" and "wherever" in English. Let us briefly study four texts in the original Hebrew to bring out the structure of the idiom and its basic meaning.

When, during the Exodus, the Israelites discover that the food from heaven cannot be kept over till the next day, the problem arises what is to be done with the portion that is to be gathered on the sixth day and kept for the next day, the sabbath. So Moses commands (Ex 16, 23): *'et ⁿšèr-tō'phû 'ēphû, uf'et ⁿšèr-t'bhašš'lû baššēlû* ("what you will bake, bake, and what you will boil, boil"). The meaning is: "Never mind how you prepare it, as long as you prepare it, one way or another." The prophet Elisha uses an analogous expression when he advises the Shunammite woman whose son he once called back to life (2 Kings 4, 8-37) to move elsewhere before an impending famine, with the words (2 Kings 8, 1): *uf gûrî baⁿšèr tagûrî* ("and go abroad wherever you go abroad"), which means: "Never mind just where you go abroad,

---

[*t*] For the following, I am deeply indebted to Th. C. Vriezen's marvelously differentiated syntactic and stylistic analysis of the idiom, in a classic essay, entitled "'Ehje 'ašer 'ehje."

as long as you go abroad." Finally, there are two thumbnail characterizations of David's travels, very similar in phraseology (both use the root *hlk* "to go"), yet wholly contrary in meaning and mood. The first occurs when David and his band of six hundred are moving about in the mountains, plundering at random, and dodging the forces of Saul, who is bent on putting an end to David's ascendancy (1 Sam 23, 13): *wayyithallᵉkhû baᵃšer yithallᵉkhû* ("and they moved about wherever they moved about")—meaning that one could never tell just exactly where they were, except that they were bound to turn up somewhere, to cause trouble for Saul. The second presents a picture of David at the nadir of his career. Having received the news that his son Absalom is succeeding in snatching the throne, David is leaving the city of Jerusalem on his way into exile, accompanied by a handful of trusty followers, among them Ittai the Gittite and his six hundred warriors. Ittai has left his home in Gath to support King David; in other words, he is already an expatriate, and joining David in exile would be an excess of devotion. So David urges him to look out for his own comfort and safety. He advises Ittai to attach himself to Absalom in the city rather than follow himself on his wanderings, which he characterizes in the melancholy words (2 Sam 15, 20): *waᵃnî hôlēk 'al ᵃšer-ᵃnî hôlēk* ("and I am moving to where I am moving"), meaning, "I am moving with no place to move to."

These four instances warrant the conclusion that the idiom, somewhat paradoxically, *combines an unqualified affirmation of the activity expressed by the verb with an expression of complete indeterminacy in regard to any particulars of that activity.*

[7] This insight gives access to the meaning of the phrase *'ehyèh ᵃšer 'ehyèh.* In light of the expressions just reviewed it must mean: "Never mind just what I am and why I am present and how, as long as I am with you" (cf. §34, 7, b). This statement is, of course, baffling and mysterious, and hence, wholly unanticipated; still, it eminently fits the question Moses anticipates the people will ask him: "What is his Name?" For in asking for the divine Name in the people's behalf, Moses is not formulating a request for theological understanding, let alone definition; rather, he is praying for assurance, both about the divine command he has just been given to lead Israel out of Egypt, and about God's promise of salvation held out to the people. The text, therefore, presents the divine Name

YHWH as the answer that must settle the people's doubts and misgivings in setting out, away from Egypt, on their journey to the Promised Land, by offering an absolute assurance of God's creative and saving presence. In doing so, the answer also places God firmly beyond all grasp or comprehension, and thus also refuses to satisfy any possible questioner's purely intellectual curiosity.

[8] In the Book of Exodus as we have it, a second great theophany is granted to Moses (Ex 33, 17-34, 10). Unlike the burning bush pericope, which comes from the Elohistic source ("E"), this latter account is the product of Yahwistic circles ("J"). Still, interestingly, it contains an echo of the episode of the burning bush, not just in the point it makes, but even in the way it makes it.

Again, the central theme is that YHWH assures Moses, and through him, the people, of an intimate divine presence, by entrusting the divine Name to them. In the sequence starting with the burning bush, this revelation of the Name was the opening move of the Covenant relationship; here, it is part of its culmination. Despite the idolatry at Sinai and the punishment that has followed, YHWH decides, at Moses' insistence, to send "my angel" (Ex 32, 34; cf. 33, 2) along with the "stiff-necked" people, now turned repentant; but with Moses YHWH deals directly, face to face, "as one speaks to one's friend" (Ex 33, 11). Still, Moses prays for an even deeper assurance about God's "ways," as a pledge of the fact that he as well as the people "have found favor" in the sight of YHWH, constituting them as a people truly "different" from all other nations (Ex 33, 13-17). In the end, the answer to Moses' prayer will be a solemn theophany: YHWH grants Moses new stone tables and confirms the grant by passing before Moses standing in a cleft of the rock face, proclaiming the divine Name and the titles detailing the divine mercy and justice, while at the same time using the divine power to shield Moses from the divine Glory (Ex 34, 1-10).

However, earlier in the account, there is a prelude to this final theophany. It has the form of a solemn divine promise to Moses, as follows (cf. Ex 33, 18-19):

Moses: Please, make me see your Glory.

YHWH: I will make all my splendor pass before you,
            and I will call out my Name, YHWH, before you.

And I will favor whom I favor,   [u*hannōtî 'et-*šer 'āhōn]
and befriend whom I befriend.   [u*rihamtî 'et-*šer *rahēm]

But you cannot see my face,
for no human being shall see Me and live.

The point of this brief prelude is that God turns down Moses' request that he be reassured by means of a revelation of the divine Glory in its naked transcendence; the intensity would be deadly. But the refusal is preceded by the offer of a revelation that is life-giving: on behalf of the whole people (cf. Ex 20, 19), Moses will receive an indirect view of the divine majesty and hear the divine Name, which it will be Israel's privilege to use to call upon its God. And in anticipation of the Name and the titles of YHWH that will be the heart of the theophany itself (Ex 34, 6-7), the meaning of the Name is already held out by way of promise, by means of a parallelism couched in a now familiar idiom: "I will favor whom I favor, and befriend whom I befriend." It means: "Never mind the what, the how, and the why of my graciousness and mercy, as long as I am gracious and merciful to you."

[9] The worshipful recognition of YHWH's utter transcendence as God Alone will be the heart of Israel's faith-assurance. It will be kept alive by prophetic narrative, like the story of the theophany granted to the prophet Elijah, driven into exile by idolatrous Jezebel, in the form of the "sound of a slight whisper" that is more telling than the turmoil of the elements (1 Kings 19, 4-18). It will be the core of post-exilic spirituality (cf., for example, the divine address to Cyrus and its continuation to Israel, Is 45, 1-25). It will be cherished as the "great commandment" in the opening lines of the Š*ma'—the profession of faith, whose recital, twice a day, by every adult male in Israel is one of the main sources of Israel's continuing sense of identity (Deut 6, 4; cf. Mk 12, 29-30 parr.):

Hear, Israel:
our God is YHWH, YHWH Alone.
And you shall love YHWH your God
with all your heart
and with all your soul
and with all your capacity.[10]

[10] Israel's sense of the divine transcendence is matched only by its deep sense of the divine presence—the divine "immanence" to

which it has been so graciously introduced. The combination is paradoxical, and the paradox is most persuasively conveyed where Israel professes, prophetically, its sense of privilege at the realization of its intimacy with the God of heaven and earth:

> Now question the days past, the days that were before you were,
> ever since the day God created people on earth.
> Let your questioning scan the heavens from end to end,
> to see if ever so great a thing has occurred or been heard of.
> Has any people ever heard God's voice
> speaking out of the midst of fire, as you have heard it,
> and stayed alive?
> Or has any god ever tried to draw near
> and to take for himself a nation from the midst of another nation,
> . . . . .
> the way YHWH your God has done all this in Egypt, before your eyes?
> You are the ones who got to see it,
> so that you might know:
> YHWH is God Alone; there is no other besides him.
>
> (Deut 4, 32-35; cf. 5, 24-26)

Here if anywhere Israel demonstrates its conviction that the transcendent God of heaven and earth, whom it worships in holy awe, is more, not less, transcendent and adorable for being so intimately present and self-revealing, and hence, more worthy of total abandon on that score (§34, 2) [u].

[11] For a further example of Israel's historic faith in the merciful presence of the transcendent God, we turn to a portrayal of Jewish faith characteristic of the Hellenistic *diaspora*. The second half of the Wisdom of Solomon (Wisd 10-19) conveys one pious Jew's meditative re-reading of Israel's distinctive, normative faith-tradition. It is couched in consistently universalist terms. What inspires the meditation is still the sense of Israel's twin privilege of having recognized the One God as the transcendent Creator of the world and of having experienced the favor of this God at close range, especially in the Exodus from Egypt. But during and especially since

---

[u] Cf. David's prayer in 2 Sam 7, 22-24 for similar (if somewhat excessive, and perhaps even manipulative) expressions of this sense of privilege. The worship-tradition of the Christian community was to incorporate this tradition. Indeed, the worshipful recognition of God Most High as the decisive transforming presence in the world is the fundamental, most characteristic trait of all three branches of Western theism (cf. §34, 2; §67, 4, b; §105, 6).

the Exile, in the *diaspora*, Israel has been increasingly exposed to a variety of gentile cultures. Accordingly, its sense of privilege at being familiar with the God of the whole world has developed into an awareness of its vocation as a mediator: through the community of the Elect, the citizens of Zion now found everywhere among the nations, the God of Heaven and Earth now clearly means to appeal to all the nations and invite them to their true home (Ps 87). And not surprisingly, while Israel's idiom has changed to suit the cultural climate, its basic faith-attitude has not. The ancient faith can now patiently speak to the culture with the politeness of cosmopolitan philosophic wisdom, in a prayer of quiet admiration addressed to a God both transcendent and immanent:

> It is always in your power to show great strength,
> and who is to resist the might of your arm?
> Yes, the world, before You, is a speck on the scale,
> and like a dew drop in the morning falling on the earth.
> Yet You are merciful to all, for You are able to do all things,
> and You overlook people's sins, with a view to repentance.
> For You love all things that are,
> and You dislike none of all that You have made;
> for You would not have fashioned anything in disgust.
> How would anything have lasted, had you not wanted it,
> or how could anything not called into being by You have endured?
> But You are considerate of all, for they are yours,
> Lord, lover of the living;
> For your imperishable Spirit is in all of them.
>
> (Wisd 11, 21—12, 1)

The writer of the creation account in the first chapter of Genesis conveyed the same universalist theological insight in a phrase that is even more anthropological—one that the Greek Fathers would not be slow to notice and adopt (cf. §75, 2):

> So God created *'ādām* in his own image,
> created him in the image of God,
> created him male and female.
>
> (Gen 1, 27)

[12] Finally, in this context, let us at least pay our respects to a much later form of Jewish faith—one surrounded by the brilliance and dominance of medieval Christianity and indeed largely eclipsed by it. The *Siddur*, the standard collection of daily prayers of the

modern Jewish *diaspora*, contains a long alphabetic poem, meant to be prayed on the first day of *Šavu'ôth*—the Feast of Weeks (that is, the fiftieth day after Passover and the predecessor of Christian Pentecost).   It was written in Aramaic by Rabbi Meir ben Isaac of France, who lived in the eleventh century, which makes him a close contemporary of Saint Anselm of Canterbury (cf. §101). The text shows how, by the early middle ages, in the alien environment of Christianity, the small rabbinical schools and the tradition of Jewish literacy associated with them have become the principal support of Jewish faith in the One True God. To the small, isolated Jewish communities, the little world of school and synagogue has become the sanctuary from which they have access to the Lord of Heaven and Earth. And so, with an appeal, as charming as it is profound, to the familiar furnishings and utensils of this microcosm, this medieval rabbi can write:

> He has boundless might,
>   and there is no end to the explanation of it,
> even if the firmament were a roll of parchment,
>   and all the reeds quills,
> even if all the seas and all bodies of water were ink,
>   and all the earth's inhabitants scribes.
> Glorious is the Master of the Heavens
>   and the Ruler of the dry Land;
> He alone established the world,
>   and veiled it in mystery.[11]

[13] Modern Western sensibility, especially in North America, biased by a conventional acceptance of monotheism as the only "reasonable" idea of the divine, is poorly equipped to appreciate the profound originality of Israel's worship of YHWH. This applies even more if the monotheism concerned is, in fact, a form of Deism—the monotheism associated with, for example, Cartesian philosophy, Newtonian cosmology, or the humanisms inspired by the Enlightenment and Romanticism. All of these translate God's transcendence into mere remoteness, and God's uniqueness into mere numerical unity, of the kind that has given rise to the quip that many modern Americans "believe in at most one God." If the monotheism of the modern era has any real conception of immanent divinity, it is located in, and limited to, that universal feature of humanity: *self-consciousness and interiority*. *That* is where God (or at least the dynamic equivalent of God) is truly experienced, though, of course, apart from any worship (cf. §17, 1, a; §25, 4, a-

d). The Deist mood, in other words, tends to take Israel's monotheism for granted, or, at best, to interpret it as a first (if still primitive) victory of normal, universal human rationality over unenlightened mythology and prejudice. Needless to say, this overlooks the crucial fact that Israel's monotheism is inseparable from its claim to a *special* relationship with the One God—an idea Deism regards as offensive or, at best, naive (cf. §28, 4, a, [d]).

All these modern biases generally overlook an historical fact of fundamental significance: Israel's worship of YHWH as God Alone is unparalleled in the entire ancient Near East [v]. The fact that it arose in the setting of a cluster of influential civilizations that were consistently polytheistic makes it unique. Unlike any of its neighbors, Israel worships, not divine powers, but *God.* In the context of the religions of its neighbors, Israel's faith in God looks like a revelation—which, of course, is exactly what Israel professes. Simple, healthy realism, therefore, entitles Israel to the ardent awareness of its own distinctiveness; far from being an example of chauvinism or of belaboring the obvious, its deep sense of privileged identity is justified.

Moreover, Israel's conception of God involves an idea unknown to the rest of the ancient world, namely *creation.* The idea accounts for a highly distinctive view of the universe and of humanity's place in it—a view bequeathed by Judaism to Christianity, and one shared by Islam as well. This, too, begs for theological reflection.

[§98] GOD, CREATOR OF THE UNIVERSE

[1] The plausibility of polytheism lies in its taking seriously the fact that the world, while splendid in its untold variety, is not entirely harmonious, but full of unresolved tensions and even conflicts. This is why, in polytheistic civilizations, the divine, though consisting of a realm of superior powers, is experienced as an ingredient immanent *within* a restless cosmos; in fact, it is experienced as an integral part of the world—always mysterious, often mischievous, and sometimes downright wanton. Divinity, therefore, is almost

---

[v] The "monotheism" promoted in Egypt by Akhenaton (*c.* 1360-1344 B.C.) is too incidental (and perhaps too "poetic" as well) to offer a serious challenge to this statement. Cf. *ER* 1, pp. 169-70; W. Brede Kristensen, *The Meaning of Religion*, pp. 76-77.

physically associated with the whole press of local and seasonal processes and concerns: underworldly, earthly, astral, climatic, organic, animal, familial, tribal, and dynastic—an immense welter e-volving, ultimately, under the sway of blind, unknowable Fate. Accordingly, religious observance consists in the whole array of the human spirit's studied intercourse (under the bewildering canopy of Fate) with the world of powers above, close at hand, and below, whether benign or ominous—an intercourse combining subservience, negotiation, and even attempts at control. This finds symbolic expression in mythological tales and religious observances in which awe, terror, struggle, devotion, and abject submission alternate with calculating deference and even adulation, but also shrewdness and outright rebellion and *hybris*. One important feature of the mythological world is that, while broadly integrated, it is jealously *divided*; since all the powers (even the highest) are *local* and *seasonal*, they all have their competencies in place and time; no wonder what little stability results from this is always tenuous. For polytheism canonizes rivalry. If human persons and communities are to help establish cosmic and human stability and peace, therefore, it is in their own interest to offer respectful recognition to the properties and territories of all the powers that be, while at the same time making efforts to keep their influence where it belongs— that is, within limits. The heart of worship, in this setting, is inevitably *negotiation*—the management of a situation laden with conflict. *Do ut des* ("I give to you, the god, so you may give to me") may be too *simpliste* a way to characterize polytheistic worship; it is not incorrect, for religious observance is inextricably tied in with the maintenance, in a world dominated by competing spiritual powers, of as much human identity and security as possible.

Historic Israel came to think of YHWH as not local, not seasonal, not particular—in fact, not even as the highest of all the powers:

> For who in the skies compares with the Lord,
> who among the mighty ones is a match to the Lord?
>
> (Ps 89, 7)
>
> There is none like You among the gods, Lord.
>
> (Ps 86, 8)

YHWH is transcendent beyond any and all powers that may be dominant in whatever place or time: "God of gods and Lord of lords" (Deut 10, 17), "Sovereign of the heavens" (2 Macc 15, 23; cf. Deut 10, 14), God "from everlasting to everlasting" (Ps 90, 2), God "of the earth and all that makes up its fullness" (Ps 24, 1). Hence,

YHWH is the God of the nations as well (cf. Ps 67).

Needless to say, this struggle for monotheism ended up, by an historic process of patient and discerning (if sometimes tumultuous) inculturation, decisively arranging (and in cases rearranging) Israel's map of the universe as well as its own position in it.

[a] The principal end result of this historic rearrangement will be the affirmation that Israel (and more broadly, all of humanity, made in the divine image and likeness) enjoys pride of place in God's affection and hence, in the universe.[12] One of the opening moves in this development is an angelology and demonology compatible with monotheism, and indeed supportive of it. Privileged to be aware of humanity's position of stewardship, and hence, called to familiarity with the transcendent God, Israel can still marvel at humanity's position, so directly *below* the *'elohîm* (Ps 8, 3-8); not infrequently, however, it will find itself conscious of being so much at the center of God's attention that the angelic powers, and even, it would seem, "the Lord's messenger" (*mal'āk YHWH*; LXX *angelos tou Kyriou*), are cast in the role of servants, messengers, and protectors (cf., for instance, Gen 19, 1; 2 Sam 14, 17. 20; Ps 34, 8; Ps 103, 19-22; Tob 12, 6-20). In the vision of the author of the Epistle to the Hebrews, this development is clinched "in these last days" (1, 2). The Son—tempted and tested like all human persons, yet unlike them, sinless—has enacted the fulfillment of what used to be the annual *Yom Kippur* celebration; in fact, in doing so he has displaced it. For, in a once and for all purification ritual of cosmic proportions on behalf of all humanity (1, 3) and carrying his own blood, he has entered the heavenly sanctuary, where he remains as everlasting High Priest, drawing humanity to himself; being the "reflection of the Glory and the stamp of [God's] Being" (1, 3), and thus decisively superior to the angels, he definitively shows, by contrast, that the angelic powers are "ministering spirits" (1, 14). This kind of christological interpretation of the subordinate nature of the angels will also help put the demonic powers in their places (cf. 1 Cor 8, 4-6).

In other words, Judaism, and in time, the Christian community as well, simply assume the existence of angelic powers. The classic Christian creeds positively affirm the *invisiblia* (the "things unseen"; cf. Col 1, 16) in God's creation; the later Christian tradition has wisely resisted the temptation to deny the affirmation (cf. DH 800; CF 19) [w]. (Yet it must be added that it has shown a certain lack of appreciation for the subtlety of the biblical picture, or, for that matter, of corresponding "pagan" pictures: it has lumped all the unseen powers together under the general rubrics of "angels" and "demons."[13]) In fact, the Christian Church (encouraged, possibly, by the Hebrew Bible's unabashed use of 'ĕlohîm to denote, not only God, but also heavenly beings acknowledged as divine by other religions: cf. e.g., Ps 29, 1; 138, 1b) was to show its continuing respect for the angels by adopting, from at least Papias on, the pagan epithet *theios* ("holy") to acknowledge the angels and their "movements" as "holy"[14] without worrying about equivocating about the transcendent holiness of God. But more importantly, both Israel and the Christian community will, with the patience of genuine resolve, reject the unseen powers' alleged claim to religious submission and especially worship. For the tradition of Jewish-Christian monotheism will, more firmly than paganism needed to do it, assign to the powers a place, not *above* the universe but *in* it. That is, while the unseen powers may inspire humanity's access to God or impede it, they do not *control* it; humanity is assured of the offer of unmediated encounter with a truly transcendent God

---

[w] Paul M. Quay's very full treatment of the question ("Angels and Demons"), concludes that the Fourth Lateran Council defines, as an article of catholic faith, the existence of unseen powers. This is unconvincing, on hermeneutical grounds. Indubitably, the decree *Firmiter* explicitly affirms (and in that sense teaches) the existence of unseen powers, and it does so in the course of a definition God's all-encompassing creatorship—a doctrinal orchestration of the creed's first article. It is Quay's intent, not only to show (as he does) how pertinent the definition was to the dualistic errors of the day, but also to argue that the decree's affirmation of the existence of the *visibilia et invisibilia* amounts to a *definitio fidei*—in other words, that its doctrinal affirmation goes well beyond the definition of God's universal creatorship. This is where I differ. For a *definitio fidei*, what is required is *definitional intent both express and specific*, and I see no evidence of this in the text of the definition. — The initiative in thematically *denying* the existence of unseen powers lies, not so much with liberal Protestantism (as Quay suggests), as with scientific rationalism, intolerant of even the thought of *invisibilia*. However, this rationalism was to succeed only in driving the issue underground, as the widespread, if largely unacknowledged, nineteenth-century and early twentieth-century interest in spiritualism and the occult was to prove. Contemporary movements like New Age come to mind as well. So does the *Engelwerk* or *Opus angelorum*, a secretive and doctrinaire, if pious, Catholic association in Austria and Germany. It appeals to revelations allegedly granted to a Mrs. Gabriele Bitterlich, and is characterized by an undiscerning claim to knowledge of the details of the invisible world; it has been the target of repeated Roman investigations. Cf. Heiner Boberski, "Das 'Engelwerk'"; also, "New examination of 'Opus Angelorum'." On angelic and demonic powers, cf. §124, 4, a-g, and notes.

undeviatingly devoted to its well-being.

Yet this encounter is marked by a cosmic struggle: humanity is both open to God and resistant to God, and it participates in a world torn between plasticity and sluggishness, between a knack for coordination and a tendency toward decomposition, between tendencies that favor the emergence and survival and growth of humanity and tendencies that jeopardize it (cf. §115). In this struggle, the Jewish-Christian tradition, supported on this score by Platonist and Aristotelian cosmologies, will respect heavenly powers as spiritual (and in that sense "personal") influences for good or evil in the world (cf. §124, 4, a). Of these, the good angels are to be held in veneration (DH 600; CF 1251)—not worshiped, nor even appeased (cf. Col 2, 18).

[b] However, in all fairness it must be pointed out that the Christian community's intellectual and hence, doctrinal tradition (unlike its liturgy) experienced some real irresolution in relation to an ancient *philosophical* conception of the powers that be, found with such appealing vigor in Neo-Platonism, in the form of the idea of the Great Chain of Being. In this world picture, all the superior powers somehow *mediate* between true deity—"the greatest God" (cf. §27, 4, b)—and humanity and the world. Thus, in referring to the Son and the Spirit as the Father's hands, instruments, and powers, and in suggesting that they are eternally "immanent" in God (*endiathetos*), but relative to creation "uttered" by God (*prophorikos*), early Christian trinitarianism did suggest that they belong to a middle realm of reality, "created so God could create." Not until some time after the obviously subordinationist Creed (or "Blasphemy") of Sirmium of 358[15] did the sustained trinitarian teaching of Athanasius and the Cappadocian Fathers succeed in recovering for Christian doctrine the full majesty of Jewish monotheism, by making it clear that "there can be no grades of deity, and God needs no intermediary to protect Himself from the world or the world from Himself" (cf. §102, 6, [q]). Gregory of Nyssa's *Catechetical Oration*, probably written in 383 A.D. or shortly thereafter, provides, especially in its closing chapters, compelling formulations of this essential theological insight.[16] The infinite qualitative distance between God and humanity and its world (cf. §82, 3, b) cannot "be bridged by inserting enough intermediate steps," but only by "the free act of a loving Creator"—that is, ultimate-

ly, by the Incarnation of the fully divine *Logos* and the Christian community's assurance of the gift of the fully divine Spirit, which the risen Christ obtains from the Father [x].

[2] Israel's road toward this balanced rearrangement of the world is a long and painful one; it is marked, too, by one incessant prophetic refrain: heavenly bodies, the powers of nature and the idols fashioned in deference to them, and the princes and rulers of the nations are not, in and of themselves, numinous; they are subject to critique; if they inspire awe (as they regularly do), they do so under YHWH, who alone is worthy of worship (Is 40, 9-26; cf. 44, 9-20; Ps 115, 2-11; Jer 10, 2-16).[17] Far from being obvious or routine, in other words, Israel's cultic monotheism is always a faith struggling against impossible odds (Josh 24, 19), jeopardized by the widespread attention paid to the powers that be. It must exert itself to survive the dynamics implicit in, respectively, its sedentarization in residually polytheistic Canaan, its need for dubious political alliances with neighboring nations, and finally, from the Babylonian Exile forward, its resolve to settle among the nations, often as an oppressed minority, forced to "praise [YHWH] in song in the teeth of the angels" (Ps 138, 1)—that is, of the gods worshiped locally.[18]

No wonder the prophetic writings, from Deuteronomy on, will brand the observances offered to the powers that make up the international pantheon as sinful (for a representative example, cf. 2 Kings 21, 1-9; cf. §124, 4, b-e). Life in Canaan, amidst residual gentiles, and especially amidst the seductive fertility of the land, must be kept in focus by the remembrance of the austere sterility of the desert as the setting where Israel was powerless to produce anything, and hence, where it allowed itself to be courted by YHWH alone (Deut 8, 12-17; Hos 2, 14-23). The farmers' homesteads and

---

[x] Quotations from Joseph T. Lienhard's review of R. P. C. Hanson's *The Search for the Christian Doctrine of God* (336). Lienhard has also suggested (in "The 'Arian' Controversy: Some Categories Reconsidered") that doctrinal clarity about the blessed Trinity, inaugurated by the application of the *homoousion* to the Holy Spirit was also the natural *theological* prerequisite for the resolution of the *christological* elements in the Arian controversy. This idea, also suggested by R. P. C. Hanson (both in Part IV of *The Search for the Christian Doctrine of God*, and in "The Achievement of Orthodoxy in the Fourth Century A.D.," p. 153), merits serious attention. Coherent trinitarian doctrine began to take shape with the *Tomus ad Antiochenos* of 362 and culminated in the Council of Constantinople of 381. The idea has the added advantage of providing those of us who teach doctrine with a sound *theological* principle to create order in the notoriously tangled thicket of fourth-century debate.

the city strongholds with their shrines and sanctuaries, those centers of festive seasonal abundance, were indeed capable of functioning as parables of YHWH's faithfulness, but only as long as the memory (a memory probably more indebted to theology than history) of the patriarchs and their successors—herdsmen precariously journeying from oasis to oasis with their families and flocks—was kept alive (cf. Deut 26, 5-11; Ps 23). The sole Lordship of YHWH as the soul of Israel's identity as a sovereign nation was to demand the gradual cleansing of the various local shrines, even those maintained under royal warrant; eventually, this involved (under king Josiah, 640-609 B.C.) their demolition in favor of the single Temple in Jerusalem [y]. Finally, at the time of the fall of Jerusalem (587 B. C.) and the subsequent Exile, the absence—first forced, then elected (Jer 29, 4-7)—of a sizable portion of the people from the Temple drove home the conviction that the true worship of the God of Heaven and Earth consists in faithfully cherishing, in the *diaspora,* God's costly Wisdom resident in the Torah (cf. §90, 5, b), and in the sacrifice of a righteous life among the nations. And those nations, too, though still ignorant of the Lord, are destined one day to participate in Israel's worship of YHWH, in a renewed Jerusalem (Is 2, 2-5; 66, 18-23).

In this way, in insisting on worshiping YHWH alone and on recasting its habits of life and thought according to this cult, Israel involved itself, not in a timeless truism, but in a long series of sensitive transcultural moves of historic significance [z].

[3]   One essential element in this history is a conviction that remains, to this day, both a fundamental assurance of stability and a

---

[y] The Temple liturgy also provided the editor of Exodus as we have it with the props for the description of the majestic displays of sights and sounds orchestrating Israel's covenantal encounter with YHWH as God Alone on Mount Sinai.

[z] On this subject, cf. H. Richard Niebuhr's classic *Radical Monotheism and Western Culture.* On a less austerely theological note, G. Ronald Murphy has given us an admirable account of the poetic sensitivity it may take to bring about a productive transcultural encounter between Christian monotheism and a coherent polytheistic culture governed by divine powers of war and wisdom, and ultimately by Fate. Cf. his translation of the ninth-century Saxon epic *Heliand* ("The Savior") and his delightful monograph *The Saxon Savior.* The epic's author, a scholar-monk, recounts the Gospel in keeping with the ethos of the Germanic warrior-world of the Saxon tribes, recently brought to heel by Charlemagne and forced to accept imperial Christianity. In doing so, he succeeds in both accepting and substantially rearranging the world picture of ancient German mythology, along with the attitudes it used to cultivate.

never-ending invitation, to Jews and Christians alike, to religious universalism. That conviction is Israel's dogged insistence that the One God has created the *whole* world (cf. §60, 1, b), and created it as *one*. This rejection of dualism, however, leaves room for the acknowledgment of the countless tensions that are inherent in the world. The unity of the universe is not a matter of self-contained perfection, but of *dynamic structure*, and hence, of *process* (cf. §2, 1; §11, 3 and [*m*]; §16, 1). Heavenly bodies, natural powers, and the rulers of the nations (as well as whatever other powers and authorities may exist or emerge in time and place) divide the world into climes and competencies and kingdoms; consequently, contest and the interplay of forces and energies (sometimes constructive, sometimes destructive) are inherent in the world —a recognition that involves the realization that human life with God in the world may demand historic *choices*. But both in principle and in the final analysis, thanks to the transcendence of the One God who has created it, the evolving world is and remains fundamentally harmonious and *one*. The consequences of this realization at the level of theological principle are enormous. Basically, it marks the difference between understanding the world as "originated" or "come about" as the result of cosmic struggle and understanding it as *created*; that is, it marks the end of (mythological) cosmogony and the beginning of (philosophical) cosmology. This bears further exploration.

[4] The world is intrinsically finite, and hence, beset by ambiguity [*aa*]. At the specifically anthropological level, the most persistent, intractable ambiguities are connected with the issues of *class, race, and sexuality* (cf. Gal 3, 28; cf. also §128, 1, a; §130, 1; 11, d; 12-13; §142, 2). Put more broadly, the issues of control, trust, and *erōs*, along with their endless permutations, combinations, and interferences, are perennial concerns, and perennially problematic ones as well. Issues of *influence* (who/what is up and who/what is down?), *inclusion* (who/what is on the inside and who/what is on the outside?), and *intimacy* (who/what gets private access to whom/what and how fast?) continually force persons, communities, and indeed whole cultures to make choices—none of them ever quite satisfactory, and hence, always up for revision, in a never-end-

---

[*aa*] Paul Tillich's broad philosophic explorations of this theme remain valuable. Cf. esp. his *Systematic Theology*, I, pp. 81-94, 147-55, 186-204.

ing interpersonal and socio-political process.[19]

In Israel's understanding of creation—that is, of the manner in which God is Lord of the universe—all these concerns are operative as symbols, yet they are all transcended, ultimately in the realization that nothing can be the opposite of a wholly transcendent God (cf. §79, 4).

[a] Precisely because the world produced by God is so obviously dynamic and energetic, the frequent, unresolved incidence of in-considerate, and even destructive, *struggle for dominance* is all the more frustrating. Yet God produces everything with a view to harmony, without forcing anything; the very real, though residu-al, cosmogonic battle imagery in Scripture (cf. for example, Ps 74, 12-17; even the pre-existing *tohuvabohu* of Gen 1, 2 may have to be read as an instance of this; but then again, cf. Ps 104, 26) tells only half the story;[20] the world is fundamentally not the outcome of a divine struggle with the powers that be or with the monster of chaos, nor the result of God forcibly having to bend into shape some intractable pre-existing matter. God does not make by force, but freely calls into being by the sovereign *word*, and out of a shapeless, unnamed chaos (Ps 33, 6-9; Gen 1, 1-31; Sir 39, 17-31); consequently, nothing in the world ultimately de-serves to be overpowered or defeated. "God creates" means: if the world is said to be *made* by God, this does not imply that something pre-existing had to be turned into the world by divine *force majeure* (cf. §79, 2). God, and only God, and nothing else, accounts for the existence of the world—that is, for the world as an integral whole ("in their whole substance ... out of noth-ing": DH 3025; CF 418). As a result, the universe is not framed for the dominance of the fittest or for class struggle. It is not even framed for the immediate victory of the righteous over the unjust. In a wonderful hymn found at Qumran, the just man beset by God's enemies sings the praise of God nevertheless. He can do so because he knows that his salvation is ultimately as-sured because "my footsteps are from You"; but at the same time he realizes that the onslaught of the unrighteous on his soul is ultimately "from You" as well. In this way he acknowl-edges that, in this violent confrontation inside creation, it is God's design to reveal the divine glory precisely through the judgment visited on the godless and the mighty deliverance of God's faithful. Thus the deepest significance of the dreadful

situation in which the author of the prayer once found himself
is the actualization of God's glory in the world.[21] Summing up:
the Jewish-Christian tradition professes that the world is created,
in the final analysis, for synergy. Ultimately, the God of the powers disarms.

[b] Precisely because the world produced by God is so obviously
ordered, its wild, unsettled profusion of *variety*, often of the disso-
nant kind, is all the more baffling. This raises the issue of inclusion and exclusion—that is to say, *discrimination*. Yet the One
God produces all things that are, inclusively, without exception;
the world, therefore, is not an unstable, unreliable mixture of
one realm of reality made by God and other realms of counter-
reality produced by opposite, demonic powers. Despite the obvious element of natural and human chaos in the world, and even
more, despite the many troubling instances of divinely authorized discrimination and intolerance in the Scriptures (the book
of Judges being a good example), therefore, nothing in the
world must, ultimately, suffer discrimination because of an allegedly alien origin (cf. §78, 2, a). No creature can lose its *natural* reference to God (cf. Mt 5, 45) [*bb*]. "God creates" means:
God *sustains* the world by having everything that exists *participate*
in the all-encompassing, all-pervading reality of the one world, of
which God is the one single, transcendent principle ("the one
principle of the universe": DH 800; CF 19); consequently, the
universe is framed for all-encompassing trust. God is the Lord
of inclusion and ultimate reconciliation.

[c]   Finally, the self-actualization and self-preservation of the
world is driven by strong forces of *attraction* seeking the equilibrium of union and intimacy as well as the gratification inherent in
the release of the tension that precedes the equilibrium. Material things seem naturally to settle into their appointed places,
plants at their peak charm and allure by dint of shade and color
and smell and taste so as to achieve a profusion of progeny, animals pursue food and mate in search of appeasement and off-
spring, men and women nervously seek to allay their hunger and

---

[*bb*] Mystics, being closest to God, are most keenly conscious of the inalienable
holiness of all creatures, which ultimately places them beyond all discrimination
and prejudice; cf. the final paragraphs of the long quotation from Ruusbroec's *Espousals* in §90, 3.

thirst for things, protection, food, and one another, to ensure survival. But the irrepressible instinct for self-actualization and self-preservation is deadly, too; nothing so furious as *erōs* thwarted. And that is not all. The erotic drive may find itself unnerved by the forces of *repulsion and hate* it turns out to conjure up; and even worse, the wearying imbalance kept up by *erōs* is capable of awakening in persons the ache for the lasting composure of death.

No wonder the cosmogonies of the ancient world teem with erotic desire, contest, conquest, generation, and extinction. In this context, what is most striking is the fact that Israel's God, though symbolized as male, is in no way associated with fertility [cc]. Equally strikingly, while more and more firmly resolving not to associate YHWH with a female divine consort, Israel steadfastly refused to reduce its God to a loveless, expressionless, impregnable monad, incapable of true self-communication [dd].[22]

[cc] In interpreting this patriarchal feature of Israel's religion, so neuralgic in the West today, the Christian tradition, as instanced by the Cappadocian fathers, will "equate divine fatherhood with motherhood because God transcends gender." While often using the language of "culturally entrenched misogyny," the great Tradition will insist that the things that are "important and definitive about the human condition, nature and moral character, are unaffected by the gender distinction," since (and here the Jewish heritage shines through with particular clarity) human differences, and specifically gender, no matter how real, are "overwhelmed by the glory of God which they have in common." Cf. Verna E. F. Harrison's illuminating essay "Male and Female in Cappadocian Theology" (quotations 442, 447, 451); cf. also Frances Young's pointed remarks in *The Making of the Creeds*, pp. 100-03.

[dd] In an unpublished paper, Francis X. Clooney has shown how, in treating the relationship between the transcendent God and a humanity involved in sexual differentiation and the ambiguities attendant on it, a South Indian Hindu theologian of the Northern Srivaisnava tradition follows a course diametrically opposite to Israel's, yet one which, curiously, gives rise to illuminating comparisons with the Jewish and Christian understanding of God. In a refined speculative effort to teach true monotheism critical of Vedic polytheism, Vedanta Desika (1270-1369) continues to recognize the goddess Sri as the Lord Visnu's Consort, but explains that (to use Christian terminology) she is wholly consubstantial with him, as well as inseparable from him in the work of salvation. What is interesting is, first of all, that both Vedanta Desika and Israel, in their very different ways, make the point that the One and Most High God is not an impassive, self-confined monad marked merely by overpowering might. On account of his union with Sri, Vedanta Desika can explain, Visnu is the fertile, all-embracing fountain of life; similarly, Israel regards YHWH as lover, groom, and husband, faithful to Israel his beloved, his spouse, and his wife, and eager to share all his delights with her (cf., among countless examples, Ez 16; Is 61, 4-5). (However, note the flexibility of the imag-

Equally relevant here is the fact that YHWH is neither the father of the gods nor engaged in the amorous exploits with gods and humans considered allowable to the head of the cosmic household in the interest of enforcing the divine rule and displaying the divine grandeur. "God creates" means: far from being the involuntary emanation of a divine being driven by inexhaustible needs for self-reproduction, the world is the free revelation of the divine goodness and liberality, as well as its beneficiary (cf. DH 3002, 3024-25; CF 412, 331, 418), *providently* framed for *fulfillment* in a union that provides integration without absorption—of the kind in which everything will be accomplished because "God will be all in all" (1 Cor 15, 28).

[d] Consequently, the Jewish-Christian tradition will consistently maintain God's absolute transcendence over the universe: God is "by virtue of both reality and essence distinct from the world ... and ineffably exalted above whatever exists or can be conceived besides God" (DH 3001; CF 327; cf. §69, 1, c; §102, 7).[23] This transcendence above, and distinction from, the universe, however, is anything but a separation from it; God is not remote (cf. §75, 2). In fact, it is precisely God's utter transcendence that guarantees not only God's gracious presence to the world, but also God's essential, because creative, immanence in the world. Yet the divine immanence, while being downright constitutive of the world, does not in any sense make God "part of" the world—that most characteristic feature of polytheism. If it is

---

ery in third Isaiah. In Is 66, 12-13 the gender roles are reversed: Israel becomes the beloved son and YHWH his comforting mother. This unconventional image, it would seem, led a nervous scribe to append an ill-fitting half-verse to verse 13, explaining that Israel's comforter will really be Jerusalem, as verse 11 had explicitly stated.) But secondly, Vedanta Desika's teaching also invites interesting comparisons with Jewish and Christian conceptions supportive of female symbolizations of God. What comes to mind are the late-Jewish conceptions of Wisdom as the female representation of God and even as God's close companion from before Creation, and of the Torah as the embodiment of this divine Wisdom. This was to have trinitarian consequences, when the Christian community began to understand Jesus Christ as Wisdom and Torah (as well as *Logos*) Incarnate. Elizabeth A. Johnson has treated and elaborated these themes, initially in an illuminating essay ("The Incomprehensibility of God and the Image of God Male and Female"; cf. the response by Mark S. Smith, "God Male and Female in the Old Testament: Yahweh and his 'asherah'"), but more recently as well as very compellingly, as part of her full-size monograph *She Who Is* (cf. esp. pp. 76-103). Finally, the Hebrew Bible's long-standing habit of casting the *mal'ak YHWH* ("the Lord's Angel") as the transcendent *persona* in and through whom God is present to and engages humanity and the world may conceivably be relevant to this issue as well.

rightly said that God is "contained in the universe and everything in it," the prior, more foundational truth is that "spiritual entities contain the things in which they dwell"; this means that God is indeed "contained" in creatures, but only as containing and encompassing them, as both Augustine and Aquinas teach.[24] Pantheism, therefore, incorporates a profound truth indeed, but only on condition that this truth is understood in a "panentheistic" sense; only a God who is wholly transcendent and all-encompassing is sovereign enough to be at the essential core of the last and least creature. Nothing in the world is so great as not to be exceeded by God's infinite greatness, nor is anything in the world so small as not to be sustained in its very being by the divine indwelling.

[e] In the final analysis, therefore, the worship of God (as well as the holiness produced and demanded by it: §47; §49) and the deepest conceivable appreciation and enjoyment of the world encourage and support one another.[25] A Latin epitaph for Ignatius of Loyola composed by an anonymous Jesuit scholastic in the third decade of the seventeenth century, printed in the *Imago primi sæculi,* a rather pretentious volume published in 1640 to celebrate the Society of Jesus' first centennial, and adopted by the great nineteenth-century German poet Friedrich Hölderlin as the epigraph of his poem *Hyperion,* captures in a fine paradox these two inseparable elements of the Jewish-Christian conception, both of God and of life with God in the world: *Non coerceri maximo, contineri tamen a minimo divinum est* ("Not to be confined by what is greatest, yet to be contained by what is smallest—this is divine").[26]

[5] The destiny of the world is ultimately governed, not by the anxious persistence of the powers that be, but by the constancy of YHWH, who grounds the true (if relative) autonomy of everything in the world according to its nature. If this is so, it is not surprising that the *values* by which Israel must learn how to live (and hence, its *ethics*) derive, ultimately, from considerate divine right—not from inexorable cosmic might. *For Israel, faith and the work of justice are inseparable.* This feature of Israel's identity is especially prominent in the large, distinctive body of *prophetic* literature it produced. The ethics demanded by the prophets are very different from the value systems derived from a mythological world view. Mythology fits a

world pervaded by divine powers running interference. Accordingly, not only does mythology serve to help human cultures claim their appointed places in the welter of the cosmos, to cherish them as sacred, and, if necessary, to maintain them to the death against any invasion; it also helps humanity derive solace from the ineluctability of the cosmic order. In this way, mythology does indeed allot and apportion and insure humanity a place under the sun, but in doing so it also exonerates, exculpates, and absolves it. Israel believes and lives differently. Committed to the *Torah*, Israel becomes the people incapable of letting itself be comforted—its conscience salved, its responsibility alleviated, its freedom tempered, and its thirst for the infinite allayed—by myths, idols, and ideologies. Israel acknowledges YHWH *both* as utterly above *all* the powers that be (that is, indeed, as their Lord and Creator) *and* as the God to whom Alone it is privileged to owe an absolute loyalty expressed in worship, reinforced by, and indeed embodied in, a demanding code of purity regulations. In this way, Israel accepts to live as a community of holiness. No wonder it also accepts to live *morally*, and to do so, not by taking its cues from "the world" and its powers, but by vowing *responsible obedience to God.* This obedience is concretized in *the freely undertaken observance of a demanding code of ethics*, which Israel understands as its path to sanctification. Thus, while Israel's communal ethic is in harmony with the natural order, which both faith and reason can discern to be a reliable guide to moral action, ultimately, Israel understands its moral life to be stably rooted in the holiness and the omnipotence and the mercy of God. Consequently, in Israel's eyes, the cosmos, restless and full of conflict and injustice as it is, is *emancipated, at least in principle, from the powers that be.* Accordingly, Israel can think of God as vowing to put an end to the "gods" and the rampant injustice they are causing in the world (Ps 82) [*ee*].

[*ee*] On this subject, cf. Johann Baptist Metz, "Theologie gegen Mythologie." Cf. also Emmanuel Lévinas, in "Simone Weil contre la Bible" (*Difficile liberté*, pp. 178-88), p. 183: "The oneness of [God's] Name means the oneness of the language and the Scriptures and the institutions. It means the end of naiveté and rootedness. The Church remains faithful to a deep-seated Jewish impulse when it seeks the religious emancipation of humanity by (as Simone Weil complains) 'imposing the Jewish Scriptures everywhere.' All speech means being uprooted. Every rational institution means being uprooted. The establishment of a genuine society is a form of being uprooted—it marks the end of an existence where 'being at home' is an absolute, where everything comes from inside. Paganism means rootedness, almost in the etymological sense of the term. The arrival of

In its interpretation of the world as YHWH's unfinished creation, Israel involves itself in a *fundamental acceptance of moral responsibility for humanity and the world*. It agrees to exercise stewardship over creation in behalf of God—that is, it accepts the call to treasure and do justice, both to human persons (with the powerless, the marginal, and the lonely and unloved as the test-case: Lev 18, 13-18!) and to the cosmos. At Israel's hands, human life in a divinely created world becomes a never-ending task of *mediation*: taking its warrant from a transcendent God, Israel understands it to be its moral responsibility to lead God's imperfect, unfinished creation out of its present state of imbalance, and thus, at long last, to bring it home to its true but hidden self, to be found only in the presence of God. Israel sees it as its never-ending responsibility to turn humanity and the world more and more into what they fundamentally are: the very stuff of the glorification of YHWH. In this way, Israel also comes to enjoy the privilege of privileges: forever to glorify the Immeasurable God while appreciating and enhancing the work of the divine hands. Thus, in the Jewish-Christian tradition, the call to faith is inseparable from hope, and both are inseparable from the call to justice. For unless it is not verified in responsible moral conduct amidst a cosmos and a humanity that remain imperfect, the worship of the living God lacks integrity (cf. §44, 2; §45, 2).

[6] Let us conclude. For Israel, the mystery of God is summed up in YHWH's utter transcendence and intimate presence combined. The combination is not a compromise; both transcendence and immanence are affirmed in all their starkness; it takes a wholly transcendent God to be so wholly immanent. The combination is also vital: the sense of the divine immanence kept Israel's faith from losing touch with worldly responsibility, and the sense of God's transcendence prevented it from turning its faith into a rigid, comprehensive, definitive, know-it-all religious ideology. Consequently, Israel's sense of the divine transcendence could also be deepened by the test of the *diaspora* experience. There Judaism learned to surmise the transcendent, mysterious presence of YHWH to a humiliation that looked, to the eye untrained in looking beyond ap-

---

Scripture means, not the spirit being subordinated to a letter, but the letter replacing the soil. In the letter, the spirit is free; in the root, it is tied down. It is on the arid soil of the desert, where nothing holds, that the true spirit descended into a text, so as to seek a universal fulfillment."

pearances, like a devastating sign of God's absence [*ff*]. Accordingly, this apparent absence ended up being appreciated as a tenderer, more intimate divine presence. All of this can be put negatively as well. Judaism retained its religious identity by learning, over and over again, not to expect the living God to be a remote, immobile Archimedean point of leverage, moving the world to its own advantage without expense to itself.

All of this enables a distinguished modern Jewish philosopher, Emmanuel Lévinas, to marvel at Israel's faith, in terms that church fathers East and West as well as Thomas Aquinas would doubtlessly have admired (cf. §79, 4, b):

How vigorous is the dialectic by which the equal partnership between God and Man is established right at the heart of their incommensurability.

It also enables him to characterize Israel's religious experience as

An integral and austere humanism, coupled with difficult worship! And, the other way round, a worship that coincides with the exaltation of Man![27]

ISRAEL'S FAITH IN JEOPARDY

[§99] THE CHRISTIAN CONCEPTION OF GOD AND WESTERN ATHEISM

[1] At the beginning of this chapter, the warning cry of a seventeenth-century Christian thinker, Blaise Pascal, served to take us back to the origin of the great Tradition: the faith of Israel. Now that this chapter is about to wind up, the faith-testimony of a contemporary Jewish thinker has returned us to our Christian (and post-Christian) twentieth century. Such a homecoming calls for a few moments of reflection. Lévinas can continue, at least for another instant, to serve as our guide.

Like Pascal, Lévinas, too, has a warning cry to utter. Read in their original context, his fine outpourings in admiration of Judaism turn out to be—surprisingly—part of a *polemic*. In praising Isra-

---

[*ff*] A good indicator of this is the following. With near-perfect consistency, the Septuagint renders Heb. *b'rît* ("Covenant"), with its connotations of mutuality, not by Gk. *synthēkē* or *synthēma* ("agreement," "compact"), which it does use elsewhere, but by Gk. *diathēkē* ("last will," "testament"), with its connotations of asymmetry, and hence, of divine transcendence. The lone exception is a textual variant in 4 Kings [= MT 2 Kings] 17, 15, where *b'rît* is rendered by *synthēkē*. LXX 3 Kings 11, 11 renders *b'rît* in MT 1 Kings 11, 11 by Gk. *entolas* ("commandments"). Cf. *ConcSept* I, 300*a*-302*b*, 479*b*, 1316*a*.

el's "difficult worship" and "austere humanism," Lévinas is insisting that the Jewish conception of both God and humanity is far superior to what its Christian inheritors have made of it. Christians, Lévinas protests, have cheapened both the worship and the humanism. Their God is no longer the God of glory and majesty, but a "children's god"—the purveyor of mere indulgence and reassuring presence. Accordingly, the God of the Christians has become, in the religious imagination of much of the West, nothing but a function of human weakness accepted as a permanent (and hence, excusable) condition. Thus hopelessly tangled up in the needs and inadequacies of humankind, this God has been drawn into complicity with human irresponsibility and injustice; the most distressing example of this is the continuing irresolution of the Christian world in regard to the Holocaust. This makes it clear that the God of the Christians is not the transcendent One who, graciously as well as demandingly, calls a humanity made in the divine image to conversion and covenanted, responsible partnership (cf. §70, 4, b, [b]).[28]

This is a serious indictment, and one that must put the Christian theologian on notice. It suggests that, having been the dominant force in the shaping of Western culture in a way Judaism has never been (cf. §64, 5), modern Western Christianity may very well have to re-learn from Judaism just how fragile and subtle a configuration of themes and emphases Israel's acknowledgment of YHWH is.

Minimally, the Christian (and post-Christian) West, as well as those sections of Judaism that have traded in the faith of Israel for forms of Western Deism and agnosticism, must reflect on their historic experience in this regard. For modern liberalism and agnosticism, whether they are found in residually Christian or residually Jewish circles, have not always appreciated the delicacy of the great Jewish-Christian Tradition's profession of faith in God. It takes a great deal of care and intellectual tact (1) to integrate, in one coherent pattern of belief, the utter transcendence of the One True God with the intimate, caring presence of that same God to humanity and the world. It is equally hard to do so in such a way as (2) to recognize that humanity and the world (and all human beings and all things cosmic) truly are what they are, yet that at the same time they are truly meant, ecstatically, to bespeak the glory of God, apart from whom they would not be. Finally, it is a real challenge to do all of this in such a way as (3) to recognize that humanity, by virtue of its special resemblance to God, is both part of the cosmos and in a position of responsible stewardship over it.

With these observations, we have, of course, raised the issue of Western religious thought as a whole. But this move at once obliges us to acknowledge *Western atheism* as well. We must take time, therefore, to explain, at least briefly, how modern atheism is in part the fruit of the decline of Christian self-understanding. This move, incidentally, is theologically sound as well: it is only right that a chapter devoted to faith in the living God should end up emphasizing once again that this faith is and remains precarious —a privilege and a grace, not an insured possession.

For reasons of clarity, let us distinguish between two types of atheism, but in such a way that the distinction will not obliterate the interrelatedness between the two.

[2] The first type is *humanistic atheism*, most blatantly exemplified by Feuerbach (cf. §70, 4, a-b). Lévinas is certainly right when he points out that a narrow preoccupation with human well-being, on the part of Western Christianity, has both compromised the divine transcendence and disgraced the inherent glory and responsibility of humanity. Large segments of Western Christianity have indeed tended to make the doctrines of human sin and divine salvation into the central themes of the Christian profession of faith (§20, 2-3). Such an overemphasis on the theme of humanity's salvation is liable, sadly, to reduce both the full sense of God as creator of heaven and earth and the appreciation of the world in a religious perspective. Fervent, even thankful, reliance on the constant supervention of divine mercy and forgiveness increasingly replace the traditional Christian conviction that humanity and world as a whole are called to participate in the divine life; Israel's (and classical Christianity's) sense of high privilege in having worshipful access to the divine Glory that permeates all of creation gradually declines. Not infrequently, the acknowledgment of God's transcendence is replaced by forms of pantheism, or by a flatly agnostic, joyless, worshipless awe before a remote, faceless, impenetrable supreme being; more often it is reduced to experiences of emotional comfort in the depth of individual self-awareness. In this way, the acknowledgment of a transcendent God to whose presence humanity can publicly respond in worship and moral responsibility has come to give way, in many quarters, to the immanent religious consciousness. And this consciousness, in turn, is often primarily appreciated, not as an attunement to the living God who is present everywhere, but pri-

marily as the (remedial or constitutive, as the case may be) core of human integrity (cf. §25, 4, d).

No wonder much of Western Christianity has lost its sense of the full extent of God's Glory, both as Creator and Savior; no wonder either that in many circles the existence of such a God has come to be viewed as a mere postulate of human weakness or immaturity (cf. §70, 4, b, [b]). To the extent that this is the case, "humanity created in the divine image" has given way to "humanity leaning on God as the projected fulfillment of human needs and anxieties."[29]

But a god who keeps humanity under tutelage, no matter how gracious and merciful, is an insult to human integrity. What is more, tutelage will not work. Human persons will not settle forever for the dubious blessings of mere fiduciality; humanity will awake, arise, and even rebel. On this perspective, Lévinas explains, atheism is "the healthiest response" on the part of all those who have ceased to believe in "a rather primitive god, [who] awarded prizes, imposed sanctions, or pardoned mistakes, and who, in his goodness, treated people like perpetual children."[30] Pious Christian overdependence on an indulgent God is a reliable road to humanistic atheism.

[3] The second type is *scientific atheism.* In favoring soteriology over doxology, the Christian West began to attenuate, and eventually to sever, the connection, as fragile as it is vital, between humanity and the world with which it is continuous. The reduction of theology to soteriology, in other words, has had notable effects on the theology of the world. In many Christian contexts since the sixteenth century, salvation has scarcely been viewed as God's gift to all creation. The cosmos has been largely reduced to a mere stage on which God deals mainly (or even exclusively) with humanity (cf. §9, 1 and [i]). But such a neutralized cosmos no longer bespeaks God; not surprisingly, it will eventually also cease to provide reliable cues to God's existence (cf. §103, 2). Further down the road, such a cosmos will also cease to inspire respect, which will open the way to the modern exploitative *use* of the world by dint of mere scientific and technological *power* (cf. §102, 10).

Theological anthropology thus having parted company with cosmology, the scientific mentality has not hesitated to return the favor. In its quest for certainty, the sixteenth century began to favor geometrical, or at least "objective," empirical ways of knowing and establishing truth—that is, it uncritically favored an epistemology that took its decisive cues from the world of objects alone. In its fondness of definition (cf. §7, 1, a-b), it also favored far-reaching dissociations, such as those between nature and grace, reason and revelation, philosophy and theology (cf. §86, 3, b-c). All these biases fell into a pattern and became a threat to Christian doctrine, already threatened by the wearisome debates that had typified both the Reformation and the Counter Reformation. Not only did the various Christian orthodoxies come to depend more and more on sheer authority to enforce their increasingly controversial doctrinal positions, they also began more and more to look to natural philosophy for reliable foundations. In the Catholic world, traditionally devoted to the understanding of the natural order (cf. §82-83), this resulted in the move that prepared the ground for *scientific* (or "cosmological") *atheism.*

[a] In his book *At the Origins of Modern Atheism,* Michael J. Buckley has given us a riveting account, both of the move and of the developments it precipitated. In Buckley's interpretation of the rise of atheism, René Descartes and Isaac Newton become the main actors in the drama that reduced the Christian understanding of God's existence to a purely rational, essentially cosmological problem. But it was early seventeenth century thinkers like the Jesuit Leonard Lessius and the Minim Marin Mersenne that made the first move. By treating the God-question fundamentally as a matter of, respectively, philosophical cosmology and modern science (cf. §56, 3; §68, 1, [*l*]; §84, 2, a, [*u*]; §90, 5, [*mm*]), they effectively authorized the conceptions Descartes and Newton were to develop. When inconsistencies in these conceptions came to the surface, disciples like Nicolas Malebranche and Samuel Clarke attempted to exorcise them, but this only hastened the moment when the "god" of the philosophers and the astronomers began to die the death of a thousand theoretical qualifications. The eighteenth century clinched the development, with Denis Diderot's conversion to loquacious unbelief and Baron Paul Henri d'Holbach's extravagant but coherent interpretation of the System of Nature as wholly chaotic (cf. §86, 1, [*d*])— an interpretation that removed the need for any god responsible for design and harmony in nature.

Having surveyed these developments, Buckley offers an interpretation of disturbing simplicity. Atheism in the Christian West is substantially rooted in a *theological* failure: by leaving the question of God's existence wholly to the emerging natural sciences and the new, geometrically-inspired philosophy, Christian theology sidestepped, at the dawn of the modern era, a fundamental part of its responsibility. This inspired the development of a new conception of god, essentially cosmological, fundamentally remote and impassive, exclusively secular, almost wholly unrelated to the Scriptures, and wholly unrelated to the life, death, and resurrection of Jesus Christ—that is, an essentially non-Christian conception of god [gg].

This new conception was made pivotal, on the one hand, to the astounding discoveries of the mechanics of the solar system, and on the other hand, to the understanding of the human mind's relatedness to the physical world. Over time, however, a concept of god so integral to the knowledge of the motions of the heavens and to the understanding of human self-consciousness also became dependent on the dynamics of that knowledge and that understanding. When pressures of scientific progress were brought to bear on both, "god" progressively receded to where it became, at first marginal, and then finally, a superfluous hypothesis.

[4]   Thus, in the end, under the canopy of geometrical and

[gg] One measure of the "success" of this reconception of God in the West is that much Christian theology in the nineteenth and twentieth centuries came to regard as "classical theism" what is actually a distorted version of the classic Jewish-Christian understanding of the living God—the understanding cherished and cultivated (even if never perfectly) by the great Christian saints and sages of the classical and pre-modern eras. In our own day, this has led to curious historical and hermeneutical spectacles. Talented as well as thoroughly responsible Christian theologians will now often look back at what they take to be "classical theism" and rightly criticize it as incompatible, not only with Christian conceptions about a loving and merciful (and triune) God, but also with balanced Christian and humane conceptions about humanity itself. In doing so, they are apparently unaware that what they are rejecting is (if not totally, at least essentially) a characteristic product of *modernity*, as Michael Buckley has shown. Let us mention two telling and significant examples out of many. Bishop John A. T. Robinson's popular *Honest to God* created a stir in 1963, especially with its rejection of the traditional "theistic" notion of a remote "God out-there" as unreal and un-Christian (cf. esp. pp. 29-44). Recently, in Elizabeth A. Johnson's notable and altogether constructive monograph *She Who Is* (1992), a pointed, scholarly feminist critique of the ingrained patriarchal biases that have affected the Jewish-Christian conception of God goes hand in hand with a broad theological critique of conceptions about God that are equally dubious but of a far more recent vintage, namely, "classical theism's" understanding of God as both remote and impassive (cf. esp. pp. 19-21, 147-49, 224-25, 230-33, 246-48). We will come back to this latter theme in §§110-11.

technological rationality, autonomous, scientific mastery of the world and autonomous, self-conscious humanism became bedfellows. The more participative, interpretative ways of understanding humanity and the world, and of understanding them in their mutual connectedness (cf. §63), became intellectually suspect. Not surprisingly, so did faith (cf. §56, 12, a, [i]; §96, 4). Eventually, suspicion turned into indictment. It was increasingly realized that neither the system of nature nor the free spirit of humanity stood in need of God (now widely thought of as a mere "stopgap god"). Such a "god," in fact, might as well be dead (cf. §70, 4, b, [c]).

"God" could now become the subject of *badinerie*, whether of the polite or the banal kind (cf. §29, 2 and note 35), in the *salons* of eighteenth-century Paris and the coffee-houses of eighteenth-century London. The mission of alleged religious liberation undertaken by these establishments has been successfully continued by many of the universities, literary circles, libraries, and scientific laboratories of the nineteenth and twentieth centuries. The delicate web of relationships that is at the core of the Jewish-Christian tradition, holding the living God, humanity, and the world together in harmony, was broken, and Western Christianity had produced its own alienation.

[5] In a classical essay, T. S. Eliot has pondered the developments just outlined under the rubric of *dissociation of sensibility*.[31] Pascal was intensely and painfully aware of it, though he witnessed only the first installment of a long and increasingly commanding process; yet he obviously felt that even that beginning could not be halted, let alone reversed (cf. §96). Dissociation was there to stay. But the depth of his pain at the dissociation indicates how deeply the established Jewish-Christian tradition had cherished its understanding of humanity and the cosmos as God's creation, and its understanding of God as the sole Creator of all that is. As a result, theology, anthropology, and cosmology had always been inseparable—if often quite properly distinguishable as well as distinguished in practice. But what the New Learning was beginning to take apart was a whole world-picture—one in which the web of connections between the experience and understanding, respectively, of God, of humanity, and of the world, while always the subject of lively philosophical and theological debate, was fundamentally never in doubt.

[6] It is time to study these connections in some detail. By the early Middle Ages, Christian faith had become one of the principal cultural factors that gave rise, in the West, to the excitements of philosophy. To some of the fruits of the reflective endeavors of the Christian Middle Ages, then, the next chapter must turn.

CHAPTER 10

The Living God:
Two Medieval Syntheses

AGAIN: THE PRIMACY OF WORSHIP

[§100] REFLECTION AND TRANSCENDENCE

[1] Much as thoughtful reflection is integral to the catholic Tradition, an urgent question arises whenever the issue of theological reflection comes up. Given the native eagerness of human intelligence, what will keep religious thought catholic—that is, both *faithful* to the integrity of the great Tradition and *open* to the challenges inevitably entailed by existence in place and time (cf. §1)? The answer must be: the central faith-experience of which the great Tradition is the most direct expression (cf. §35, 1, c). The Christian understanding of God must reflect the tradition of *Christian worship*—both its practice and its authoritative forms (cf. §23, 1). It is primarily in worship that the organic connection between God, humanity, and world become a matter of lived experience, of the kind that can support genuinely catholic thought.

In this regard, Christianity is, again, but the heir of Israel. In the *tôdāh*-tradition common to both Jews and Christians, all public profession of belief and all reflection on it is rooted in the act of worship, which is also the context of all profession of shortcoming and sinfulness (cf. §34; §36, 3; §45; §97, 2, [j]).

Now worship fundamentally consists in the never-ending sacrifice of praise and thanksgiving offered to God, in a world that bears witness, both to the glory of the God who made it and to its own continuing imperfection. Thus praise and thanksgiving generate the supplication that befits a community aware both of its privileged access to God and of its deep inadequacy in the presence of God. In that presence, the worshiping community gathers up itself, along with its scattered experience in the world, so as to offer up to God both itself and its experience, to be integrated and made whole as well as holy in the offering, in anticipation of the world to come.

In doing so, the community both actualizes its creatureliness and attains its responsive identity, while also immediately returning both of them to God in thanksgiving and hope. Why? For all the mutuality that worship in the Jewish-Christian tradition involves, it is an experience of radical asymmetry. Much as worshipers gain identity and integration from the act of responding to God with all they are and have, they know that the focus of worship is neither their response nor the identity or the integration they attain, but in the God who prompts and enables the response. In the *perichōrēsis* of transcendent divine presence and divinely empowered creaturely response, the living, all-holy God is and remains sovereignly dominant (cf. §23, 4, b; §35, 1).

[2] This chapter will study two classic instances of the Christian West's reflection on the living God. From what has just been explained it follows that the first test of the adequacy of these instances will have to derive from worship. The instances discussed in the present chapter—texts by Anselm and Aquinas—will turn out to stand that test. This is not surprising; the instances have been selected with the test in view. But the test itself must be called to mind, if only to make this clear once again: any authoritative Christian conception of God must so place the world and humanity in relation to God as to do justice, not only to the inherent dignity of creation, but also to that which alone prompts true worship: the presence of a wholly transcendent God (cf. §35).

[3] At the same time, we should be careful not to push our suspicions vis-à-vis thought and reflection to excess. After all, worship itself gives rise to thought, and with more vigor than most other experiences. In fact, could this deep yearning for theology betray a deep affinity between worship and thought?

On the one hand, let us recognize that it is part of human intellectual integrity to wish to challenge, understand, interpret, and explain a phenomenon like worship, at once so all-embracing and so mysterious, and so disconcertingly *concrete*—so thoroughly *positive* and *particular*. Particular things as such cannot be adequately captured by means of universal concepts—*individuum est ineffabile*. And precisely because the particular and the obvious resist complete domestication by the idea, they leave us no rest, whether by dint of charm or by chronic intractability; they keep impinging on us; they

are and remain the primary challenge offered to the human mind.[1]
Frustration is inherent in intellectual understanding.

But on the other hand, let us recognize that there is relief in
thought as well. It is precisely by bumping up against the relentless-
ly occurring particular that our minds are also driven to the discovery of their universalizing capacity, which allows us to take a mea-
sured distance from the wear and tear of the particular (and, at
times, from its boredom). Philosophy consoles. Why is it that meditative persons will acquiesce in being kept unquiet by the never-
ceasing ebb and flow of things? Because they have come to realize,
by dint of reflection, that their identity is ultimately not at the mercy of the swirl of the ever-particular, ever-changing phenomena.
Even more, they often realize that in reflection they enjoy a deep
affinity with an eternal, as-yet-unattainable order of stable truth—an
order ultimately anchored in God. Thus, at bottom, the intellectual
life is an exercise in both human identity and ecstasy.

Let us conclude. Of all particular things and activities, worship
tends to be especially irritating to the universalizing human mind
(cf. §27, 4); hence, too, it tends to drive the mind to reflective
thought with special insistence. But if it is true that reflection is
one of the truly profound human responses to the divine immanence and transcendence, then those who primarily profess their
faith in worship are justified in expecting, not only challenge, but
also deep support from reflective endeavor. For in the end, reflection on God is intellectual worship, not only on account of its divine subject-matter, but also on account of the God-given thirst for
understanding with which the divine subject-matter is pursued (cf.
§8, 8).

[4] The great Tradition has indeed proved that the practice of
Christian worship, the profession of Christian faith, and intellectual
reflection fundamentally require and support one another (cf. §12,
1, a). The next two sections of the present chapter will exemplify
this. We will first discuss the *Proslogion,* in which Anselm of Canterbury develops what is usually called the *ontological argument.* We will
then turn to the *Summa theologiæ* of Thomas Aquinas to study his
"five ways" to demonstrate God's existence.

[5] A final preliminary caution. Appreciating the thinking of past
masters, especially masters as distant from us as two great medieval
Western theologians, is a demanding exercise, not only in theological reflection, but also in historical and cultural hermeneutics.

Thus it is important, in advance, to stop at a few observations relevant to the sound interpretation of the texts we are about to study.

[a] *Any* form of knowledge and *any* level of intellectual accomplishment (as well as any level or form of commitment to responsible living) are capable of stirring the human mind to a reflective awareness of both itself and its native attunement to God.[2] However, much as the mind's self-awareness and its aspiration to the transcendent are its birthright, both are worked out under the conditions of place and time. This means that only with such tools as are culturally and historically available will the human mind ever give an account of its affinity with higher truth (cf. §101, 7). Thus all *expressions* of the mind's reflective self-awareness and its aspiration to the transcendent will bear the traces of such forms of knowledge and such shapes of responsibility as have given rise to the self-awareness and the aspiration themselves. That is, *all* expressions of self-awareness and aspiration to the transcendent must be *interpreted.* This must be done in a spirit of hermeneutical modesty, openness, and sensitivity to cultural differences, in the conviction that this side of the eschaton there is no single universal, perennial, or definitive way of insuring, or giving valid expression to, either the mind's self-discovery or its itinerary to God (cf. §64, 3; §91, 3; 4, a).

[6] With these observations in mind, then, let us turn to the Christian Middle Ages, when Western thought first began to discover the profound intellectual congruence of the Christian faith—the faith it was still broadly aware of having inherited from Israel— with the dynamics of the human mind operating to the full extent of its reflective capacity.

THEOLOGY, ANTHROPOLOGY, COSMOLOGY

[§101] ANSELM: FAITH SEEKING UNDERSTANDING

[1] The ontological argument comes to us from the small but intellectually spacious world of the monasteries and cathedral schools of the tenth and eleventh centuries. In those cradles of modern Western civilization, the liberal arts first flourished, in the form of elementary curricula grounded in grammar, logic, and rhetoric—those permanently indispensable tools of interpretation and understand-

ing, trivial only in name [a].

The author of this great early medieval attempt at developing a reflective, truly intellectual insight into the Christian faith-awareness of God, was Saint Anselm of Canterbury (c. 1033-1109), a Benedictine monk born in Lombardy. After unsettled *Wanderjahre* in Italy and France he had attended the monastery school at the famous Abbey of Le Bec in Normandy in 1059, where he had become a monk, and soon after, the community's prior. Kept busy by a truly original intellectual talent as well as a way with people, he was a teacher, a writer, a spiritual guide, an administrator, as well as a vigorous correspondent. In 1078 he became the monastery's abbot, only to be called to England in 1093, to succeed Lanfranc, the great church administrator who had also been his tutor at Le Bec, as Archbishop of Canterbury.

The ontological argument as it is generally known occurs at the beginning of Anselm's *Proslogion*. This brief, highly original work was written in 1078, shortly after the *Monologion*, which already displays the author's characteristic interest in the exploration of the faith by means of strictly intellectual meditation, though it remains far more deeply indebted to Saint Augustine's analysis of desire.[3] Anselm's biographer, Eadmer, tells the story of the difficult birth of the insight that lies at the root of the *Proslogion*—an insight that was to exercise the Western mind for centuries to come:

> ... it occurred to him to inquire if it would be possible to prove by one single, brief argument what we believe and preach about God, namely, that he is eternal, unchangeable, omnipotent, all present everywhere, incomprehensible, just, kind, merciful, truthful, truth,
> 5   goodness, justice, and some other things; and to show how all these are one reality in him. And this, as he himself would say, gave him great trouble, partly because this thinking took away his desire for food, drink and sleep, and partly—and this bothered him more—because it interfered with the attention which he ought to pay to mat-
> 10   ins and to the other divine offices. When he became aware of this, and still did not succeed in entirely gaining a hold on what he was seeking, he supposed that this kind of thinking was a temptation of

---

[a] "Trivial" derives from *trivium*, the three-layered lower end of the medieval liberal-arts curriculum, consisting of grammar, logic, and rhetoric. For a touching thumbnail sketch of one early school, cf. R. W. Southern's brief account of Fulbert of Chartres and his band of disciples, in *The Making of the Middle Ages*, pp. 188-94. The entire fourth chapter of this book ("The Tradition of Thought") is relevant to our theme.

15 the devil and he tried to banish it far from his mind. But the more strenuously he worked at this, the more this very thinking continued to plague him. And behold, one night, during the night office, the grace of God shone in his heart, and the matter became clear to his understanding, and it filled his innermost being with measureless joy and exultation.

To keep a record of his precious insight, Anselm had, precariously, taken notes on wax tablets. They very nearly got lost, by the kind of mishap that invariably threatens (at least in biographies) the survival of great ideas. Finally, however, from a reconstructed version of his notes securely transcribed on parchment, Anselm

20 ... composed a volume, small in size but great in gravity of discourse and most subtle contemplation, which he called the *Proslogion*. For in this work he addresses either himself or God.[4]

[2] Few arguments in the history of Christian thought have provoked so much commentary and have so captivated the philosophical imagination of the West as Anselm's ontological argument. Itself the record of an intuition, it has triggered many more [b]; but like all intuitions, it has left a great many minds dissatisfied, and hence, more than a little eager to articulate the reasons why the argument does not pay off in the end. Thus the argument's "effective history" (*Wirkungsgeschichte*) is so impressive as to make many modern interpreters doubtful about the possibility of recovering its "original" meaning from underneath the mountain of historic endorsements, interpretations, critiques, and outright rejections [c].

---

[b] One of the more memorable ones, quoted by R. W. Southern (*Saint Anselm and his Biographer*, p. 58), is Bertrand Russell walking down Trinity Lane, Cambridge, on his way home, tossing a tin of tobacco he had just bought up in the air, and exclaiming, "Great Scott, the ontological argument is sound." The year is 1894.

[c] R. W. Southern offers an historian's perceptive (but almost wholly non-philosophical and non-theological) interpretation in *Saint Anselm and his Biographer*, pp. 57-66. For a competent discussion that pays attention to some important interpretations, including Karl Barth's, cf. the introduction and commentary in M. J. Charlesworth's edition of the *Proslogion*, pp. 1-99. Thomas C. Oden (*The Living God*, pp. 174-79) briefly reviews the argument and gives bibliographical references to its principal interpretations. For Karl Barth's full explanation, cf. his *Fides quærens intellectum* (ET *Anselm: Fides Quaerens Intellectum*). For a series of modern responses, including (again) Karl Barth's, cf. *The Many-Faced Argument*, edited by John Hick and Arthur C. McGill. Most recently, Iris Murdoch has added her (atheistic) interpretation of the ontological argument and its effective history to the record: *Metaphysics as a Guide to Morals*, pp. 391-460.

[a] The hermeneutical problem starts right with Eadmer's account of the argument's origin. As Southern rightly observes,[5] Eadmer's account construes Anselm's treatment of the divine attributes, which occupies chapters 6-13 and 18-26 of the *Proslogion*, as the heart of the work (ll. 3-6). In doing so, however, Eadmer seems to overlook, at least at first blush, the fact that the opening chapters, which contain the ontological argument, are wholly unprecedented and original, and hence, far more likely to have moved Anselm in the manner described than the remainder of the work. Yet what gives Eadmer's account great credibility (so much so that it must be considered a decisive hermeneutical key to the *Proslogion*'s original meaning) are the following two features. First of all, Eadmer mentions Anselm's intention to offer a concise but conclusive *intellectual* argument to settle the issue of the divine nature and attributes *as understood by the Christian faith* (ll. 1-2). There is no suggestion, in other words, that in pondering God's nature and attributes Anselm meant to prescind from the Christian faith; consequently, it is even less likely that he thought that God's existence needed demonstration by rational argument. In fact, the opposite is true. For (and this is the second feature) Eadmer situates the entire argument's gestation period and birth in the context of the *opus Dei*—the monastic practice of praying the divine office in common. Moreover, he uses the language of spiritual discernment to describe Anselm's experience: while at matins with his community, Anselm received the gracious gift of intellectual certainty, not so much about God's nature and attributes as about God's *actuality*—that is, what is involved in God being *God*, or in God's "existence." This gift takes the shape of a profound experience of harmony and consolation in the soul (cf. §79, 2, a), for which Anselm had been prepared by his faithful endurance of a period of desolation and doubt (ll. 6-18). In this way Eadmer suggests that Anselm's argument, taken as a whole, is inseparable from three themes: the communal praise of God, the Christian's need for confirmation in the faith by being assured of God's presence, and the congruence between faith and reason. Anselm's own wording confirms these suggestions (cf. §101, 4-7).

[3] Anselm writes:

[c. 1] ... I acknowledge, Lord, and I give thanks for it, that you have created this image of yours in me, so that mindful of you I

might think of you, love you. But [your image] is so worn down by
the abrasion of vices, so beclouded by the smoke of sins, that it can-
5   not do what it is made for, unless you renew and restore it. I do not,
Lord, attempt to penetrate your eminence, for I judge my understanding in no measure adequate to it; but I do wish in some measure to understand your truth, which my heart believes in and loves.
For I do not seek to understand so that I may believe, but I believe
10   so that I may understand. For I believe this, too: "unless I believe,
I will not understand" [cf. Is 7, 9 Vg]. ...

[c. 2] Therefore, Lord, you, who endow faith with understanding,
grant to me that I may understand (insofar as you know it to be
profitable) that you *are*, as we believe, and that you are what we be-
15   lieve. Now we believe that you are something so great that it is impossible to think of anything greater. Or are we to infer—since "the
fool has said in his heart, there is no God" [Ps 14 (Vg 13), 1; 53 (Vg
52), 1]—that there is no such nature? But surely, when this very
same fool hears just what I say, "something so great that nothing
20   greater can be thought of," he understands what he hears; and what
he understands is in his understanding, even if he does not understand it to *be* in reality. For it is one thing for something to be in
the understanding, and another thing to understand something to
be. For when a painter thinks in advance of what he is going to
25   make, he indeed has it in his understanding, but he understands that
there is no reality yet to what he has not made yet. But once he has
painted it, he both has in his understanding what he has made and
he understands it to be real. Thus even a fool must grant that "something so great that nothing greater can be thought of" is at least in
30   his understanding, for when he hears it he understands it, and whatever is understood is in the understanding. Now surely what is so
great that nothing greater can be thought of cannot be in the understanding alone. For if it is indeed in the understanding alone, it is
possible to think of it as being in reality as well, which is greater.
35   Thus, if what is so great that *nothing* greater can be thought of is in
the understanding alone, then the very thing that is so great that
nothing greater can be thought of leaves the possibility of thinking of
something greater. But surely this cannot be. Indubitably, therefore,
something so great that no one is capable of thinking of anything
40   greater *exists*, both in the understanding and in reality. ...

[c. 3] Now, naturally, this [something] so truly *is*, that it cannot
even be thought of as not being. For it is possible to think of something as *being* that cannot be thought of as not being; and this something is greater than something that *can* be thought of as not being.
45   ...   Therefore, something so great that nothing greater can be
thought of *is* so truly that it cannot even be thought of as not being.
And this you are, Lord our God. You *are* so truly, Lord my God,

that you cannot even be thought of as not being. And rightly so.
For if there were a mind capable of thinking of something better
50   than you, the creature would transcend the creator, and sit in judgment on the creator—something utterly absurd. And indeed, anything else that is can be thought of as not being, except you alone.
Therefore, you possess being most truly of all, and hence, most of
all; for whatever else there is possesses being not so truly, and hence,
55   less. Why, then, is it that "the fool has said in his heart: there is no
God," since it is so obvious to the rational mind that you *are* most of
all? Why, except because he is stupid and a fool? ...

[*c.* 4] But how is it that he "has said in his heart" what he has
been unable to "think of," or how is it that he has been unable to
60   "think of" what he "has said in his heart," since "saying [some-
thing] in the heart" and "thinking of" [something] are the same?
If (or rather, since) he truly has *both* thought of it (since he has said
it in his heart) *and* not said it in his heart (because he has not been
capable of thinking of it), it follows that there is more than one way
65   for something to be said in the heart and thought of. For it is one
thing to think of the word that refers to a reality; it is something else
to understand what that reality itself is. For clearly no one who understands what God is can think of God as not being, even though
he may say these words in his heart, either without any meaning or
70   with some outlandish meaning. For God is "what is so great that
anything greater cannot be thought of." Whoever understands this
well will certainly understand that [God] is just this, in such a way as
not to be capable of being thought of as not being. Whoever, therefore, understands God to be in this way is incapable of thinking of
75   him as not being.

I thank you, good Lord, I thank you, for what I used to believe by
your gift I now understand by your enlightenment, in such a way
that, if I should not want to believe that you are, I would be unable
not to understand it.[6]

This fascinating text begs for commentary. By way of opening
moves, three sets of observations, already suggested by Eadmer's account of the *Proslogion*'s genesis (§101, 2, a), come to mind.

[4] The first concerns the place of *praise and prayer* in the first
chapters of the *Proslogion*. Anselm's whole argumentation is encompassed and permeated by *worship*: he begins by praying for understanding (ll. 12-15) and ends by giving thanks for it (ll. 76-79). This
is consistent with the original title of the *Proslogion*, which was *Fides
quœrens intellectum*: "Faith Seeking Understanding."[7] This splendid
phrase, ultimately of Augustinian inspiration,[8] now occurs right at
the end of the first chapter, where it marks the precise point where

explicit prayer turns into prayerful theological reflection. This is consistent with the fact that from the outset, Anselm regards the understanding he is seeking as a *grace*—a God-given gift of intellectual enlightenment. Far from suggesting that he is going to offer a rational argument that is both free-standing and conclusive, he insists that the understanding he is seeking is not independent of faith (ll. 9-11), let alone adequate to the reality of God (ll. 5-7; 13-14; cf. 49-51). Anselm, in other words, is attempting *an intellectualization of the Christian faith-experience of God's presence and attributes* (ll. 13-15)—the experience shared by Christians in worship and common life, at the Church's proclamation, yet always imperiled, too, by failure and sin.

[a] This interpretation is confirmed by an alternative approach to the text. From a literary point of view, the opening chapters of the *Proslogion* can responsibly be read as a worshiper's meditative struggle, first with the text, "the fool has said in his heart, there is no God," and subsequently with the question what a fool could possibly mean by "God" in saying this. According to the *ordo* of the divine office as set out in the eighteenth chapter of the Rule of Benedict, this text, the opening verse of both Pss 14 (Vg 13) and 53 (Vg 52), occurs twice a week: in the second vigil of the office of Matins on Tuesday, and in the office of Prime on Thursdays.[9] If we combine the prominence of the fool's words in the *Proslogion* with Eadmer's insistence that Anselm was so preoccupied by his intellectual worries that his ability to participate in worship was sorely tested, is it fanciful to suggest that this indicates the extent to which theological reflection, in Anselm's mind, is inextricably linked with worship—the basic shape of faith (§35)?

[5] The second theme is *the believer's need for confirmation in faith.* What is the point of the intellectualization offered by the *Proslogion*? Anselm is very explicit on this point. Our knowledge and love of God are rooted in our native attunement to God—in our being created in God's image and likeness. But given human weakness and sinfulness (both of them well exemplified by the fool in the Psalm), our native affinity with God is diminished, and hence, our knowledge and love of God have become precarious (ll. 1-5). Only God can renew the divine image in us, and one way in which God can do so is by graciously granting us the kind of understanding (*intellectus*) that illuminates, and thus supports, our knowledge and

love of God. In Anselm's view, therefore, reflection on the faith serves to confirm the faith, by enhancing the believer's affective awareness of God's presence. The point of the argument, therefore, is not any proof of God's mere existence, but the recovery and reinforcement, by means of reflective understanding, of the believer's sense of God's *reality*—a reality understood to be so intense as to be unique. Hence, its impact on the believer is wholly unlike the impact of other beings, all of which, being finite, can be *thought of* as non-existing (l. 44; ll. 51-52). Yes, it is nothing short of folly to think of so real a God as non-existing.

> [a] The final statement of the argument (ll. 76-79), therefore, must not be interpreted to mean that Anselm expects firm understanding simply to supplant feeble faith. In context, it is to be read as a hyperbolic affirmation of a commonplace in spiritual theology: the experienced gift of inner enlightenment and understanding can be so comforting that certainty of conviction (especially when summed up, as in this case, in a riveting formula) seems henceforth impregnable, even in the teeth of the possibility of future doubts about the faith [d].

[6] Thirdly, there is the most important theme of the *Proslogion*: the *congruence between faith and reason*. But just what kind of understanding is Anselm seeking? That question is, of course, inseparable from the question as to how he understands the word *cogitare* ("thinking of") in relation to God.

Once again, Anselm is unequivocal about the fact that the understanding (*intellectus*) he is seeking cannot conceivably be adequate to God, for God is transcendent (ll. 5-7; cf. 49-51). In fact, his text suggests that he is not really looking for a conception of God at all. The main reason for this is that he already has one—the one furnished by faith: "that which is so great that nothing greater can be thought of." What, then, *is* Anselm seeking to achieve? He says: an understanding (not strictly of God as such, but) *of God as Christians believe God to be* (ll. 13-15).

---

[d] For a much later parallel, cf. the following hyperbole from the autobiography of Ignatius of Loyola (nr. 30; *St. Ignatius' Own Story*, p. 23): "These things which he saw [=inner visions of Christ and of the Blessed Virgin] gave him at the time great strength, and were always a striking confirmation of his faith, so much so that he has often thought to himself that if there were no Scriptures to teach us these matters of faith, he was determined to die for them, merely because of what he had seen."

Anselm's search, therefore, is for a genuinely intellectual *understanding of the faith* (*intellectus fidei*). Now it is in keeping with the intellectual aims of his search that he should not resort to the authoritative language of *faith*—the Creed, Scripture and the great Tradition. Faith has *prompted the search* for understanding; it is not the *answer* to it. Thus, characteristically, he looks elsewhere. He appeals to an age-old, central theme of Augustinian anthropology, couched in a no less central Augustinian idiom—the word *cogitatio* and the ideas associated with it.

In the seventh book of the *Confessions*, Augustine recalls how, long before his conversion, he had noticed that he had begun to prefer things incorruptible to things corruptible. Now, in light of his present faith, he can interpret this elementary philosophic experience and describe it as a first, implicit affirmation on God, borne on the wings of aspiration:

... thus I was acknowledging that, whatever you might be, you were incorruptible. For no soul has ever been, or will ever be, able *to think of* [*cogitare*] *anything better than you*, for *you are the highest and best good of all.* Now since it is absolutely true and certain that the incorruptible is to be preferred to the corruptible, and since I was now attempting to exercise that preference myself, I was now trying to be able to attain, in thought [*cogitatione*], something better than you, my God, unless you were incorruptible.[10]

When Anselm prays for an understanding of what he believes, he already knows what he believes, namely (and here it is imperative to note his vocabulary), that God is greater than anything we can "think of" (*cogitare*). Whatever thoughts our accumulated and integrated experience of the past may awaken in us,[11] and whatever higher ideas and aspirations our hearts' desires for future happiness may inspire in us, we know that no *cogitatio* of our own can ever involve the full knowledge of God. Yet we *are* aware that *the dynamism that prompts thoughts* in us is inexhaustible; we will spontaneously move on and on, in the direction of the ever-greater; our souls are kept restless by the pull of perfection; this dynamism is so real that, in order to doubt our being drawn by a reality beyond any reality that could possibly occur to us in our *cogitationes*, we would have to deny our very self-awareness. That reality beyond any reality, therefore, is real; it simply must be. And it must be God [*e*].

[*e*] In interpreting Anselm's use of *cogitatio* in terms of its Augustinian antecedents, the present treatment implies that Karl Barth is correct in claiming that, at Anselm's hands, the Name of God is a given of *faith*; hence, it never becomes

[7]   It is precisely at this point that the occasion for specifically *conceptual argumentation* arises.   To develop it, Anselm naturally grasps for such theoretical tools as he has at hand (cf. §100, 5, a). However (as we will argue), the tools will prove to be interesting rather than adequate to the task of articulating his intuition in such a form as to make it philosophically compelling.

No wonder that it is also precisely at this point that disagreement with the *Proslogion* was instantaneous.   It took the form of a rough and ready piece entitled "Somebody's Reply to This on Behalf of the Fool," written by a fellow-monk, named Gaunilo, of the Abbey of Marmoutiers, near Tours, in France.[12]   While not uninteresting in themselves, Gaunilo's objections badly needed refinement, and refined they were, as well as authoritatively endorsed, almost two centuries later, when Thomas Aquinas offered, in both of his *Summas*, precise refutations of Anselm's argument (or at least of Anselm's argument as he knew it, in its standardized, simplified form).[13]   Thus it is to Aquinas that the tradition owes the most articulate expression of its running battle with Anselm's ontological argument.   Let us briefly investigate and interpret the problem.

[a]   Anselm's argument is based on two theses.   The first is in the area of *grammar*, which deals with the *true meaning of words* (ll. 65-67: "thinking of a word is not the same as understanding the reality the word refers to").   Here, Anselm maintains that *the meaning of the word "God"* is: "something so great that it is impossible to think of anything greater"* (ll. 15-16); this understanding, he thinks, being shared by Christians, is a viable basis for conceptual argument.   The second thesis is in the area of *logic*, which deals with the *structures of reasoning*.   Here, Anselm maintains, *real existence adds something to the idea*: if the thought of God is "in the understanding alone, it is possible to think of it in reality as well, *which is greater*" (ll. 33-34).

---

an issue for purely rational debate, in the sense of an independent "natural" intellectual inquiry *displacing* (or *suspending*) faith, as Charlesworth seems to argue (cf. *Proslogion*, pp. 40-46).   But our interpretation also implies a criticism: Barth overlooks Anselm's indebtedness to the Augustinian idea of humanity's *native*, and in that sense, *natural* desire for God.   Anselm is relying (not just on faith and revelation, as Barth would have him do, but) also on anthropology, except that this anthropology does not anticipate the intellectualism of Aquinas and scholasticism; rather, it harks back to Augustine's theological interpretation of *natural desire* (cf. §67, 1).

[b] Aquinas begins by agreeing with Anselm on several points, although he is not slow to identify a few problems connected with the two propositions as well. First, our native desire for happiness does indeed suggest the existence of God. But (Aquinas explains) it does so only vaguely; it does not *demonstrate* it; we have to remind ourselves that there are those who think of happiness in terms of mere riches or self-indulgence.[14] Secondly, Aquinas agrees that *the concept of God in and of itself* does imply God's existence, for God is "being itself";[15] in this regard, the idea of God is unlike the concept of any other reality. (Anselm would agree: ll. 41-43.) However, Aquinas continues, *our understanding of God* is necessarily inadequate.[16] (Again, Anselm would agree.) So far so good.

Now comes the parting of the ways. Because of the inadequacy of our understanding of God, *we* cannot draw any adequate conclusions from any *conception* of God that *we* might have, not even the conclusion that God is bound to exist. In fact, from a purely grammatical and conceptual point of view, even the understanding of God as "something so great that it is impossible to think of anything greater" is debatable. Catholics are likely to understand and agree with it, given the meaning and significance of the word "God" established by virtue of faith-tradition and usage; but again, there are others (equally endowed with intelligence!) who have thought differently about God; some of them have even denied the existence of God altogether.[17] Finally, there is a basic epistemological problem: we may have a *conception* of something, but this does not entitle us to form synthetic judgments about it *by virtue of that conception alone* [*f*].[18]

[c] First of all, therefore, Anselm's application of *grammar* turns out to fail. His proposed signification of the *word* "God" suffers from a lack of *wider credibility*. The phrase "something so great that nothing greater can be thought of" does indeed convey the *Christian sense of God*, but it does not represent a *conception of God* that is likely to have *universal* appeal. Anselm, in other words,

---

[*f*] Immanuel Kant (who, like Aquinas, knew Anselm's argument only in its reduced, standardized form) was to add to this that real existence adds nothing to the content of an idea. By way of parallel, one could say that ten dollars are ten dollars, regardless whether they are real or not; all their real existence does is put the amount in my pocket. For Kant's explanation, cf. *Kritik der reinen Vernunft*, B 620-31, A 592-603, esp. B 626-29, A 598-601 (*Werke*, ed. Weischedel, vol. 2, pp. 529-36, esp. 533-35; ET [Smith], pp. 500-07, esp. 504-06).

has not committed himself yet (as Aquinas was to do) to the habit of *dispassionate, precise definition* of words; he still understands
the word "God" with its entire Christian retinue—with the fuller
resonance it enjoys in worship, where it helps draw the whole
person, and even entire communities, into the abandon proper
to faith [g].

Secondly, the *logic* of Anselm's argument founders. It is based
on the axiom that "what is absolutely eminent in thought cannot but exist in reality." Now even if it should be granted that
the axiom applies at all, it suffers from a lack of *wider applicability.*
It applies only within the limited universe of discourse shaped by
the Christian experience, and within that universe, only to the
one isolated case of the concept of God [h]. But it so happens that rules of logic are authoritative largely because they can
be marshalled in the service of universal, or at least widely
shared, understanding. Consequently, a reasoning that only
applies to God cannot be said to satisfy the demands of broadly
shared intellectual understanding—that is, of the kind of understanding that we wish to enjoy, not only in relation to God, but
in relation to realities other than God as well [i].

---

[g] Again, there is an echo of Augustine here. In the course of a discussion of
the appropriateness of the use of "person" and "hypostasis" in speaking about
God, Augustine had indicated that language is but the lowest tier of a graded
structure of total understanding that includes thought and, in and beyond
thought, reality itself: ... verius enim cogitatur Deus quam dicitur, et verius est
quam cogitatur ("There is more truth in thought of God than in speech of God,
and God more truly *is* than can be thought"; *De Trinitate* VII, 4, 7; *PL* 42, col.
939). By contrast, Aquinas' epistemology primarily operates, not on dynamism,
but on *definition.* However, by the norms of appreciative hermeneutics, Aquinas
must be said to have failed, in rejecting Anselm's argument, to appreciate the connotations of Anselm's *cogitatio,* by simply equating it with *intellectus.* (Incidentally,
Anselm had made some such distinction in his Reply to Gaunilo, *c.* 4: Schmitt I,
pp. 133-34; Charlesworth, pp. 176-77.)

[h] In his Reply (nr. 6), Gaunilo had suggested that if Anselm were right, then
the peerless "Lost Island" from the world of fables had to exist as well, by virtue
of its very superiority to all islands. Anselm replied *ad hominem* (*c.* III): if the logic
of his argument applied to such an island, he was prepared to go and find it and
give it to his opponent. But of course, he observed, from the very nature of the
proposition, the logic of the idea of "a reality so great that nothing greater could
be thought of" could apply only to God. Cf. Schmitt I, pp. 128, 133 (in Charlesworth's edition, pp. 162-65, 174-77).

[i] Recall that it is typical of the great Western monotheisms to require a link
between their understanding of God and their understanding of everything else
there is to understand (§67, 4, b).

[8] The significance of the opening section of the *Proslogion*, therefore, lies in the conceptual challenge it poses rather than in the way it meets it. Anselm is a pioneer, even if his technical skills as a philosophical theologian are inadequate to the task of approaching God and the Christian faith with the full freedom and integrity that human reason is inherently capable of. Only this latter kind of approach is likely to be recognized and respected, by believers and unbelievers alike, as truly intellectual and universalistic, and hence, as worthy of both humanity and God [*j*].

[9] Still, the story does not end here. Curiously, both Aquinas and most of the tradition after him seem to have overlooked the fact that Anselm's own argument is still incomplete at this point. In their eagerness to point out that the opening sections of the *Proslogion* do not hold water in rational-philosophical terms, they have interrupted Anselm in mid-argument and left him there. As a result, most readers of the *Proslogion* have joined the tradition in remembering Anselm's argument only in a standardized, curtailed form, by overlooking a text a few chapters further down in the work —one that is integral to Anselm's inquiry. In fact, it is precisely this neglected passage that makes of the *Proslogion* a landmark of lasting importance in philosophical theology, for it reflects a conception of God that is the fruit of an experience of divine transcendence so towering as to engage the deepest integrity of human persons.

Right in the middle of his prayerful meditations on the divine attributes that follow the part of argument already formulated, Anselm interrupts himself and returns to prayer. He writes:

> [*c.* 14] Have you found what you were seeking, my soul? You were seeking God, and you have found him to be something that is the highest of all—*so good that it is impossible to think of anything better.* ...
> But if you have found him, why is it that you do not experience what
> 5   you have found? Why is it, Lord God, that, if my soul has found you, it does not experience you? ...
>   Lord, my God, you who have formed and reformed me, tell my desiring soul *what you are beyond what it has seen,* so that it may in all purity see what it desires to see. It is straining to see more, and
> 10   *beyond what it has seen it sees nothing but darkness;* or rather, it does not see darkness (for there is none in you), but it sees that, due to its own darkness, it cannot see more. Why is this, Lord, why is this? Is

---

[*j*] Maurice Blondel and Karl Rahner were to make analogous points many centuries later (§85, 3-4; §25, 2, a; 3, a; §87, 2, a).

15   its eye darkened on account of its own infirmity, or is it dazzled by
      your refulgence? But surely it is both darkened of itself and dazzled
      by you. ... What purity, what simplicity, what certainty and reful-
      gence is there! *More, for sure, than can be understood by creatures.*
      [*c.* 15] *Therefore, Lord, not only are you so great that it is impossible to*
20   *think of anything greater; you are something greater than it is possible to*
      think of at all. For given that it is possible to think of something of
      this latter kind as really being, *if you are not this very thing, it would be*
      possible to think of something greater—which cannot be.
      [*c.* 16]   Yes, Lord, this is the inaccessible light in which you
25   dwell.[19]

In this passage, Anselm takes a decisive step beyond the ones he
has taken in the opening chapters of the *Proslogion*, and with it, he
puts the whole quest for intellectual understanding definitively in
its place. Such intellectual clarity as he has achieved so far, Anselm
has to admit to himself, fails to satisfy his quest for God. This is
hardly surprising, for *God's greater-than-thinkable greatness consists pre-*
cisely in God's not being able to be thought of at all. In the final analysis,
therefore, the definition "so great that it is impossible to think of
anything greater" pushes the quest for understanding beyond all
articulate, conceptual thought (cf. ll. 7-12; 19-23); with that, the
original definition of God pushes itself over the edge as well. In a
paradoxical move (but one familiar to those who believe: §67, 4),
Anselm's quest for intellectual understanding attains its completion
in the very act of passing beyond the furthest thinkable limit; the
divine attributes Anselm has set out to detail in the *Proslogion* turn
out to be rooted in pure transcendence.

It is precisely here, however, that Anselm's intellectual journey
rejoins the Christian tradition of educated ignorance about God
(§67), rooted in the conception of both God and humanity revealed to Israel, treasured by it, and bequeathed by Israel to the
Christian Church (§§97-98). That conception recognizes humanity
as natively attuned to the utterly transcendent reality of God. But
this God is also the One who graciously seeks to establish the divine
presence at the heart of humanity, by a self-communication that will
both baffle and deeply enlighten the human understanding, and fill
with "measureless joy and exultation" the innermost being of believers and worshipers—people like Anselm himself (cf. §101, 1).

[a]   It is precisely this outer edge of the ontological argument
that is the most reliable touchstone wherewith to test the philosophic mettle of the ontological argument's retrievals in the

modern era, with its penchant for an idealism based on the
"turn to the subject." Of the many significant versions, none
are as clear and as symptomatic of the modern tendency to
weight the relationship between divine transcendence and human inwardness in favor of the latter as the version developed by
René Descartes.

Descartes reasons as follows. I observe, innate in myself, the
certain idea of infinite substance. Since I myself am but a finite
substance, my observation forces me to affirm that the idea proceeds from an actual infinite substance. Now since the word
"God" is to be understood to denote "some infinite, independent, most intelligent, most powerful substance, and one by
which I myself as well as whatever else (if anything) exists are
created,"[20] I am driven to the conclusion that my self-consciousness involves an innate consciousness of God that comes from
God. Now "existence" (as Descartes will clarify later on in the
Meditations) is as integral to the idea of God as "valley" is to the
idea of a mountain;[21] real existence is inseparable from the idea
of God;[22] hence, God cannot but exist—my self-consciousness
demands it. For it would be senseless for me on the one hand
to accept that I exist as I do, namely, endowed with an innate
idea of a wholly perfect God, and on the other hand to think of
God as not existing; either everything about the experience of
my self-consciousness in relation to God is fraudulent, or it is
wholly reliable. Only the latter makes sense, and hence, it calls
for a moment of contemplative adoration. After that, the meditations can be resumed.[23]

[b] Given the intellectual climate in which he found himself
and to which he felt committed, Descartes probably did the best
he could when he tried to give expression to humanity's native
attunement to God. Still, his version of the ontological argument suffers from the typically seventeenth-century dress it wears.
While clearheaded, it is bald, for it is laid out in the form of a series of rational operations quite mechanically performed by a
self-centered subject detached from the world of matter, and intensely conscious of rational method as the only reliable way towards all understanding (cf. §55, 13, [j]). No wonder the argument has lost every association with Augustine's analysis of desire
(cf. §67, 1). Anselm would hardly recognize it, for it dissociates
the progress of thought from the experience of the practice of
worshipful faith, which it treats as only one operation among

many. Most importantly, as Pascal was to insist, the argument's connection with the God of Abraham, Isaac, and Jacob, and, of Jesus Christ, has evaporated, for the divine transcendence (which ultimately defies definition) has been replaced by mere remoteness (cf. §96, 4, b; §97, 12; cf. also §28, 7, [h]), of the kind that invites a purely conceptual, utterly harmless definition of God. No wonder the *Wirkungsgeschichte*—the effective history—of Descartes' ontological argument will produce a whole series of instances of the idealist replacement of the living God by professions of godliness: the living, adorable God will be displaced by an autonomous (and, frankly, quite manageable) human consciousness of the divine (cf. §17, 1, a; §25, 4, d).

[10] Let us return to the Middle Ages. In accepting the challenge of the search for understanding posed by Anselm, yet in rejecting his argument (at least in the standardized, curtailed form in which he was familiar with it), Aquinas took it upon himself to reflect on the two great themes of Israel's faith—God and God's relationship to humanity and the world—in an intellectually more satisfactory fashion. To his reasoning we must now turn.

[§102] AQUINAS: FAITH PROMPTING REASON TO SEE THE WORLD AS GOD'S

[1] Saint Thomas Aquinas (1225-1274) presents the so-called *quinque viæ* or "five ways"—five proofs of the existence of God—at the beginning of the first part of his *Summa theologiæ*. Having first furnished the student, in the first *quæstio*, with a general introduction, in ten articles, to the "science" (that is, the scholarly discipline) of theology, Aquinas opens the *Summa* proper with a lengthy treatment (*quæstiones* 2-43) of the doctrine of God. The opening gambit of this masterpiece is the treatment of the problem of God's existence—*an Deus sit*; it takes up the entire second *quæstio*. In two consecutive articles, Aquinas first explains why Anselm's ontological argument is unsatisfactory, and why God's existence must be demonstrated *a posteriori* (that is, by recourse to its ascertainable effects). Hard on the heels of these explanations, he brings the *quæstio* to a head in the third article, whose lengthy *corpus* details the arguments for God's existence.

The text of the *quinque viæ* in the *Summa theologiæ* represents not only the most polished version of the proofs in all of Aquinas' *oeuvre*; it is also the only complete one.[24] Intimations, suggestions, sketches, and full statements of each of the five ways are scattered, in a variety of contexts, throughout Aquinas' works, from the earliest commentaries on; the argument in the *Summa theologiæ* is obviously intended as a complete, fully coherent argument— the fruit of a lifetime of reflection matured in the broad-minded setting of the medieval university.[25]

[2] Aquinas writes:

> That God *is* [*Deum esse*] can be demonstrated in five ways.
>
> The first (and most obvious) way takes its cue from change [*motus*]. For it is certain, from observation, that there are things in this world that are in process of change. Now whatever is in process of
> 5 change is being changed by something else, for the following reason: nothing *is changed* except to the extent that it has *potential* for the state toward which it moves when being changed. Now something *causes change* inasmuch as it *actually* is [in a certain state]; for causing change is nothing but making actual what used to be potential; now
> 10 something can be carried from potentiality into actuality only by means of something that is in actuality, just as what is actually hot (say, fire) causes wood, which is potentially hot, to be actually hot, and in doing so, moves and alters it. Now it is not possible for one and the same thing to enjoy both potentiality and actuality in the
> 15 same respect ... Thus it is impossible for something both to cause change and to be changed in the same respect and to the same extent—put differently, to change itself. ... Hence, all that is in process of change *has* to be changed by something else. Something follows from this. Suppose the thing by which something is changed
> 20 is itself in process of being changed; then it, too, must be in process of being changed by something else, and the latter by something else again. But here it is impossible to go on indefinitely, for that way there would be no first agent of change, and consequently, no other agent of change either; for secondary agents of change do not pro-
> 25 duce change except in virtue of their being moved by a first agent of change ... Consequently, we are bound to come down to some first agent of change—one being changed by none; and this is what all understand by God.
>
> The second way takes its cue from the nature of the efficient cause.
> 30 For we find, in this observable world, that efficient causes occur in sequences; we do not find cases (in fact, such cases are impossible) in which something is its own efficient cause—it would have to pre-exist itself, which is impossible. Now it is impossible to go on indefinitely in the line of efficient causes, for in all efficient causes, se-
> 35 quential as they are, what is first is the cause of what is intermediate, and what is intermediate is the cause of what is last, whether there be several intermediate causes or only one. But if any cause is re-

moved, its effect is removed as well. Thus, if, in the case of efficient causes, there is no first to start with, there will be no last, nor will
40 there be anything intermediate. But if we go on indefinitely in the line of efficient causes, there will be no first efficient cause, nor any intermediate efficient causes, which is clearly false. Consequently, we are forced to posit some first efficient cause—which is what all call God.

45 The third way draws upon the distinction between the possible and the necessary, and runs as follows. We encounter, in reality, things that *may* be and *may not* be; some things, we find, come into being and decay—which shows that they *may* be and *may not* be. Now it is impossible for all of this latter kind to be in existence all the time,
50 for something that *may not* be sometimes, in fact, is not. Therefore, if all things are such as *may not* be, there was a time when there was nothing in reality. But if that is true, then there would be nothing now either, for whatever is not in existence, does not begin to exist except by means of something that is in existence; thus, if there was
55 a time when there was nothing in existence, it was impossible for something to begin to exist, and in this way, there would be nothing in existence now, which is patently false. Hence, not all things that are are of the kind that *may or may not* be; there has to be something in reality that *must* be. Now whatever *must* be either derives its ne-
60 cessity from elsewhere or it does not. Now it is not possible to go on indefinitely in the line of those things that *must* be whose necessity is derivative, any more than in the line of efficient causes, as was demonstrated above. Consequently, we are forced to posit something that *must* be in and of itself—something that does not derive
65 its necessity from elsewhere, but from which other things derive their necessity, which is what all call God.

The fourth way draws upon the gradation found in reality. For in reality we encounter things that are more and things that are less good, and true, and worthy of notice, and so forth with other things
70 of this kind. But "more" and "less" apply to different things according as they approximate, in different degrees, something that is "most"; for example, something is hotter as it comes closer to what is most hot. Thus there is something that is most true, and best, and most notable, and consequently, most *being*, for things that are most
75 true most fully *are*, as we read in the second book of the *Metaphysics*.[26] Now what we call "most" this or that in its kind is the cause of whatever belongs to that kind ... Consequently, there is something that is, in respect to all things, the cause of being, goodness, and whatever perfection; and this is what we call God.

80 The fifth way draws upon the fact that there is management in things. We observe that there are things that lack knowledge (namely, material things found in nature) that behave purposefully; this is

clear from the fact that they always, or at least more often than not, behave in the same manner, in such a way as to achieve what is best; from this it is clear that they attain their goal, not by chance, but by design. Now things that do not have knowledge do not strive toward a goal unless directed by one that has knowledge and understanding—if an arrow has aim, it does so because of the marksman. Consequently, there is an intelligent being by which all natural bodies are directed to an end; and this is what we call God.[27]

[3] Much like Anselm's ontological argument, if not more so, Aquinas' *quinque viæ* have proved to be a classic. It is hard to interpret this elegant, tightly written text without being influenced, consciously or unconsciously, by its centuries-long *Wirkungsgeschichte.* That effective history has been mixed. It has involved considerable distortion and misinterpretation, as we will see (cf. §103). But it has also been a delightful history of *clarifying and enlightening commentary.* Generations of students have entered into Aquinas' argument, only to experience how it can force—delightfully—to the mind's surface a number of profound insights unstated in the text but integral to its meaning and probative force. We must develop the most important.

[4] The first issue concerns the way in which *God's transcendence is both safeguarded and conveyed by the structure of the argument.* The second, inseparable from the first, concerns Aquinas' universalist proposition that *the human mind is in and of itself capable of understanding and interpreting the world as it really is.* Aquinas' argument has been faulted on both counts in modern times; consequently, it is best nowadays to start the interpretation of the *quinque viæ* from a negative point of view, as follows.

Given its crucial importance, let the first issue be our point of departure. It has long been an axiom in logic that conclusions are only as valid as the premises that support them. Premises whose validity rests on the finite cannot bear the weight of conclusions involving synthetic judgments about the transcendent infinite. Now Aquinas' arguments for God's existence are based on realities observed in a finite universe. Hence, whatever conclusions regarding "a really existing god" these arguments may yield, such a "god" can never be more than a *part* of the universe. In fact, it may well be its highest part—its pinnacle (*apex mundi*). But still, such a "god" is at best an unknown superior force—one that remains inextricably identified with the cosmos it produces or has produced, and hence, *finite and not God.*

For reasons like these, a modern thinker like Paul Tillich can, with characteristic incisiveness, offer a characterization of Aquinas' arguments as he knows them, and proceed to argue that all they do is raise the essential *question about God* that is implied in human existence (§83, 3) and no more. In other words, they can yield no truth-statement about God at all:

... if *we derive God from the world,* he cannot be that which transcends the world infinitely. He is the "missing link," discovered by correct conclusions. ... [such a] God is "world," a missing part of that from which he is derived in terms of conclusion. This contradicts the idea of God ... The arguments for the existence of God ... are expressions of the *question* of God which is *implied in human finitude.* This question is their truth; *every answer they give is untrue.*[28]

This statement, no matter how true (or even profound) in itself, is a misinterpretation of Aquinas' argument. Four sets of observations are in order to clarify the issues involved.

[a] It is unwise to assume, almost *a priori,* that Aquinas is likely to compromise the divine transcendence so readily. In fact, he gives clear evidence to the contrary. He knows and appreciates the objection that we cannot grasp, by means of definitions or propositions, a wholly transcendent God: "... the pivotal term in any demonstration is a definition—*what something is.* But in the case of God we do not know what he is, but only what he is not ... Hence, we cannot demonstrate that God is."[29] This, however, in Aquinas' view, does not settle the issue at all. He explains that there is a difference between *deductive* forms of argumentation and *inferential* ones; for Aquinas, the spirit of geometrical deduction does not yet reign supreme. In inferential arguments, *effects can function as the equivalent of definitions;* real effects are indicative of the existence and nature of real causes. Now the infrahuman cosmic order displays ever so many characteristic phenomena that strongly suggest that the cosmos must be interpreted, in the final analysis, precisely as an effect. That is, the cosmos witnesses to a cause—one that is itself in no way an effect: the cause commonly known as "God." It is tacitly understood that, to be such an uncaused cause, God must wholly transcend the cosmic order. Yet on the other hand, this transcendent God is rightly (if far from adequately) praised and named by means of names derived from things that exist, inasmuch as all things caused by God are proportionate to him (cf. §67, 2).

For the purposes of his argument, therefore, Aquinas does not need such an impossible thing as a definition of God; all he needs is the *word* "God," with its commonly accepted meaning [k].[30]

Contemporary Christian theology must make a distinction here. On the one hand, it is well advised to leave all Platonism and Cartesianism and mere existentialism behind, and follow Aquinas, along with many modern scientists and theologians, in their firm resolve to take seriously the philosophical and theological challenges the cosmos offers to humanity, being part of it (cf. §9, 1, [i]) [l]. On the other hand, we can no longer fol-

---

[k] This enables Aquinas to write, in the text of the argument: "... this is what *all understand* by God." By writing this, Aquinas joins a long patristic tradition of pointing out that the religious world view, and hence, an awareness of God, however indistinct and imperfect, has the support of the common consent of humanity (cf. Thomas C. Oden, *The Living God*, pp. 152-55, for a survey). Aquinas' world picture was, of course, confined to Western monotheism, even though it included a reading awareness of polytheism and the classical philosophical theisms of the West (cf. §27, 4, a) and their errors. The eighteenth and nineteenth century discovery of the uncharted variety of world religions rekindled the issue of humanity's common understanding of "God" in a wholly new way. Scholars like Wilhelm Schmidt, S.V.D. (1868-1955)—the author of a massive twelve-volume series of monographs (1912-1955) entitled *Der Ursprung der Gottesidee* ("The Origin of the Idea of God")—and Friedrich Heiler (1892-1967) accepted the challenge. Ethnographical data convinced them of the validity of "ethnological arguments" for God's existence: the history of religions warrants the conclusion that all human religions are developments of a primitive monotheism—even of a primitive self-revelation of God. The mood of these schools of thought is well expressed in the death-bed proclamation of a great ecumenist: bishop Nathan Söderblom (1866-1931): "There is a living God; I can prove it by the history of religions" (Thomas C. Oden, *The Living God*, p. xxviii). However, more recent practitioners of ethnography and ethnology, more empirically inclined and less given to generalization, are finding it harder to endorse such universal professions of faith. They are more impressed by peoples whose languages have no words for "god," and cultures that appear not to have even rough equivalents of the idea of God. An example is the Yahgan tribe of Tierra de Fuego (of whom the young Charles Darwin wrote that "if they are not actually the missing link, they are not far removed from it"). Thomas Bridges lived among them, an ineffectual missionary for forty years; he wrote of the Yahgan that they "had not the faintest idea of a god or any expectation of future life." When Bridges died in 1898, all he had to show for his efforts was an unfinished Yamana dictionary, a manuscript containing 32,000 entries, which was edited and published in Germany in 1933; the manuscript got lost but resurfaced in 1945, and has been kept in the British Museum since 1946; by this time, however, the Yahgan themselves had become extinct (cf. G. Bomans, *Capriolen*, pp. 216-22; quotations pp. 218, 220). But the mythology of the tribe had been recorded, between 1918 and 1924, by two capable collaborators of Schmidt's, Martin Gusinde, S.V.D., and Wilhelm Koppers, S.V.D.; cf. Johannes Wilbert, *Folk Literature of the Yamana Indians*.

[l] The work of Pierre Teilhard de Chardin obviously comes to mind, but so do

low Aquinas in his reliance on the *word* "God," or, for that matter, on any single word, idea, or thought-system claimed to be universally meaningful and valid.

Let us pursue the latter point for a moment. For reasons of principle, explained long ago (§63), we must maintain that even the most reliable human knowledge of humanity and the world as a whole (and thus *a fortiori* of God) is, and will always remain, perspectival and interpretative. That is, such knowledge will elude all articulations that are claimed to be exhaustive or final.

While raising the issue of inculturation in all its sharpness, therefore, the modern unreliability of the word "God" neither definitively undercuts Aquinas' arguments for God's existence, nor need it be a cause for fundamental theological despondency, for two reasons. First, Karl Rahner, in a masterful retrieval of Anselm's meditation on the word "God" (cf. §101, 7), has shown that modern idioms suggesting universalism are available. Such idioms may be capable, in today's global situation, of evoking an awareness of the presence of an ineffable mystery encompassing and confronting the human person. In this way, he has fairly accommodated the sensibilities of those non-Christians and post-Christians for whom the word "God" is either non-existent or semantically vacuous, but who are open to its dynamic equivalents, or at least to aspects of it.[31] Secondly, philosophical-theological reflection on the existence of a truly transcendent God is still free to appeal to what *is* a universal human trait: a native ability and propensity to communicate across cultural divides, in the expectation that attentive mutual interpretation of the particulars of our different religions will give us glimpses of a truly universalist perspective (§64).

[b] Tillich (along with a host of modern interpreters) misreads Aquinas' arguments in one crucial respect. Aquinas concludes that God must exist, *not* because the world leaves gaps to be filled or missing links to be supplied or puzzles to be solved, but because this finite world *actually is and moves and changes* [*m*],

---

works like Werner Heisenberg's *The Physicist's Conception of Nature*, with its illuminating discussions of causality and of the limitations of Newton's method. And for all the ways one could take issue with the quaintly Newtonian ideas about God and creation delivered by Stephen M. Hawking in his *A Brief History of Time*, the fact that he brings the problem up is admirable.

[*m*] "Change" throughout the first way (ll. 2-28) renders Lat. *motus* ("movement"). In Aquinas' mind, *motus* comprises, not only *motion*, but also, and espe-

gaps and missing links and puzzles and imperfections and all. In other words, it is *not the imperfections* of things and the need to compensate for them that provide Aquinas with the premises for his demonstration, but *things themselves inasmuch as they are and move* [*n*].

For Aquinas, things in the world undeniably exhibit a dynamic actuality, while at the same time being undeniably finite and imperfect. Thus, for all their actuality and dynamism, things fall short of being unambiguous and self-explanatory; much as they are real, their quality of being is mixed; they fail to give a fully intelligible account, either of themselves or of the web of dynamic coherence in which they exist and move; they are *puzzling*. They must, in the final analysis, depend on a reality whose dynamic actuality is so original and so full as to account, not only for whatever else is dynamic and actual, but also for its own transcendent self.

Now as a matter of fact (and leaving aside processes of change and causal activity), we do find phenomena that *rather more positively* point in the direction of such a transcendent reality. If we look at the arrangement of the world as a whole, we spontaneously, and quite realistically, construe the world on a calibrated scale of increasing ontological intensity. This suggests that reality involves different degrees of resemblance to, and indeed, par-

---

cially, *alteration*; this is borne out by ll. 11-13: "what is actually hot (say, fire) causes wood, which is potentially hot, to be actually hot; in doing so, it moves and alters [*movet et alterat*] it." It is important to note this in view of the fact that from the sixteenth century on, Aquinas' argument will tend to get interpreted in purely *neutral, mechanical* terms; *motus* will be taken to mean *motion* and nothing else; all efficient causality that produces *qualitative* change will be viewed in terms of mere *locomotion*. In due course, this understanding will—disastrously—deny all divine immanence and remove God to the beginning of the world, where an omnipotent but foreign and (especially) neutral creator is needed to provide creation with its initial impulse (cf. §28, 7, [*h*]; §96, 4, a; §103, 1). The principal author to come to mind in this context is, of course, Descartes.

[*n*] This interpretation is least self-evident in the case of the first way. Despite its being "the most obvious" (l. 2), or perhaps precisely because of it, the first way strongly invites a mistaken "God-of-the-gaps" interpretation, because its initial point of departure is a phenomenon characterized by *passivity*: the undergoing of change (ll. 3-5). To interpret the first way correctly, therefore, it must be carefully noted that towards the end, the argument takes a positive turn: it hinges on the observation that worldly *agents* of change, *while effective*, do not account for themselves (ll. 19-22). Thus the first way eventually joins the second in arguing that God is to be understood as the first unchangeable agent of change, not because God fills the explanatory void left open by their passivity, but because God ultimately accounts for the actual causal activity of worldly *agents* of change (ll. 33-44).

ticipation in, a transcendent reality of the highest ontological intensity (ll. 67-79) [o]. Besides, ever so many things that have no intellectual powers turn out to exhibit, on closer inspection, a constant purposefulness in the way they function (at least for the most part); this constancy suggests a *native* preparedness for meaningful purpose—that is, a sense of direction implanted in their very nature by a transcendent intelligence (ll. 80-90).

[c] In all of this it must be understood that Aquinas' qualifying superlatives—"first" agent of change (l. 27), "first" efficient cause (l. 43), "most" being (l. 74)—are to be interpreted with caution. God is neither the "first" in a series nor "topmost" in a hierarchy; God is indeed "first" and "most," yet not in a relative or comparative sense, nor even in a superlative sense, but absolutely. A similar caveat concerns the causal sequences mentioned in the course of the argument. To use a familiar colloquialism, God stands neither for the first chicken in relation to any egg, nor for the first egg in relation to any chicken; God accounts for all chickens as well as all eggs, as well as for their mutual causal relationships.

Thus the examples suggested by Aquinas are not adequate; they must be taken as *approximations.* Thus the fire is *only relatively* transcendent in relation to the wood which it finds and proceeds to fire (ll. 11-13); in the end, the two belong to one and the same cosmic sequence of causes. God, however, is absolutely transcendent—*extra seriem* ("outside the sequence of causes"), as the scholastic tradition has insisted. But God is also immanent in each causal agent inasmuch as God is the ultimate source of its ability to cause change; this can be couched in the inelegant but accurate phrase, "God causes all causes to cause." Similarly, a marksman (for all his superiority to his arrow) is part of the same causal system as the arrow he releases (l. 88), yet he

---

[o] If anywhere, it is in the fourth way (ll. 67-79; cf. note [q]) that Aquinas clearly shows that he is arguing, not from the deficiencies of finite things, but from their being *real.* Thus, he can write (*S. c. G.* I, 13, *Potest autem*): "In *Metaphysics* II, [Aristotle] demonstrates that 'things that are most true most fully *are* as well.' But in *Metaphysics* IV he demonstrates the existence of something that is most true, as follows. We see that of two untrue things, one is more untrue than the other; this necessarily also means that one is more true than the other. Now this is because of its approximation to something that is simply and maximally true. From all of this we can furthermore conclude that there is something that maximally *is.* And this we call God." For Aristotle's text, cf. *Metaphysics* IV, 4, 1008^b33-38 (*Arist-BWks*, p. 743).

also remains, in a real sense, foreign to the arrow itself. God, however, is both wholly transcendent in relation to the creatures that are guided to their ends and truly immanent in them inasmuch as their *nature* (which is the principle of their natural purposefulness) depends directly on God (cf. §82, 3, b).

[d]   Still, the question remains: how can language borrowed from our understanding of the world convey knowledge of the transcendent? The modern skepticism with regard to truth-claims involving the transcendent and the modern demand that they be verified empirically deserve to be taken seriously. In his elegant monograph *Religious Language*,[32] Ian Ramsey has done so, by offering a classic analysis of the "odd logic" by which we must "place" the "religious phrases" employed by the Tradition and instanced by Aquinas. To interpret these phrases correctly, Ramsey explains, we must systematically realize that phrases like "first cause" and examples like the marksman shooting an arrow are *models*, applicable to God and God's relationship to the world only by means of suitable *qualifiers*. Far from being sure-fire devices to convey one and the same meaning automatically and apart from any situation, such phrases convey their meaning only within the context of empirical situations in which they are appropriately used. Their meaning, therefore, depends on an insight: the religious "disclosure" typical of religious situations. If and when this disclosure comes off, however, the whole universe of understanding widens and new truth emerges, in the form of "fuller discernment": the suitably qualified model will begin to "preside" over the whole area of discourse governed by it [*p*].[33]

Thus, in the case of our examples, once an intuitive insight into God's transcendent, encompassing causality and providence occurs in a religiously or theologically significant situation, the

---

[*p*] This is where the understanding of the divine attributes becomes an issue of theological epistemology. The Tradition has insisted, rightly, that God is uncreated, infinitely perfect, exalted above all, incomprehensible, simple, eternal, immutable, pure spirit, infinite, omnipresent. The affirmation of these classical divine attributes remains meaningful, but only on condition that its nature is correctly understood. That correct understanding involves the realization that the divine attributes are not simple predicates applied to a known quantity; that they are models borrowed from the world as we know it, which, suitably qualified, apply to the transcendent God by virtue of the correct functioning of the "odd logic" proper to religious situations; that (since worship is the "religious situation" *par excellence*), these models are best understood in worship-situations.

insight will also become the occasion for a deeper appreciation of the activity observable in the entire cosmos, including its sub-human realms: a dynamism so wild and profuse of sweep yet so constant and reliable of purpose will begin to point to God.

[5] In his own way, Aquinas is keenly aware of the issue treated by Ian Ramsey. To insure both the transcendent reference and the truth of the language in which we couch and convey our knowledge of God, he has an important explanation of his own for one particular kind of "odd logic" found in religious language. He terms it "analogy."[34]

Analogy in this strict sense is to be distinguished from metaphor. In the case of metaphors, it is clear that they properly apply, not to God, but to realities in the world: it is with reason that we name God "Rock," but we remain aware that "rock" properly refers to material things called "rocks" and not to God.[35]

However, besides metaphorical titles, there is a more intriguing category of divine names. Like metaphors, they are borrowed from created reality, but unlike metaphors, they seem to express what God really *is*: true, good, worthy of notice. These predicates, Aquinas explains, do indeed properly apply to God, but not "univocally"—that is, not in the sense in which they might equally well apply to a creature; we would implicitly deny the divine transcendence if we were to call God "good" in the sense in which we might call any creature good. On the other hand, when we call God good, we are not affirming something totally unrelated to the goodness of creatures; we are not "equivocating." When applied to God, therefore, predicates like "good" and "true" certainly do not mean the same as when applied to creatures, yet they do not mean something entirely different either. In other words, they mean *both* the same *and* something wholly different. That is, they are applied *analogously*.

Now it is important to observe (and here we touch upon Aquinas' fourth way) that *we notice this analogy first of all within the cosmos itself:* not all creatures are good in the same, univocal sense; in the world as we know it, basic properties like goodness come on a range—an ascending scale extending from "less good" through "pretty good," "quite good," and "very good," to "the best." But, Aquinas says, thus measuring and calibrating (say) goodness on an ascending scale makes sense only if we assume, at least implicitly, that there is a *maxime tale* (a "most" in its kind): something "maximally good" or "absolutely best"—the true criterion of all goodness as well as the source of whatever is good in any measure at all.

There is a range of goodness we know; within it, we have the authority to make measurements and judgments. But the range also suggests (yet does not include) a crowning reality that is "maximally" (that is, transcendently) good. Nothing is to be called good apart from it; it "presides" over the whole realm of goodness; if we know it, we do not comprehend it; it measures our measurements; it judges our judgments. That reality we call God (ll. 67-79).

[6] In this argument, Aquinas has taken a decisive step. Just what is it that makes something (or rather, anything) true, or good, or worthy of notice? Aquinas answers: the fact that it *is*. Things are known and acknowledged as true and good simply by virtue of the actuality of their *being*. This is a matter of straight *proportion*: to whatever extent something *is*, to that extent it is good and true, *and discernible as such* (as well as desirable). But this means that the cosmic analogy that leads the human mind to God is fundamentally a matter, not just of *knowing and interpreting* the world and (ultimately) God by means of predicates applied analogously, but also, and more fundamentally, of being in touch with (that is, participating in) the world's *reality* as well as, ultimately, God's. Thus the fourth way elaborates Protagoras' seminal insight that "humanity is the measure of all things."[36] Its backbone is the *participative experience* of the analogy of being (*analogia entis*). It involves this: *the knowing and discerning human spirit is attuned to reality in all its ordered forms, and in and beyond them, to God as to the transcendent Form of all that is.* There are two facets to the human spirit's deep awareness of the reality of the world and of God, and of its own position in that reality.

The first facet is that God is unqualified being. Wholly unlike anything in the world, where things may and may not be (ll. 46-50), God is (albeit "in some kind of perplexing fashion": §67, 3; §107, 1; cf. §107, 4) fullness of pure, unmixed actuality of being: *actus purus*—Being subsistent in and of itself. Accordingly, should we insist on using abstract, second-order-reflection terms like "nature" or "essence" in relation to God, we must stretch them to the breaking-point and say that God's "Nature" or "Essence" is, not this or that, but "Being as such," or "Being Itself" [*q*].[37]

[*q*] From this, the later scholastic tradition has drawn the conclusion that the analogy of being is an *analogy of proportionality*. One way (out of many) to clarify this is the following. A finite being can *be* only insofar as its nature (or its essence) will allow it to be; *what it is* fundamentally limits its capacity for *actuality of*

As for the second facet, Aquinas leaves it entirely implicit, but well over seven centuries after Aquinas (and even more, well over three centuries after Pascal), we simply *have* to make it explicit: *"unqualified being" is not equivalent to neutral being.*[38] "Being," for Aquinas, is anything but the indifferent, purely factual "existence" of faceless things moved around by other faceless things and, in turn, moving other faceless things around *tout bêtement*—mindlessly, meritlessly, aimlessly. For all his impartial rationality in regard to the cosmos, "being," for Aquinas, has everything to do with "quality of being"; whatever is comes with *inherent attributes*: truth, goodness, worthiness of notice (ll. 69, 73-74).

These three attributes are connected. The discovery of the inherent truth and goodness of the world—including the whole material world—is the fruit of treating the world as "worthy of notice." It takes the loving regard of responsive contemplation to *see* the real world—that is, to find its structures meaningful and its dynamics attractive. While neutral observation has it merits (cf. §56, 12, a), it does not do full justice to the world. And since, for Aquinas, reality in all its gradations is not neutral but worthy of notice, *the existence of God is not a neutral fact,* but a matter, first and foremost, of "reverent affection" (cf. §67, 3).

Thus the experience of analogy essentially involves doxology (cf. §35, 4, b); God's fullness of being and God's existence as the creator of the world prompt praise and thanksgiving. And, from the creature's point of view, far from being merely the basic fact that accounts for the functioning of the system of nature, God's existence is a blessing. In fact, it is *the* fundamental blessing that rests on

---

being—its "ontological intensity" (cf. *S. Th.* I, 3, 5, *ad* 2). We can mathematically symbolize a finite being (or a class of finite beings) by a *proportion*, with the numerator representing "nature" or "essence" and the denominator "actuality of being." (God cannot be symbolized by a fraction, of course, except, perhaps, by $\frac{1}{1}$, conveying that the divine nature simply *is* the full actuality of being.) On this basis, it is possible also to symbolize the dynamic analogy that prevails on the ascending scale of being—the analogy used by Aquinas, in the fourth way, as a way to God viewed as the prime analogue. We can do so by means of a *sequence of proportions* (hence the term "proportionality"), as follows: $\frac{1}{2}, \frac{2}{3}, \frac{3}{4}, \ldots \frac{n-1}{n}, \ldots \to 1$. In this model, the increasing value of the fractions suggests that creatures exist on a truly ascending scale of being, and thus bear a truly increasing resemblance to God. Still, the fact that the values only approximate the value 1, without ever reaching it, suggests that, much as there are grades of *being*, "there can be no grades of deity" (§98, 1, b). God, while truly the point of reference of all that is finite, is and remains outside the series, as the absolute fullness of being, truth, goodness, and nobility; in that fullness, all finite beings participate, without diminishing it, let alone exhausting it; as such, it remains transcendent.

humanity and the world, since God's transcendent Truth, Goodness, and Worthiness of Respectful Attention guarantee their inherent intelligibility, value, and nobility. This is what Aquinas means when he writes that the degrees of goodness and truth that we observe in the world point the way to God who simply *is*.

[7] Language thrives on affirmation. But in expressions like the ones just used, the dynamics of analogy begin to drive the language of affirmation to its limit and beyond, into the park of paradox. It is not surprising, therefore, to watch Aquinas, along with the Tradition, explain analogy, in the last resort, by formulating an essential paradox. The paradox, again, is not neutral; it does not formulate a mere epistemological or logical surd; rather, it functions in the service of *awe*. In the presence of God, the creature's experience of its divine likeness must always revert to the deeper realization of an unlikeness that will forever remain greater; in every nameable respect, the relationship between the creature and its God is, and will forever be, asymmetrical. If theology is to be a reliable reflection of this, it must participate in that (ultimately ineffable) asymmetry. The way of affirmation must lead to, and crest in, the way of the fullest *remotio* (§67, 2; cf. §109, 4; 6; 10-11).

Accordingly, Aquinas can close one of his smaller treatises with a nearly literal quotation from a decree promulgated at the Fourth Lateran Council held in 1215 A.D. (DH 806; cf. CF 320; cf. §69, 1, c; §98, 4, d), and write:

Still, the measure of human and divine perfection is not the same. For no likeness, no matter how great, can obtain between the Creator and the creature, without there being found right there [*ibi*] a greater unlikeness. This is so because the creature is at an infinite distance from God.[39]

[8] The analogy of being is mainly pertinent to the fourth way; still, it is an unacknowledged presence in the first three ways as well. This can be shown as follows.

The argument of the first three ways is based on the actual occurrence of change (ll. 2-28) and efficient causality (ll. 29-44), and on the actual existence of things that in and of themselves might not have existed at all (ll. 45-66). That is, the first three ways argue from the *dynamic actuality of finite being*. Now Aquinas maintains that this dynamic actuality irresistibly points beyond itself towards a reality so actual that it accounts for all causality and for all that moves and changes. On what ground?

The answer is implicit in Aquinas' appeal to *understanding*. Human intelligence and discernment, the fourth way implies, are reliable guides to *reality*; that is, human understanding can be trusted to do justice to things as they *are*. There are the puzzling patterns of mutual dependency among cosmic change agents and efficient causes; there is the puzzling fact that things actually exist despite their contingency. In the face of this, human intelligence finds it "impossible to go on indefinitely" (ll. 22, 33-34, 60-61). Why? Because (and here Aquinas implicitly relies on an argument that is still applicable to the world picture of modern science: cf. §115, 5, a-e) *an indefinite regress explains nothing*; far from being an exercise in understanding, settling for such a regress is the abandonment of all thought; hence, settling for regress is tantamount to being out of touch with reality. Human understanding must be taken seriously when it demands that in and beyond the things that move and change, and in and beyond the actual existence of what might very well not exist at all, it acknowledges a transcendent, incomprehensible, self-sufficient actuality of dynamic being on which all change depends.

[9] But this realization, in turn, opens the way towards a deeper understanding of the fifth way as well. Like the first three ways, the fifth way argues on the basis of phenomena observed in the non-human cosmos: natural things incapable of intellectual understanding display, surprisingly, a form of natural intelligence. They do so by their consistent striving for meaningful purposes that are beyond them. This natural drive toward meaningful, intelligible ends suggests a connection between nature, intelligence, and self-transcending finality—a connection for which infra-human things themselves, not being self-conscious, are not intentionally responsible. Such natural intelligence and finality, therefore, must derive from God, the author of nature (cf. §80, 2-3).

This ostensibly cosmological argument is, in fact, wholly dependent on an implicit anthropology; the fifth way, that is, *combines the themes of dependence and analogy*. What enables Aquinas to make this case, if not a tacit awareness of the native finality of beings that *are* capable of intellectual understanding? How would we ever be able to notice intelligence and self-transcending finality in non-intellectual agents, if we were not conscious of enjoying them ourselves, in the form of knowledge and desire? Like knows like by virtue of participation, says the law of analogy. The human spirit recognizes an intelligent urge toward transcendence in the lower domains of reality precisely inasmuch as it experiences *in itself* (at first unthematically, of course, but then, upon reflection, also thematically) an analogous tendency. That tendency is the immanent, natural desire for the God who is both the transcendent power on which all beings depend for their native dynamism and the transcendent end in which all beings are prompted to seek fulfillment by virtue of their very nature (§87, 2, a) [r].

[10] *Experience of dynamic interdependence, experience of analogy, experience of immanence reaching for transcendence:* these three lend philosophical coherence to the *quinque viæ* as a whole. God is acknowledged, first of all, as the transcendent *causa prima* of the whole network of cosmic causality. This causality is most strikingly observable in processes marked by *efficient* causality. That is, the powerful phenomena produced by efficient causation furnish Aquinas with the most palpable *material* for his argument, and thus with his most obvious, most suggestive, and in many ways most powerful point of departure: *the experience of interdependence.* All contingent things are in process of change, dependent on contingent agents of change that in turn depend on other contingent agents of change.

But there are more subtle things to be observed in the world than cosmic transmutation and the actual existence of things that might not have been at all. To the sensitive observer, the cosmos also displays patterned gradation and natural purposefulness. In and behind these two, the specifically *human* presence, sensing an affinity with itself, discerns the deeper structures that reveal that cosmic movement and change are endowed with both *order* and *higher purpose.*

These latter structures are, of course, anthropological rather than cosmological. But then again, this is hardly surprising. Is humanity not part of the cosmos? Does this not make it natural that even the material cosmos should invite an anthropological interpretation? After all, from a truly human point of view, things are not just dumb things. Whatever exists is not just available for mere use and exploitation by dint of objective comprehension and technological *force majeure* (cf. §99, 3). In virtue of their participation in the whole range of being, things also inherently and positively lend themselves to skillful coordination by virtue of human *discernment;*

---

[r] Needless to say, if cultural biases obscure or deny the human mind's intelligent urge toward transcendence, they will also narrow the scope of the mind's capacity to know. Consequently, such a culture will also lose sight of the native attunement to transcendence found in infra-human beings, and proceed to exploit the cosmos without regard—mindlessly, meritlessly, and aimlessly.

and in virtue of their innate tendencies, they inherently lend themselves to adjustment to higher ends by virtue of human *management.*
Hence, *formal* and *final* causality are integral, not just to humanity
and the spiritual world, but to the universe as such (cf. §94, 5, a).
The appeal to these two causalities, therefore, constitutes the inner
structure of Aquinas' argument, giving it its momentum.[40]

The *first* anthropological element in the argument is *the experience
of analogy,* represented by the fourth way. It consists in the human
spirit's attunement, by virtue of participation in being, to whatever
is. Humanity, by virtue of an immanent authority, can take the
measure of things, and to the extent it finds them good and true,
to that extent they *are* so, as well as knowable (and desirable) as
such; to that extent, too, they bear a formal likeness to God. We
knowingly know, and realistically realize, that *reality and intellectual
understanding are fundamentally attuned, both to one another and to God.*
No wonder Aquinas can write:

Being is what first comes within the ambit of the intellect, for to the extent
that something actually *is,* it is knowable.[41]

And (cf. §2, 1; §96, 3):

The human soul becomes, to an extent, all things, in virtue of sense and
intellect, by which all beings that have knowledge approximate, in a way,
the likeness of God, in whom all things pre-exist.[42]

The *second* anthropological element in the argument (which, as we
will see, is in reality properly theological) is left implicit, yet it is
present, as the integrating factor, in Aquinas' fifth way—his interpretation of cosmic finality. The human spirit is immanently, *a
priori* attuned (by natural desire) to the transcendent God. This attunement is both pervasive and dynamic: it suffuses all our acts of
knowing, as well as everything we know; its ultimate shape is our
native tendency towards God, our authentic desire for God, and
even our native ability to love God more than ourselves, which is
the point where grace can attach, in such a way as to perfect nature
(cf. again §80, 2-3). It is this tendency and this desire of the human spirit that enables Aquinas to affirm, in a different context (cf.
§8, 8; §95, 10):

... all those who know know God implicitly in whatever they know.[43]

This second anthropological element—the dynamism of the human spirit towards transcendence—is no less integral to the *quinque*

viæ for being left implicit. For it quietly enables the human mind to observe the dynamic intentionalities of the cosmos, to interpret them in light of its own experience of immanence reaching out to transcendence, and thus to draw explicit *a posteriori* arguments for God's existence from them [s]. As Maurice Blondel writes,

... for us, the world is the ordinary and necessary point of departure for the demonstration of [the existence of] God; but at the same time the [human] spirit's deep-seated and congenital ability to know and desire God is the initial and supreme ground of the whole movement of both nature and thought; as a result, our certainty about being is based on Being Itself.[44]

But this means that this second anthropological element, implicit in the fifth way, is properly *theological* in the last resort: the human spirit's dynamic attunement to God, left implicit in the argument, serves to detect that cosmic realities are similarly attuned to God. Thus, in a real sense, the progression of the *quinque viæ* as a whole is an ascent: *cosmology* → *anthropology* → *theology*. And the one motor force that drives the ascent is the attraction universally exercised by the transcendent God, who accounts for the dynamisms of both cosmos and humanity, as well as for their natural affinity with, and mutual attunement to, each other.

[a] Readers familiar with classical Greek thought will have noticed that the interpretation of the *quinque viæ* here proposed discerns, behind Aquinas' sturdy cosmological bias derived from Aristotle (cf. §80, 3), the faint traces of an older, more traditional philosophical conception with an intensely anthropological bias:[45] the "trichotomy" (or tripartition) cherished by the Stoa and Platonism, and, in the latter's wake, by the third and fourth century Greek fathers, most notably Origen. Gregory of Nyssa, for instance, puts the trichotomy to very effective use in his philosophical-anthropological treatise *The Constitution of Humanity*.[46] Trichotomists understand human nature as a unity of spirit, soul, and body (*pneuma, psychē, sōma*; cf. 1 Thess 5, 23). (Incidentally, this conception bears a broad resemblance to the *rûᵃh—nè-feš—bāśār* anthropology of the Hebrew scriptures.) By virtue of these components, integral humanity has theological, anthropological, and cosmological concerns to deal with; that is, it must

---

[s] In this regard, the *quinque viæ* show the same tendency at work in Aquinas' thought as the analysis of natural tendency discussed in §80, 2-3: the mature Aquinas insists on drawing *cosmology* into the ambit of the Christian faith.

balance three sets of dynamic relationships: to *God,* to *itself* as immanently predisposed to growth and development by way of active self-direction, and to the *cosmos.* Among Christians, trichotomism began to wane in the mid to late fourth century, when Apollinarius appealed to it to argue that in Christ the divine *Logos* replaces the spiritual soul (*psychē logikē*)—a move Apollinarius made to ensure Christ's inalienable holiness, but one in which he implicitly denied the completeness of his humanity. No wonder, in the increasingly Aristotelian climate of the Middle Ages in the West, trichotomism came to be, first discredited, and eventually repeatedly condemned, by means of more and more robust affirmations of the "dichotomist" thesis that the spiritual soul *by itself* informs the body—an idea rooted in Aristotle's *Peri Psychēs* (*De anima* or "On the Soul"), but in many ways the result of a Christian, theological appropriation of that masterpiece (cf. §109, 9, c, [z]; §115, 9; DH 159; CF 159; DEC I, 175 [11]; DH 900; 902; CF 405; DH 2828; 2833).

Despite this unfriendly environment, however, trichotomism quietly survived, especially in the residual Augustinianism of the Franciscan school. A fine example of its vitality is Bonaventure's *The Soul's Journey into God,* which brilliantly succeeds in putting a consistently tripartite anthropology to the task of giving a theological analysis of the Christian life that combines intelligent speculation with the experience of prayer.

[b] Jan van Ruusbroec is heir to this tradition. The second book of his chief work, *The Spiritual Espousals,* is devoted to the analysis of the life of inner desire for God. To anchor his treatment in anthropology, Ruusbroec begins by explaining that human beings are possessed of a natural *unity,* on three scores. First and foremost, he states, unity occurs by virtue of the spiritual soul inasmuch as it is the *locus* of a human person's unity with God in *being.* By virtue of the soul, human beings *are;* but this *being* is a subsistence, not just *in* themselves but also (and more importantly) *above* themselves, in God. Inalienable, unmediated union with God (Ruusbroec calls it "essential": §90, 3-4) is the core of everything human beings are or can be, regardless even of their moral standing; if this union were to desist, they would lapse into nothingness. There is a second, lower form of unity in human beings; it is of the effective, or (as Ruusbroec terms it) the "actual" kind (§90, 3, [kk]). Its locus is, once again, the human soul, except that it here functions as the seat of human

(that is, moral: §115, 2, [v]) *activity.* For the soul (often called "mind" in this context) is the single substrate ("substance") in which are rooted the three "superior faculties": memory (*i.e.*, capacity for consciousness of oneself as a permanent subject), intellect, and will. It is precisely by these faculties that human beings are immanently capable of self-actualization by means of deliberate, that is, properly spiritual acts of virtue. The third and lowest form of unity occurs, again by virtue of the soul, at the biophysical level. Here, Ruusbroec explains, the soul "informs" the living body (cf., again, §109, 9, c, [z]), and especially the heart, the body's vital center and source of all physical, sensible activity. Ruusbroec sums up: "These three unities naturally exist in human beings by way of one sole life and one sole domain. In the lowest we are sentient and animal; in the middle we are rational and spiritual; in the highest we are sustained essentially."[47]

This trichotomist anthropology provides Ruusbroec with the framework for his theological understanding of the Christian life as a whole, elaborated in *The Spiritual Espousals* and explained in terms of a *threefold elevation by supernatural grace.* Ruusbroec sums it up in three short sentences: "Now these three unities are supernaturally adorned and possessed, as one domain and one everlasting dwelling-place, [first of all] by means of moral virtues [practiced] in charity and by means of the life of action. And it is even better adorned and more honorably possessed by means of interior practices over and above the life of action. But it is most honorably and blissfully adorned by a life of supernatural contemplation."[48]

It is not difficult to recognize in this progression the tripartite scheme of increasing transcendence that also underlies Aquinas' five ways. The process starts humbly. *Cosmological,* biophysical human life finds itself trained and disciplined and thus moved toward completion by being integrated into humanity's immanent tendency towards transcendence over the cosmos, in the deliberate, moral life (cf. §§129-131). That properly *anthropological* privilege of humanity which is the deliberate life finds itself in turn liberated and moved toward completion, as the virtuous life turns out to aspire to a life beyond virtue (cf. §122; §137, 4-5). The moving power of this is natural desire awakened by the gracious appeal that comes from God—desire to gather up moral accomplishment and offer it to God, desire to live for God, desire to be united with God by the gift of self-transcending charity (cf. §137, 1, a-d). The source and precondition of this desire is, of course, none other than humanity's distinctively *theological* attunement to God—the echo, in the depths of self-consciousness, of every human person's essential unity with God seeking consummation in self-abandon. This, finally, opens the way to the total fulfillment. Human beings find themselves graciously enabled, by total self-abandon, to do what, by definition, is entirely beyond them: returning to God the ineffable favor which is their own being. With that, identity finally turns fully responsive: human beings find themselves doing justice to the God with whom they have been inalienably united by virtue of their very subsistence, by a gift of self so total that the life of the triune God becomes their life, embracing and inundating them by sheer love. At last, human beings are empowered to do the impossible; swept up, in loving contemplation, into what Ruusbroec calls "superessential" union with God, they find, in unmixed joy, their true, undivided, everlasting selves—"knowing as they are known" (cf. 1 Cor 13, 12).

[11] It is time to conclude. At the very least, the treatment here offered and the final comparison with Ruusbroec's theological anthropology demonstrate that Aquinas' five ways invite *interpretation.* They do so because they are themselves the fruit, not of deductive reasoning of the quasi-objective, scientific kind, but of interpretation. In other words, this immensely insightful series of arguments becomes intelligible only to those who appreciate the broader agenda that inspired them: Aquinas' effort to develop a novel, far-flung, exciting philosophical theology of *creation,* but one that would integrate an inherited, primarily anthropological theology inseparably connected with the ascetical, moral, and spiritual-mystical theology he cherished (cf. §67, 2; 4).

These realizations must inspire a concluding set of observations on Aquinas' "proofs." They concern *the conditions for the intelligibility of the arguments that make up the five ways.*

[a] This is directly related to a point made before. It was stated (§93, 9, c) that Aquinas' proofs are creative philosophical approximations of the doctrine of creation that Christianity inherited from Israel; in that sense they are part of the catholic tradition of natural theological reflection. This means they are not free-standing; they are not a-historical or a-cultural; they call for revision and reinterpretation, especially in the light of modern

science (cf. §115, 5, a-e).

This leads to a conclusion: nineteenth and twentieth century neo-scholastic rationalism was wrong when it absolutized them, as if, taken by themselves, they were universally appealing, perpetually valid natural preambles to the Christian faith (cf. §84, 2, a, [*u*]; §86, 5; 6, c). This chapter must not end without an inquiry into the prejudices behind this historic misunderstanding.

RATIONALITY AND THE FORCES OF DISSOCIATION

[§103] AQUINAS' ARGUMENT REDUCED TO RATIONAL COSMOLOGY

[1]   Aquinas' text must be placed in the context of the historic beginnings of the modern Western curiosity about the cosmos, combined with confidence in impartial rationality (§80, 2). In fact, it testifies to both of these with such vigor and resolve that the less impartial *anthropological* themes of *participation in being* and *natural aspiration to God*—the substance of the theological anthropologies of Augustine and Anselm—are simply left unstated.

Modern readers, taking the argument at face value, are likely to overlook this. They are unlikely to appreciate the argument's crucial supposition, namely, that there prevails *a basic affinity and coordination between humanity and the cosmos* (§102, 10).

[2] In view of this, any disruption of this affinity and coordination must be expected to damage the *theological* persuasiveness of the argument at the root. The New Learning confirmed this with a vengeance. The mechanization of the world picture (which owed some of its inspiration to nominalism's emphasis on God's *potentia absoluta* in relation to creation) drastically modified the relationship between humanity and the cosmos; the New Learning's methodical resolve, signalized by Pascal, to treat the material cosmos as essentially neuter (cf. §56, 12, a and [*i*]) cast suspicions of irrationality and prejudice on all knowledge of the non-geometrical, non-empirical kind (§96, 4). The recasting of cosmology in exclusively geometrical and mechanical terms led to a complete re-reading of the *quinque viæ.*

The first step in this process occurred when the fascination with geometry and especially mechanics began to reduce Aquinas' entire argument to the cosmological argument, especially in the form of the *prima via*—the argument from motion, but now narrowly inter-

preted as mere locomotion (§102, 4, b, [m]) [t]. Not surprisingly, God's existence came to be viewed mainly as a rational, *cosmological* problem. But as the God-question got reduced to the need for
a purely cosmological explanation, God's existence got minimalized,
and God's significance even more. The universe could pretty well
be counted on to function on its own. Accordingly, the key question progressively became: how much of a God do we *minimally require* to account for the world of things as we know it?

Not surprisingly, once the initial religious wonder at the intricacy
of the universe wore off (cf. §27, 3, a), nature's God got mar-
ginalized even further. Eventually, God became the "deity"—a
fixed entity remoter than the remotest stars; and divine causality in
regard to cosmic motion was reduced to the mere imparting of an
initial impulse (cf. §28, 7, [h]; §96, 4, b); it looked as if the universe
were a clockwork wound up for good in the beginning and left to
run on that divinely imparted store of energy [u]. The *deus oti-
osus* of antiquity was back, only now in the form of the cosmic artificer, absolutely omnipotent but remote, looking on from afar, presumably contented, invisible arms folded [v].

---

[t] A characteristically eighteenth-century thinker like William Paley (1743-1805),
the author of an influential *Natural Theology*, is a good example. At his hands, the
fifth way (the "argument from design") gets transmogrified into a purely mechanical proposition. Very interestingly, Paley's argument for God's existence is
drawn from the *organic* world: the structures and behaviors found in plants and
animals. Nevertheless, the key to interpret these data as evidence for God's existence (developed in the two introductory chapters, pp. 1-13), is *mechanical.* If
someone, walking out in the countryside, should chance upon *a watch*, Paley explains, the discovery that it is a "contrivance" that serves an intelligent purpose
would force him to conclude that there exists a "contriver." Thus Paley's key
example is an artificial, non-natural device that employs mechanical, purely uni-
form motion in the service of the purely numerical measurement of time; accordingly, it has nothing in common with its maker other than cleverness. This suggests that Paley's God is a "first artificer," not the Creator.

[u] The obvious philosophical problem with this is, of course, that such an initial
mechanical impulse would have been merely the first in the whole sequence of
cosmic impulses, and hence, not transcendent *in kind.* Consequently, a god
thought of as imparting the first impulse to the universe is a "stop-gap god" and
not God.

[v] With regard to "the god(s) with nothing to care about," cf. Cicero's question (*De natura deorum* 3, 93): what is there about the divine mind that allows gods
to be idle and unconcerned about human affairs? Minucius Felix confirms this
notion where he points out that Epicurus thinks of gods in terms of either idleness
or (what comes down to the same) non-existence (*Octavius* 19, 8). By Tertullian's
time, the tables seem to have been turned, witness the way he mocks Marcion (cf.
§40, 3, d; §78, 2, a) for treating the God of the New Dispensation as *deus ille otio-
sus*—the god who had nothing to do with what occurred and was announced

Eventually, even the initial impulse became a superfluous hypothesis from a scientific point of view. With this move, the probative force of the paramount argument for God's existence—the argument from motion—was wiped out; all cosmological arguments were now felt to have been discredited (cf. §99, 3, a), as a succession of thinkers, led by David Hume and Immanuel Kant, began to point out. The natural world as scientifically observed and known had ceased to support the existence of God (cf. §86, 1).

The only part of the cosmological argument—the first three ways in Aquinas—now left standing was the bare *idea* of God as "necessary being"; that idea would soon become a mere conundrum for the ratiocinating mind (cf. §107, 2-3).

[3] The radical response to these extraordinary abstract propositions of natural theology was, of course, a return to fideism. Not surprisingly, given the eighteenth and nineteenth centuries' leanings towards extremes, it took the form *pietism*, accompanied by its natural ally, traditionalism (cf. §12, 1, a). After centuries of hot, wearying doctrinal debate in the wake of the Reformation, followed by the cool formalism of the Christian Deists and the rationalists' removal of God to the margins, both of the universe and of the mind (cf. §28, 1; §72), the severance of all ties between faith and reason looked downright attractive. Irrationality was now free to become the hallmark of genuine faith. God and Jesus had to be a matter of *direct experience*, of the kind available to the individual heart alone. Roman Catholic devotionality (often tinged by Jansenism) could now succeed where heavy-handed ecclesiastical authority and theological rationality had obviously failed. So could Johann Sebastian Bach's Cantatas and Passion Oratorios in Germany, and the preaching and the hymns of John and Charles Wesley in England. Yes, reason and learning were blind—illusive to the point of despair; the balm of shared feeling was needed to regain the sense of God. A devout English Evangelical, William Cowper, on the verge of yet another attack of insanity, could convey the central theme of pietist spirituality in lines of classic simplicity:

---

during the time of the Old Dispensation, or, for that matter, with time itself. Do we not have the witness of the New Testament to assure us that God was preparing the fullness of time and teaching people to wait for it (*Adv. Marcionem* V, 4, 3; *CC* 1, p. 672)?

Judge not the Lord by feeble sense,
But trust him for his grace;
Behind a frowning providence
He hides a smiling face.

. . .

Blind unbelief is sure to err,
And scan his work in vain;
God is his own interpreter,
And he will make it plain.[49]

[4] Still, human intellectuality dies hard. The story of theological reflection on the living God turned out to have a future after pietism. The misinterpretation of Aquinas' *viæ* forced the development of the modern, purely anthropological "proofs" of God's existence (§104), among which John Henry Newman's proof from conscience holds pride of place (§105). And eventually (as well as far more importantly for the continued life of the great Tradition), there is, in our own day, the recovery of the twin themes of Christian witness and God's powerlessness (§§106-111). The next chapter must tell that story.

CHAPTER 11

The Living God: The Modern Quest

THEOLOGY AND ANTHROPOLOGY

[§104] THE TURN TO THE ANTHROPOLOGICAL ARGUMENT

[1] If we discount the option of radical pietism, the triumph of rational, scientific, and technological understanding and manipulation of the world left human reason in the West only one alternative—one which it took: it resigned itself to the separation of nature and freedom (§80, 3, [c]; §87, 2, d, [gg]; §94, 6, a). That is, in order to recover its full range of creativity, it made its *Wende zum Subjekt*—its turn, away from the exterior world of mere objects, to the inner world of the subject. C. P. Snow's "two cultures" became an entrenched cultural fact in the West (cf. §87, 2, a, [x]). The more traditional circles, devoted to the arts and to "humane" science, began to flaunt *Geisteswissenschaft* as true humane learning, while decrying *Naturwissenschaft* and the spirit of enterprise and progress associated with it (though often secretly admiring as well as fearing both of them). Eventually, in the twentieth century, this humanist, anti-scientific mood was to produce the existentialist movement; in fact, some schools of existentialism tried to make the contest between objectivity and subjectivity a matter of principle, while at the same time deciding it in favor of the latter, by simply (and, it must be added, often quite condescendingly) tarring science ("thing-thinking") with the brush of "inauthenticity."

The turn to the subject accounts for the rise of a new and (despite its strongly Augustinian features) typically *modern* type of "proofs" of the existence of God. What characterizes these proofs is their avoidance of cosmology and of demonstration by recourse to causality (and especially efficient causality), and their reliance on *anthropology* alone. The general tenor of these arguments is as follows: there are certain distinctively *human* experiences and phenomena (of the kind at best indirectly related to the world of things) which make sense only if they are understood to imply the existence of God as a postulate. Such human experiences and phenomena, these anthropological arguments usually point out, are inherently marked by irresolution and even conflict (especially in the form of the never-ending struggle around the issues of influence, inclusion, and intimacy: cf. §98, 4, a-c); but in the end these conflicts and imbalances "drive us into the arms of God." Not surprisingly, therefore, the arguments frequently contain explicit, and highly characteristic, elements of *katharsis* and, and, hence, of *fiduciality*. Put differently, the anthropological arguments tend to be analyses of the implicit human *longing for God* rather than "demonstrations" of God's "objective" existence; on closer inspection (so the arguments go) deep, "existential" human experience presupposes an implicit *trust* in God as the condition for its own possibility. By virtue of this implicit trust believers can conquer their impasses and their anxieties, recover wholeness, and (in Paul Tillich's celebrated phrase) find "the courage to be"; in this fashion they end up finding both God and their authentic selves, as well as true human community.

[a] It is not farfetched to connect the anti-cosmological mood, the emphasis on anthropology, and the predominance of fiduciality in these arguments with the Reformation, or at least with the intellectual atmosphere associated with it. The Reformation's personalist bias—its stress on the human experience of salvation from the sinful human predicament as the center of the Christian profession of faith—shared the New Learning's tendency to dissociate cosmos and humanity, by objectifying the world and setting humanity apart from it as the proper object of God's concern (cf. §20, 1-2). Thus the enrichment of the great Tradition furnished by the anthropological proofs is ultimately of Protestant (and especially neo-Protestant) extraction. No wonder the Catholic world, dreading Protestant "subjectivism," was long wary of them: not until anthropology came to be understood in terms of dynamic attunement to true transcendence (Blondel played a crucial role here; cf. §§85, 87) did theological anthropology of the "transcendental" kind find acceptance in Catholic circles.

[b]   On a quite different score, it is possible to interpret the
ethnological argument (§102, 4, a, [k]) as an anthropological argument, inasmuch as it relies on evidence pointing, beyond attempts at mere survival, in the direction of a cultivated sense of
human transcendence, and thus presumed to be universally and
characteristically human (development of authority structures,
burial customs, offerings to unseen spiritual powers, the cultivation of etiological myths about the cosmos, etc.; cf. §41, 1-2).[1]
The same can be said for the so-called "eudaemonological"
argument, which argues that humanity's innate, never-ceasing desire for ever-greater happiness—an extrapolation from humanity's immanent penchant for self-transcending growth (cf. §87,
2,a)—postulates the existence of God.

[2]   Immanuel Kant (who denies the validity of any rational arguments for God's existence, whether ontological or cosmological; cf.
§63, 1, a; §107, 2-3; 5, b-c) gives us a most representative sample of
this new type of argument. The essential human experience of *free,
conscientious moral choice, resolve, and action,* he explains, implies the
postulate of God's existence. This postulate is a matter of practical
reason, which operates not by natural determinism but by human
freedom. Practical reason, therefore, is above pure reason; accordingly, the postulate is inarguable. Yet in practice it can be accepted
as a true metaphysical insight.[2] For whenever we act out of genuine moral conviction (that is, not merely to fulfill a moral obligation imposed on us from outside), we find ourselves implicitly wish-
ing that the interior "maxim" *we* are *freely choosing to follow* should
really be a *universal* law; this shows that we are deciding and acting,
and doing so reasonably, on an imperative that is not predicated on
our limited personal experience, but on one that is unconditional
and "categorical." This imperative can be formulated as follows:

Act only according to that maxim which enables you at the same time to
wish that it should become a universal law.[3]

This combination of universality and unconditionality in the experience of the free, autonomous (!) moral conscience making choices
is understandable only if we take it to imply, as a necessary postulate, the reality of God.

Implicit in this experience, Kant goes on to explain, are two further postulates. Both are roundly fiducial. First, there is the fact
that in the world as we know it, virtue and happiness are all too often separated. Yet the moral conscience demands that they should

ultimately coincide. Now the essential link between conscience and God suggests that they will so coincide, even if the manner in which this will be accomplished is not open to human understanding, let alone verification. Thus the experience of moral conscience supports the anticipation that *eternal happiness will be the reward of virtue*—an anticipation only God can fulfill. This first postulate is related to a second one. To make this eternal reward possible, the experience of moral conscience must be taken to imply the assurance of *individual immortality*[4]—a postulate that can be fairly called one of the Enlightenment's hobbyhorses,[5] and in many ways its substitute for the living God.

[a] This last, somewhat scornful observation is made to raise a question—one that Kant fails to answer adequately. In Kant's analysis, which is beholden to which? Is the conscience beholden to God, or God to the conscience? In other words, is God not reduced to a mere function of the autonomous conscience? That is, is transcendence not reduced to immanence? To arrive at God as *real*, do we not somehow have to pass beyond a postulate for God's existence based entirely on human self-assurance, and proceed to an acknowledgment of God as a transcendent Reality that encounters us and prompts worship? In other words, how does Kant's analysis show, not only that God is a function of the human conscience, but also (and even more) that conscience is a function of a truly transcendent God?

[3] With his argument, Kant has moved to within a stone's throw of the religious and theological experience of Romanticism. For Kant, "the starry heavens above us and the moral law within us" are the *loci* of genuine religion. The former is symbolic. Geometrical and technological reason have assigned to God a place beyond the fixed stars—beyond the remotest reaches of the knowable cosmos; religion, therefore, is not a matter of rational knowledge, whose proper subject-matter is the cosmos and its workings. The second is practical. Religion, Kant maintains, is a matter of an earnest, self-motivated upright moral life under the categorical imperative, inspired by the anticipation of everlasting happiness.

[a] However, to reach the fullness of the Romantic vision, what the spirit of the Enlightenment had left to achieve was one more, final displacement. That displacement involved two realizations: first, that moral norms are culturally determined, and secondly, that the sense of obligation we experience in the moral

conscience is not innate and categorical, but acquired and hypo-
thetical. Enlightened socio-political reason took responsibility
for this move; the sense of duty (or the categorical imperative),
it began to declare, is not implanted from on high, but simply
motivated by the social contract; consequently, true judgments
about what is and is not moral are shaped only culturally, and
encoded by means of enlightened laws. In this way, much to the
relief of many conscientious unbelievers, it could become clear
that people no longer had to be religious to qualify as moral.
Humanity, it began to be widely perceived, is morally autonomous.

[4] Thus the spirit of the Enlightenment succeeded in secularizing
the human world as definitively as it had demystified the cosmos.
In this predicament, where will intelligent, responsible, self-conscious individuals turn to account for the sense of God?

This is precisely the question Friedrich Schleiermacher poses in
the second of his *Speeches*. His answer is as simple as it is profound:
truly enlightened people, Schleiermacher explains, find the sense
of God in the depth of their own self-consciousness. The evidence
for God, in other words, is purely anthropological; every connection
with the world of things has been severed. For this reason, the
Speeches deserve pride of place among the anthropological arguments; arguably, they represent the prototype. In typically (and, in
fact, radically) Romantic manner, Schleiermacher scorns the idea
that the basis of religion is a conventional mixture of knowledge of
the world and morality. How could cosmological metaphysics (with
its account of God as the ultimate explanation of the universe) and
ethics (with its intimations of a happy life hereafter as the reward
for stern virtue practiced in the present life) add up to a sense of
the transcendent God? Schleiermacher writes:

... you can mix and stir all you want; this is never going to blend; you are
playing a futile game with materials that resist combination; all you will
ever get is what you have: metaphysics and morality. This mess of opinions
about the supreme Being or about the world, and of precepts for a human
life (or even for two)—you call that religion? And the instinctive drive
that hunts for these opinions, and also for the dark intimations that are the
ultimate sanction of these precepts—you call that religiosity? But what
causes you to mistake a mere compilation, an anthology for beginners, for
a proper masterpiece, for something particular—something with an origin
and a power all its own?[6]

Thus, to draw the modern "despisers of religion" back to the original and proper sense of God without having to fob them off with pietism, Schleiermacher refers them to the deeper, reverential piety that lies at the core of human self-consciousness itself (cf. §24, 3). *There* is the primary evidence of the reality and actuality of God. Whoever pays attention, contemplatively, to the majesty of the universe as a whole will discover an *inner* "feeling" of reverence and total dependence that corresponds to it. This discovery also involves a most profound experience of self-identity, affective as well as luminous. In it, human persons find the original *locus* of the awareness of God. It is an awareness of both self and God; it is indebted to nothing and nobody; it is unmediated and entirely self-authenticating.[7]

No wonder the second of the *Speeches* was never conceived as an argument for God's existence. God-consciousness may conceivably have to be pointed out to people who are unaware of possessing it in themselves; the reality of God is itself beyond demonstration. But, very importantly, God-consciousness is nothing but the deepest, constitutive feature of human self-consciousness itself. In the Christian profession of faith, this is exemplarily (*vorbildlich*), and indeed, archetypically (*urbildlich*) recognized in the person of Jesus, acknowledged as the actualization of humanity at its most mature— fully self-conscious and spiritual. In that capacity, Jesus is also the original exemplar of God-consciousness; in that capacity, he is its universal mediator as well.

It is unnecessary to point out the brilliance of this theological conception; unnecessary, too, to point out that it (again) raises the unsettling question whether the living God is not here being replaced by a mere human sense of God (cf. §9, 1, a; §24, 1-4; §25, 4, d; §35, 3, a) [*a*].[8]

[*a*] In our own day, the anthropological, "experiential-expressivist"[9] approach continues to dominate the demonstration (not so much of God's existence, as) of the essential relevance of religious experience to human existence.[10] Reflective, "transcendental" anthropology is manifest, not only in classics like Ru-

---

[*a*] On the interpretation of "feeling" in Schleiermacher's analysis of religion, cf. Richard R. Niebuhr, *Schleiermacher on Christ and Religion*, pp. 116-34; F. J. van Beeck, *Christ Proclaimed*, pp. 454-65. On the misunderstanding between Schleiermacher and Hegel on the subject, cf. Nicholas Lash's sensible discussion in *Easter in Ordinary*, pp. 125-28.

dolph Otto's *Das Heilige* (ET *The Idea of the Holy*) and William James' *The Varieties of Religious Experience* (cf. §35, 3), but also in modern works by great systematic theologians. There is Paul Tillich's idealist-existentialist analysis—in short works like *Dynamics of Faith* and *The Courage to Be*, but also in the first volume of his *Systematic Theology*—of the human predicament as an existential "quest," to which the divine answer is "the New Being" (cf. §83, 3). There is also Karl Rahner's transcendental-Thomist *Hörer des Wortes* (ET *Hearers of the Word*) and the opening chapters of his *Grundkurs des Glaubens* (ET *Foundations of Christian Faith*). The idea also shows in a host of "minor" works. Examples are Hugo Rahner's elegant *Der spielende Mensch* (ET *Man at Play*), Peter Berger's *A Rumor of Angels*, John Coulson's *Religion and Imagination*, Ray L. Hart's *Unfinished Man and the Imagination*, John Macquarrie's *God-Talk*, Paul van Buren's *The Edges of Language*. All of these show, by means of careful analysis, how elements of transcendence are integral to characteristically human experience. And as for the fiducial element in the anthropological arguments, note how crucial the category of *trust* is to Hans Küng's strategy in *Existiert Gott?* (ET *Does God Exist?*).

Quite recently, however, Nicholas Lash, in an admirable monograph entitled *Easter in Ordinary*, has proposed a careful and welcome recovery of the classical balance between subjectivity and objectivity (that is, between humanity and the world we live in and are part of), by showing that transcendental anthropology alone cannot and will not account for religious experience.

[b] It must indeed be conceded that the loss of connection with cosmology has been seriously detrimental to catholic theology [b]. Yet it must also be conceded, thankfully, that the turn to anthropology, one-sided as it may be, has also been very productive. The catholic decision, first advocated by thinkers like Blondel, to join the culture in doing justice to the subject (cf. §85, 4) has borne fruit. Reflection on such typically anthro-

---

[b] It still is, and it remains especially painful in the continuing irresolution of the part of the Christian community as a whole to come to a truly discerning evaluation of the blessings that science and technology have undeniably given to the world. The chasm fixed between Christian ethics and the world of modern medicine and life science is only one very troubling instance of this. The task of integration remains enormous. Think of the entire area of global injustice brought about by scientific and technological inequalities, to say nothing of the issues involved in the preservation and restoration of the environment.

pological themes as "immanence" and "transcendental a priori" has marvelously stretched our theological awareness of the range of available human experience; in doing so, it has helped demonstrate the depth and the breadth of humanity's capacity, both for inner fulfillment (§28, 6, d) and for deep authenticity, so necessary in the midst of a bewilderingly differentiated world. It has led to the retrieval of the traditional catholic insight that the native attunement of the person to Transcendence is the fundamental invitation to human maturity—intellectual, ethical, and ultimately mystical.

The next section must elaborate a striking example of this.

[§105] JOHN HENRY NEWMAN'S ARGUMENT FROM CONSCIENCE

[1]   It is fascinating to discover, in the midst of the sophisticated humanism of the nineteenth century, so ardent in its glorification of Nature as a source of authenticity and so studiously attentive to human sensitivities, yet so out of touch with humanity's deep physical involvement in the material world [c], one anthropological argument for God's existence that stands out for the way it succeeds in blending sincere Protestant self-conscientiousness and firm Catholic "objectivity": John Henry Newman's argument from the analysis of conscience. It is a handsome piece of theological mediation in another respect as well: it shows, on the one hand, a deep affinity with Romanticism and the anthropological concerns typical of

---

[c] When dealing with nineteenth-century Western European culture, it is always good to bear in mind that dissociation of sensibility is characteristic of the higher *Bildungsschichten.* The dissociation takes the shape of a deep rift between (among other things) human interiority and the material world, soul and body, and further down the line, anthropology and cosmology. But beyond this, it is good to be aware that there is a powerful and ugly social side to the dissociation as well. The curious, detached unworldliness of both the Rationalist and the Romantic mind is not unrelated to the ugly chasm fixed between the rich and the poor. On one side of this indefensible dissociation between what amounts to two kinds of humanity, there are the upper classes and the *bourgeoisie.* They are marked by aloofness from coarse matter and a differentiated, individualized consciousness, and they taste the cultural delights (as well as the neuroses) their situation of detachment confers. On the other side, there are the industrial and rural proletariates—the disadvantaged, downtrodden masses, leading wholly sub-human lives, alienated from integral humanity and depersonalized by virtue of having been turned into mere workers, immersed in the process of sheer material production. Small wonder that both Christian faith and atheism should have become class issues. And, it must be added, for all the hardship suffered by the poor that emigrated to the New World, they escaped at least this plight.

the age, and on the other, the theological freedom characteristic of genuine faith (cf. §14, 3).

[2] In its developed form, the argument is found in the *Grammar of Assent*, published in 1870,[11] in the form of a full-fledged phenomenological analysis *avant la lettre*. It represents a lifetime of reflection, for attempts and insights pointing in the direction of the mature argument are found in some of Newman's earlier works,[12] especially in the *University Sermons* [d].

Newman begins by simply settling on the experiential principle "that we have by nature a conscience." On that basis, he sets out to explain how "we gain an image of God," and how we "give a real assent to the proposition that He exists."[13]

[3] Conscience, Newman points out, has two distinguishable yet inseparable elements: a *moral sense* and a *sense of duty*; both of them are integral to the full experience of conscience. By virtue of the former, we make specific moral choices; we discriminate between what is good and what is evil. This is conscience viewed as "the rule of right conduct"; it is the part of conscience where human understanding, both of humanity and the world, plays an essential role, and hence, the part where *change*, both for the better and the worse, can occur. The latter element—the sense of duty—is the *stable* element in the experience of conscience. For in every experience of conscience we are aware of something not subject to either negotiation or revision; it is not mediated by the moral culture to which we belong; it is the inalienable and permanent element of human moral consciousness as such. That element is the authoritative "dictate"—the straightforward sense of obligation to do what is good. Having explained this distinction (which will turn out to be, in due course, of crucial significance to the distinction between ethics and religion), Newman declares he will leave the former alone and pursue the latter.[14]

[4] There is, Newman points out, a curious feature to conscience taken as the *sense of duty*. Unlike, say, the sense of beauty,

---

[d] Nicholas Lash writes: "The *University Sermons* remain the indispensable companion to the *Grammar of Assent*." This is supported by Newman's own testimony, in a letter written just after the completion of the manuscript of the *Grammar*: "I began [the inquiry] in my Oxford University Sermons." Cf. *Grammar of Assent*, (ed. Lash), pp. 1-2.

... conscience does not repose on itself, but vaguely reaches forward to something beyond itself, and dimly discerns a sanction higher than self for its decisions, as is evidenced in that keen sense of obligation and responsibility which informs them. And hence it is that we are accustomed to speak of conscience as a voice, a term which we should never think of applying to the sense of the beautiful; and moreover a voice, or the echo of a voice, imperative and constraining, like no other dictate in the world of our experience.[15]

Newman recognizes, implicit in the phenomenon of this commanding inner voice [e], two distinctive features of the experience of conscience.

The first of these is *personalness*:

... it is always, what the sense of the beautiful is only in certain cases; it is always emotional. No wonder then that it always implies what sense only sometimes implies; that it always involves the recognition of a living object, towards which it is directed. Inanimate things cannot stir our affections; these are correlative with persons.[16]

The second is *transcendence*. The depth of affect stirred up by conscience, in the form both of negative feelings of remorse, compunction, confusion, foreboding, and self-condemnation, and of positive feelings of peace, security, self-abandon, and hope, gives rise to the following reflection.

If the cause of these emotions does not belong to this visible world, the Object to which [a person's] perception is directed must be Supernatural and Divine; and thus the phenomena of Conscience, as a dictate, avail to impress the imagination with the picture of a Supreme Governor, a Judge, holy, just, powerful, all-seeing, retributive, and is the creative principle of religion, as the Moral Sense is the principle of ethics.[17]

---

[e] Heidegger has observed the same "voice," witness §57 in *Being and Time*, devoted to the experience of conscience. He writes (*Sein und Zeit*, p. 275; cf. ET, p. 320): "For the call is never ever either planned, or arranged, or deliberately performed *by ourselves*. »It« calls [»*Es*« *ruft*], contrary to expectation and even contrary to volition. On the other hand, the call indubitably does not derive from someone else in the world with me. The call comes *out of* me and yet *upon* me [*Der Ruf kommt* aus *mir und doch* über *mich*]." Heidegger rightly explains that it is understandable but also methodologically precipitate that the voice should have been interpreted in terms of "an alien [*sic!*] power forcefully thrusting itself into human existence from elsewhere [*einer in das Dasein hereinragenden fremden Macht*]," construed, say, "as a self-manifesting person (*i.e.*, God) [*als sich bekundende Person (Gott)*]." Instead, he very characteristically (and very much unlike Newman) regards the voice as an *impersonal* feature of *Dasein*.

[5] Thus conscience, in Newman's analysis of it, does squarely involve the moral sense; concern about the right ordering of human life in the world (and consequently, the careful study of ethics) is integral to the conscientious life. But for true *guidance* the moral sense must rely on the sense of duty—the experience of superior obligation. Now far from being an empty moral form, the sense of duty is both *dynamic* and, in the final analysis, properly *religious*. This has consequences. Newman had dwelled on the most important in his Anglican days, long before he wrote the *Grammar of Assent*, in one of the *University Sermons* (cf. §49, 2, c):

Conscience implies a relation between the soul and a something exterior, and that, moreover, superior to itself; a relation to an excellence which it does not possess, and to a tribunal over which it has no power. And since the more closely this inward monitor is respected and followed, the clearer, the more exalted, and the more varied its dictates become, and the standard of excellence is ever outstripping, while it guides, our obedience, a moral conviction is thus at length obtained of the unapproachable nature as well as the supreme authority of That, whatever it is, which is the object of the mind's contemplation.[18]

In this way conscience, understood as the sense of duty, turns out to be an authoritative inner guide—one that demands that it be cherished and taken seriously; followed, not manipulated (cf. GS 16; DH 4316; cf. §131, 2 and a-b). If heeded, it will take a person on a journey into territories of responsibility and disciplined self-denial whose horizons are apt to recede further and further. The journey will prove to require gifts of progressive clarity of moral vision, nobility of moral purpose, and subtlety of moral appreciation. Surprisingly, though, the person on the journey will turn out to muster these gifts as the progress demands. The moral life turns into a gentle yet demanding school of true virtue, yet in such a way that the call to virtue, while ever close at hand, is limitless. That is, its measure can only be a Reality of transcendent justice and holiness that eludes every grasp.

[6] Interestingly, Newman's analysis of conscience recalls the passage in the *Confessions* in which Augustine relates his former ignorance of the difference between mere moral custom and the inner sense of justice that attunes one to God's law.[19] More fundamentally, however, it is a timely recovery of a constitutive element in the Jewish-Christian tradition: that characteristic cluster of connections by which the living God is related to a humanity that is both part

of the world and responsible for the world to God. Humanity once again turns out to be natively oriented to, and invited to respond to, a God who never ceases to call for greater virtue, thus remaining ever greater than the call. Thus the sense of duty is found to lead the person beyond mere morality; it offers a challenge that is measureless; that distinctively human pursuit, which is the sustained moral life, turns out to be squarely set within the force field of holiness (§49). Accordingly, the deepest blessing that may befall the truly moral person is an experienced increase—not diminishment!—in devotion; as human persons grow in intimacy with God, they will find themselves imbued by a deeper sense of awe in the presence of the God who Alone is Holy and who Alone is *semper maior* (cf. §34, 2; §97, 10, [u]). For this is how and where the tables are turned. What started as a human quest and a postulate of the moral conscience has turned into an encounter with the living God. Transcendence has disclosed itself and begun to "preside" over the developments that led up to the awareness of it (cf. §102, 4, d).

[7] So we have caught the great Tradition astir once again, in the act of coming alive (§55, 4), becoming aware of the unconditional yet all-enabling Presence that is so transcendent as to move our innermost immanence (§95, 10). Humanity once again turns out to be so wholly encompassed by the "divine milieu" that it is touched to the core by it: human conscience senses transcendence—its appeal as well as its majesty.

And as a result, while it is not surprising that there should be theology in all anthropology, it is even less surprising that anthropology should prove to be steeped in theology. That decisive Jewish-Christian asymmetry again.

THEOLOGY BEYOND THE POWER OF BEING

[§106] ESTABLISHED CHRISTIANITY AND THE NEGLECT OF WITNESS

[1] There is one feature of the Jewish-Christian understanding of the living God that is not mentioned, let alone treated as crucially important, by either Anselm or Aquinas. Pascal does mention it; in fact, he emphasizes it as the very thing that sets the living God—the God of the Jewish-Christian Tradition—apart from the God of the New Learning. God is the *God of the witnesses* (§96, 1; 5-6; cf. §95, 7; 10-11):

God of Abraham, God of Isaac, God of Jacob,
not of the philosophers and the men of learning.
God of Jesus Christ.

Viewed from the vantage point of Pascal's *Mémorial*, does it not seem curious that two of the Christian West's greatest reflective theologians should have relied so much, for their thoughts on the nature of God, on the allegedly universal human ability to interpret humanity and the cosmos, and so little on qualified witnesses [*f*]?

[a] Witness is indeed integral, not just to the origins of Israel's faith, but to its entire faith-tradition [*g*]. This is entirely in keeping with the fact that Israel thinks of God as utterly transcendent: while intimately present to Israel and, indeed, immanent in the world, God is in no way part of the world. Consequently, those who truly believe find God represented and witnessed to by things and events in the world, and most of all by men and women of faith. Accordingly, countless passages in the Bible testify to the fact that Israel is accustomed to appeal to the obvious majesty of the cosmos to profess its sense of God (examples are Ps 19, 1-4; Is 40, 26. 28; Jer 5, 21-22), and the Jewish wisdom tradition is dedicated to elaborating and orchestrating the theme (cf. Sir 42, 15 - 43, 33). But most importantly, in all its history, Judaism never abandoned its reliance on qualified human witness, whether for the cultivation of its faith-tradition inside the community or for its dialogue with those outside. Even the most universalist traditions in Judaism will affirm that it takes a special, prophetic gift of affinity with God to interpret the

---

[*f*] In fairness to Aquinas it should be pointed out that his treatment of witness as a theological (as against forensic or moral) theme mainly takes the shape of a careful analysis of *prophecy* (cf. especially *S. Th.* II-II, *quæstiones* 171-74). Aquinas associates prophecy principally, not with the understanding of the nature of God, but with particular instances of divine revelation transcendently accorded to privileged individuals, corresponding to inner illuminations produced by the Holy Spirit.

[*g*] A famous passage in one of the prophets sums it up as well as any. When the authorities are planning the murder of Jeremiah, they salve their consciences by assuring each other that the dispatching of one prophetic troublemaker is not likely to jeopardize the customary exercise of authoritative witness to the living God: the teaching of the Law, the cultivation of wisdom, and the prophetic utterance of the word of God. So they say, "Come, let us plot against Jeremiah, for the priest will never be short of instruction [*tôrāh*], nor the wise person of counsel, nor the prophet of the word" (Jer 18, 18).

world as it demands to be interpreted (cf. Sir 17, 8; cf. Wisd 13, 1-9; Rom 1, 19-20). The secure possession of the truth, in other words, is the fruit of divine inspiration of one kind or another and its careful cultivation. Only what is positively attested by God can be congruent with the natural, and hence, real; the alternative to dependence on Torah, prophecy, and wisdom, therefore, is not trust in worshipless natural reason, but deceitful, idolatrous vanity and folly [h].

[b] The theme of witness pervades the New Testament writings as well, as a glance at any New Testament concordance will bear out [i]. The New Testament casts, not only the Baptist and Jesus' disciples, but also the Old Testament authors, in the role of witnesses. Most importantly, of course, Jesus himself is "the loyal and true witness" (Rev 3, 14; cf. 1, 5; cf. 1 Tim 6, 13). Even the Holy Spirit and God are cited and referred to as witnesses. The theme, while ubiquitous, is especially prominent in the fourth Gospel, the Johannine letters, the Lukan writings, and the Apocalypse. In fact, it is so powerful and many-sided that a biblical theologian might well describe the entire Christ-event as treated in the New Testament in terms of a dynamic network of witnessing relationships.

[c] For the full revival of the theme of witness in catholic theology, we must go to the modern period. Pascal's vehemence on the subject, in the mid-seventeenth century, indicates that he is making an unfamiliar point. But by the early nineteenth century, Newman is treating the theme as a commonplace one, though still with a noticeable sadness. His *Lectures on the Prophetical Office of the Church* of 1837 are based, as are so many of the *Tracts for the Times*, on the Tractarian conviction that the nation is apos-

---

[h] For a New Testament example of the contrast, cf. 1 Cor 3, 20, where Paul quotes Ps 94, 11. Incidentally, it may be pertinent to remind ourselves at this point that the reluctance to engage in *forms* of worship that is so characteristic of modern religious universalism of Deist extraction (cf. §25, 4, c; §30, 5) was unknown among the ancient universalist philosophers, at least in the sense that they considered practices of meditation and of philosophic prayer to, say, the *Logos* integral to the philosophic quest for a purer, more spiritualized humanity. Cf. Pierre Hadot, *Exercices spirituels et philosophie antique.* Cf. also the suggestions in Peter Brown, *Augustine of Hippo,* pp. 165-68.

[i] "Witness" is of very frequent occurrence in the New Testament writings, both the nominal (Gk. *martys* and *martyria/martyrion*) and the verbal (*martyreō/martyromai*) senses.

tatizing, and hence, that the Christian establishment can no longer count on the culture for support. The Christian community will once again have to witness to its faith freely and deliberately, in the face of widespread unbelief.

For Newman, witnessing to the truth is far from identical with the affirmation of objective truths; not surprisingly, therefore, the distinction between affirmation and witness is never very far from the center of his thought. In a culture dominated by rationalism, the idea of witness turns up with special clarity in Newman's careful distinction between notional assent and real assent, between affirmation based on cogent, strictly intellectual apprehension and affirmation sustained by personal commitment.[20] Newman treats the subject of *Christian* witness explicitly and at length in an early sermon entitled "Witnesses to the Resurrection." It points out, quite ominously, that those are "few in number" who are "on the side of *Truth*." If this holds for the general body of Christians, in which the saints are invariably hidden, it applies all the more to the world at large, where error is so prevalent as to threaten to lead true believers to despond.[21] Christians, in Newman's mind, clearly cannot count any longer, for the profession of their faith, on any normative cultural-religious climate, not even among themselves.

[2] All of this is remarkable enough to invite reflection. The facts suggest that Anselm and Aquinas had come to count on the cultural milieu (and on the mind shaped by that milieu) to represent the Christian conception of God so assuredly that they could simply appeal to universal reason to support it. Personal witness no longer came to mind as a prime source of the knowledge and understanding of the God in whom they believed. If this hypothesis should be true, serious questions arise.

Could it be that the establishment of Christianity served, not only to shape and refine Western culture as well as Western culture's conception of God, but also, in the longer run, to blind it to its fundamental reliance on witness, and hence, to impoverish it (cf. §74)? And since any establishment is a matter of *cultural dominance,* could it be that the conception of God in the West has, ever since the Constantinian era and the subsequent Christianization of Europe after the fall of the Roman Empire [j], suffered a lapse of

---

[j] For a few suggestions, cf. F. J. van Beeck, *Loving the Torah More than God?*, pp.

memory as a result of its association with power, as Gerd Theißen suggests (cf. §64, 5)? And hence, could it be that—in the Providence of God—the Christian community has positively *needed* the modern victory of both scientific and technological reason and autonomous, secular humanism over Christian faith and theological anthropology? And did the Christian conception of God have to be *forced* to recover its roots in witness?

Again, at the very least, all of this invites reflection. To get a sense of the dimensions of the issue, let us turn to two texts. One is by Aquinas; it was touched upon earlier in this volume. The other one is a passage, not quoted thus far, from Immanuel Kant's *Critique of Pure Reason.*

[§107] GOD BEYOND AFFIRMATION: AQUINAS AND KANT

[1] When Aquinas describes how we ascend to the knowledge of God by way of *remotio*, he writes (§67, 2; cf. §102, 7):

... when we proceed towards God on the road of removal, we first deny everything corporeal of God. Then we go on to deny everything spiritual as it is found in creatures, such as goodness and wisdom. At that point, all that is left in our minds is that God *is*, and nothing else; thus God *is* in some kind of perplexing fashion, so to speak. *Last of all, however, we remove from God even this very being according as it occurs in creatures.* At that point, God is left to dwell in a kind of darkness of ignorance; yet *after the manner of this ignorance*—at least as long as we are on our present way—*we are best united with God*, as Dionysius says. This is a dark cloud of sorts, in which God is said to dwell.[22]

[2] To appreciate what is happening in this passage, written about the year 1255, let us contrast it with a passage written well over five hundred years later, by Immanuel Kant. It first appeared in print in 1781, in the first *Critique.*

Towards the end of the book, while discussing the cosmological argument, and specifically the argument from necessity (Aquinas' third way: §102, 2, ll. 45-66), Kant suddenly (and quite uncharacteristically) sounds a highly personal note. He writes:

Unconditioned necessity, which we need as the ultimate bearer of all things, to the point of being unable to dispense with it, is the true abyss for human reason. Even eternity, so dreadfully sublime ..., does not make so

70-75.

vertiginous an impression on the mind; for it only *measures* the duration of things—it does not *carry* them. We cannot help thinking (yet we cannot stand thinking it either) that a being that we also envisage as the highest among all possible beings should, as it were, say to itself: I am from eternity to eternity; aside from me there is nothing, save what is something by virtue of my will alone; *but where, then, am I from?* Here everything drops out from under us, and the greatest perfection as well as the least is up in the air, discomfited, before speculative reason alone, which considers it no matter to let both the one and the other vanish away, without the slightest hindrance.[23]

[3] From a neo-scholastic point of view, it is not difficult to find fault with this passage. No Thomist or neo-Thomist would ever allow that we "envisage" or "portray" (*uns ... vorstellen*) God, let alone that we envisage the transcendent God merely "as the highest among all possible beings." Aquinas himself, along with the Tradition, would have agreed with Kant that the conception of God involves the affirmation that God is both eternal and the sole creator of all things;[24] still, he would in all likelihood have been offended by the picture of God self-consciously going over these attributes and rehearsing them, as it were. In the great Tradition, neither divine self-assurance nor divine self-absorption or self-preoccupation, let alone any need for self-perfection on the part of God, are the motive and the goal of creation, but only the free sharing of the divine goodness *with others* (cf. §98,7 4, c).[25]

Still, in fairness to Kant, critical comments like these are mere nigglings in the face of the extraordinary purport of the text as a whole. If we wish to *understand* it, we must not debate, correct, or refute, but *interpret.* For in this passage, Kant is not just making a few embarrassing logical errors, which then deservedly prevent him from developing a sound conception of God; he is conveying, and conveying dramatically, the religious experience of the modern mind, self-confined as it is to the rational, scientific study of a neutralized, almost wholly objectified material world, and to the rational, technological manipulation of it. That experience is one of *radical bewilderment at the very thought of the living God.*

We are torn, Kant is saying; the one notion we cannot live without is the very notion we cannot live with either. For on the one hand, we badly *need* the sovereign self-sufficiency ("unconditioned necessity") of God, to assure us that the world of things we know about and manipulate is *real;* in fact, we need this assurance all the more since we realize that the world's essential nature ultimately eludes our rational understanding. But on the other hand, the very conception of God we so desperately need wholly perplexes us. What else could a sovereign, self-sufficient God be except *self-asserting*? But, disconcertingly, the picture of God asserting, to his own satisfaction, the divine eternity and omnipotence stirs up in us, not certainty or assurance, let alone awe in the face of transcendence, but an instinctive reaction of *anxiety*. The reason for this is simple: it is quite beyond us to imagine how self-assertion can be prompted by anything but basic disquiet about one's own being: *but where, then, am I from?* By the late eighteenth century, the only thinkable, imaginable, and hence *real* self has become (at least in polite circles) the *anxious* self—the self that feels compelled to account for itself. The experience of the *divided self*, in other words, has become the normative experience of spirit (cf. §95, 1, a, [*jj*]) [*k*]. Unnervingly, we moderns do not succeed in imagining *as real* a self-sufficient, omnipotent God that is free from explicit, thematic self-assertion—that is, a God unmoved by that most distinctively modern (and hence, we tend to feel, deepest) experience of identity: *self-questioning self-consciousness.*

Stop right here at the edge, says Kant. This is too much to take. This is where everything crumbles. At this point, what difference does anything make any more? At the thought of this preoccupied God, all things, the most tenuous as well as the most substantial, turn into mere ideas and essences, ethereal, without anchorage in reality. At the very thought of God, that is, far from acquiring ultimate coherence and stability as anticipated, the world order disintegrates. Aquinas could not have been more wrongheaded. He argued that reflective attention paid to an active but orderly cosmos paves the way to the true God. The shoe is entirely on the other foot: the speculative attempt to ascend from the world to the conception of God seduces reason into the nightmare of cosmic collapse. The conception of God should never have been attempted. Go back to where you came from. After all, your mind is not responsible for the world as a whole; it is meant to deal with *things*; it can afford, without any cost to itself,[26] to drop the subject of absolute perfection as immaterial.

Thus speculative reason conceiving of God finds itself faltering

---

[*k*] J. H. van den Berg's *Leven in meervoud* (ET *Divided Existence and Complex Society*) remains a fascinating exploration, guided by a wealth of artistic and literary detail, of the extent to which self-doubling and self-dividing forms of human self-awareness have become part and parcel of modern Western culture.

at the very point where it is attempting to understand what it most needs to both understand and affirm as understood. But in endeavoring to make the affirmation, the mind finds itself treading on the quicksand of indefinite regress and losing its foothold. The Ground of Being turns out to be an abyss; the Power of Being turns out to awaken a deep sense of ineffectualness. Under the circumstances, all the mind can do is to admit complete defeat and give up.[27]

[4] By contrast, far from becoming dizzy and irresolute at the thought of God, Aquinas (like Anselm before him: §101, 9) seems to come home when he travels beyond affirmation. This is, in fact, exactly what happens. After removing from God whatever is merely cosmological ("everything corporeal") and anthropological and angelological ("everything spiritual ... in creatures"), he arrives at the naked affirmation that God, "in some kind of perplexing fashion," simply *is*. But that done, without a trace of hesitation, he boldly steps forward into the void:

... we remove from God even this very being according as it occurs in creatures.

In this way Aquinas makes it clear that the mainspring of his intellectual inquiry and its ultimate guarantee is neither the desperate need to know God articulately, to the mind's own satisfaction, nor the need to be assured that in his questioning and understanding he is dealing with reality. Ultimately, what Aquinas wants is what he already knows from the community of faith: having his desire for God nourished in the kind of worship that implies abandon. Unthematically, he has trusted God all along to sustain his natural intelligence as far as it has taken him in the graded order of being. He knows that, at the point where his mind will encounter the limits of the visible world, he will lose his foothold in articulate understanding. But that is precisely where he will find, in the emptiness of his mind, not a maze of mental corridors luring him on into indefinite regress (cf. §102, 8), but the door to the sanctuary. There the to and fro of reasoning and judging is left behind and ultimate *unity of understanding and will* is found. There, too, he can do that most realistic of all things, which is: give himself over to the Sovereignly Real—the transcendent God, whom he has been more than content to worship all along, in the footsteps of both the ancient philosophers and the great Tradition, with their habits of spiritual exercises and liturgy in honor of the unattainable Transcendent,[28] as the transcendent Prompter and Sustainer and Accomplisher of his life's journey, including the itinerary of his mind (cf. §67, 2-4).

[5] What we have here is a stark contrast indeed. Still, curiously, it can lead to a common theme. For that reason, the contrast deserves further reflection. Not surprisingly, this reflection will turn out to involve both the conception of *understanding* and the experience of *reality*. Put broadly, the contrast is between participation and distance, between the concrete and the abstract, between the real and the conceptual.

[a] For Aquinas, neither the world nor the fact of its existence are neutral, whether anthropologically or theologically. For him, the material world is still vitally related to humanity and *vice versa*; consequently, the normative understanding of the world is an exercise, not in purely geometrical and empirical objectivity, but in responsive contemplation animated by appreciation, ultimately learned in the school of "reverent affection" (cf. §67, 3; §102, 6). In this way, Aquinas' intellectual quest is most deeply rooted in dependence on God, who is best known not in articulate thought but in the unifying experience of worship that is responsive to God beyond all rational understanding. This transcendent God is God the establisher—the Source and Sustainer not only of a dynamic, true, and good universe entirely worthy of contemplation, but also of the human understanding of that universe, and of all certainty and assurance in that understanding.

This means that the efficient causality displayed in the powerful processes of cosmic change and in the actual existence of things that might very well not exist is not a matter of faceless cosmic *force* enigmatically exercised by things that simply and unaccountably *exist* and, in their inexorable objectivity, throw their weight around. It is, rather, a marvelous spectacle of dynamic, interdependent being, attractive by virtue of inherent truth and goodness, and ultimately driven by native thirst for God.

[b] For Kant, by contrast, the rational, basically geometrical, schematizing approach to *the world of things* (a world that was soon to include plenty of human "things" as well) treated, in principle, *empirically*, as *neutral objects*, has become the normative

form of understanding [*l*]. In a centuries-long series of ges-
tures of apparent epistemological superiority, the critical, inves-
tigating Western mind has succeeded in setting off the cosmos
against itself as a huge and fascinating collection of usable objects. Excitingly, a world full of matter and movement has presented itself, to be observed, examined, described, talked about,
compared, tested, defined, picked up and put in place, picked
apart and put back together, or worked around or avoided as
necessary; more and more things have been, and are being,
made available for human inspection, ordering, comprehension,
manipulation, and use.

For their part, things have largely obliged; they have turned
out to be objects that obey, for the most part, the beautifully
geometrical laws of nature, which, thanks to science, are getting
better understood every day. It is true, things have taken a re-
venge of sorts; having been simplified, they have also turned
elusive; they now baffle any deeper, more discerning, more interpretative understanding. But then, this is how the mind has conceived and set up the relationship in the first place: by distanc-
ing itself from things, it has *made* them into just that—things; it
is only natural that things should have reciprocated, by hiding
their nature from the rational approach as something opaque;
das Ding an sich has become an *ignotum x.*[29] Still, the mind has
persuaded itself that whatever the "nature" of things may be, it
is bound to be something marginal or merely residual—that is,
intangible, immaterial, non-operational, non-utilitarian, equiva-
lently unreal.

Occasionally, of course, the mind will find itself wondering
why things continue to surprise and inconvenience us, with an
unanticipatedness and an intractability that remains as perplexing as it will turn out to be, time and again, scientifically exciting. Also, the occasional onset of a mysterious sense of the unknown, or a puzzling experience of beauty, or the realization of
the imminence of death and of the transience of everything, or
an odd sense of alienation with regard to the cosmos as a whole
will prompt questions about what things really *are.* But scruples
like these are only to be expected; a little doubt or uneasiness is
but a small price to pay for the spectacular successes of the cul-

-----

[*l*] Put differently, Kant is facing the outcome of the developments that made
Pascal apprehensive: cf. §96, 3-4.

ture of empirical rationality. Let the philosophers, the theologians, and the poets worry. The resourceful rational mind has every reason to be very pleased with its mastery over the outside world, and increasingly, over the human world as well [*m*].

The problem is, of course, that while the deep-seated human desire for deeper understanding can be suspended and suppressed, it will not be stifled forever or wholly disavowed. Natively dissatisfied with limited, schematized, objectifying, empirical knowledge about more and more things and with its mere ability to use and control them, the human mind will (in the higher, more refined, more purely intellectual reaches of the *ratio superior*) insist on fuller, deeper truth. Kant is a philosopher; he experiences that demand. He feels it, on the boundary of his reasoning mind, as a desperate need for final certainty and assurance and contact with reality; the notion of "unconditioned necessity ... as the ultimate bearer of all things" is indispensable. But on the threshold of the concept of a transcendent God, he finds that the mind, *thrown back as it is upon itself and upon its self-imposed, merely rational norms for certainty and assurance* (cf. §17, 1, a), will reel and faint. Just as Pascal was afraid it would, the fascination of a never-ending series of cosmological problems has lured human knowledge into the measureless reaches of space and time, where it has gotten the knower lost (cf. §96, 4).

[c] At this point, Kant might have resorted to a headlong leap into pietism or fideism. Or, giving in to the sheer urgency of the need for a concept of God, he might have pulled himself together in a final, *forced* attempt at theological affirmation. Or, like Spinoza (and a host of less eminent adherents of the New Learning), he might have concluded that the potent dynamics of cosmic change suggest that the God of the cosmos simply *has* to be an absolute, remote, omnipotent, utterly determinative power even more faceless and even more forceful than the natural world produced and moved by it [*n*].

[*m*] For a pointed, perceptive phenomenological analysis of the cultural phenomena touched on in these paragraphs, cf. J. H. van den Berg, *De dingen* (ET *Things*).

[*n*] Theo de Boer perceptively suggests that, when "being" gets neutralized to mean "bare existence," *omnipotence* (understood as absolute *force*) becomes the prime divine attribute. He cites Spinoza as the classic example. Every being, Spinoza writes, strives to persist in being so far as it lies in itself to do so; in fact, this "striving to be" (*conatus essendi*) coincides with a being's very essence (*Ethica*, III, Prop. 6-7 [*Opera*, 2, p. 146; ET pp. 498-99]). In this way, *being is identified with effi-*

Much to his credit, Kant does none of this. Instead, overcome by faintness, he admits defeat. After all, rational reason does not really *understand* the cosmos, its nature, and its dynamics; it merely knows *about* it; consequently, it cannot extrapolate from its knowledge of the cosmos to the reality of God.

Kant is aware, of course, that the mind does have an idea of God. However, he is forced to think that this idea is just that: an *idea* and no more. It is "transcendental"—that is, purely *a priori*; it is simply part of the way the human mind goes about the business of thinking. What the idea of God does for us is to enable our minds to place all possible ideas of any other things in the world in an all-encompassing context. But the idea of God does not connect us with the *reality* of God any more than our idea of any thing connects us with the reality of the thing itself.[30] This is confirmed by our experience: as soon as we try to envisage or portray God as *real*, we find that we are attempting the impossible; the human mind will quail at the thought of a God without any weakness. Any affirmative concept of nature's God caves in under the crushing weight of the idea of the divine self-sufficiency [*o*].

---

cient causality, and its only agenda is self-maintenance at the expense of whatever is in the way. Put differently, *pushing power* has become the quintessence of "being." Now according to Spinoza, all things that exist are but the necessary, inexorable modifications of the eternal, infinite God—the one that is identical with the universe as a whole (*Deus sive Natura*). Thus the forceful striving with which each being asserts, maintains, and promotes itself in being is directly reducible to God. Not surprisingly, therefore, Spinoza can write: "God's power is God's very own essence" (*Dei potentia est ipsa ipsius essentia: Ethica* I, *Prop.* 34 [*Opera*, 2, p. 76; ET p. 439]). This God is bound to become the supreme, faceless rationale for the *status quo* enforced by whatever is most powerful. No wonder the Amsterdam rabbinate opposed Spinoza tooth and nail; how can such a God be expected to become manifest in a burning bush, in the interest, of all things, of showing mercy to a powerless, displaced, marginal people? Cf. *De God van de filosofen en de God van Pascal*, pp. 54-55. Incidentally, it is fascinating to watch Aquinas, in his *Quæstiones disputatæ de potentia*, scrupulously maintaining God's "absolute" power, while at the same time carefully refusing to *identify* God with effective power.

[*o*] It should be pointed out, of course, that Kant, in turning away from the cosmos as a source for theological affirmations, does not renounce all affirmativeness about God. True power, he will suggest, is *moral* power. The God who is truly God is not an all-powerful, self-sufficient ruler needed as the designer and enforcer of laws of nature, in the interest of the *cosmos'* ultimate stability; God is the Lawgiver, the Preserver, and the Judge of a conscientious, free, responsible, disciplined *humanity* (cf. *Die Religion innerhalb der Grenzen der bloßen Vernunft*, B 211, A 199; ed. Weischedel, vol. 4, pp. 806-07). Not the mind worried about what is behind empirical truths about things, but the human conscience attuned to moral duty will find a God worthy of the name. The religious life is based on "the

[6] Given these considerable differences, what room do Aquinas and Kant leave for mutual understanding? Not a great deal, but they do agree on this much: the transcendent God is beyond any simple, unqualified affirmation. For Kant, this is a matter of intellectual weakness: reason's capacity for knowledge is limited to contingent being, and hence, understandably, the mind will involuntarily faint if it attempts to go beyond contingent being. For Aquinas, it is a matter of the faith professed by the great Tradition: he gradually strips away (serenely because voluntarily) all affirmativeness, until he advances, beyond the removal of "being according as it occurs in creatures," into the elected silence that is the soul of all worship.

[7] In our day, this Tradition of awed, wordless, non-affirmative Christian worship has an exquisite opportunity to extend a gesture of recognition and reconciliation to the wavering modern mind. Bold evangelization and authoritative witness to normative Christian truth, supported by worship (cf. §46, 3; §48, 4) and by the witness of an attractive, disciplined life (§32, 2; §42, 1, a), is and remains the primary task (cf. §31, 5-6), as Pope John Paul II has consistently and forcefully reemphasized, not only in his encyclical on the Church's missionary vocation, *Redemptoris missio*, but in a great many other documents and addresses as well.[31] Yet the Christian community must never forget that an integral part of its witness (and perhaps, in cases, the more persuasive part) has always consisted in serenely and patiently agreeing to profess its faith in the living God by way of "unsaying"[32] and even by outright silence—a subject to which we must return (§109, 12) [*p*].

To the extent that the great Tradition will continue, in the public conversation about the living God, this practice of unsaying and silence, it will also adopt, and be seen to adopt, a posture that the modern mind understands all too well from its own experience of attempting to think about God as real: *weakness*. And (fortunately from the point of view of a theology dedicated to the fullness of the great Tradition) the recovery of weakness will also yield a retrieval of the full significance of the central Christian theme of *witness*. This proposition deserves further analysis and reflection.

---

appeal to the moral conscience, and [on] a virile, austere ethic of duty, obedience, and motive—doing the good for the sake of the good" (Hans Küng, *Menschwerdung Gottes*, p. 105; cf. ET, p. 78).

[*p*] On Newman's conception of such a "silent Church," cf. John Coulson, *Newman and the Common Tradition*, esp. pp. 132-47.

[§108] POSITIONS, WEAKNESS, AND THE RECOVERY OF WITNESS

[1] Our central task in this section is an inquiry into the fundamental liabilities of *all* positive affirmations and commitments, or,
as we will call them for present purposes of analysis and argument,
positions.[33] Let us begin this inquiry by taking a socio-philosophical
approach—one to be shortly followed by a properly theological one.

Positions, including the Christian profession of faith as a whole,
as well as its specific affirmations concerning the nature of God, are
determined and particular. Hence, they are limited; they involve
boundaries. In any position we adopt, therefore, we inevitably involve ourselves in implicit *exclusions* or *denials* of some kind, at least
hic et nunc: this is the case (and not that); *we* (and not some other
community) take this position. But no boundary is ever an absolute. In fact, things that find themselves on opposite sides of one
and the same boundary determine and connote one another;
hence, they at least partly *identify* one another. Positions, therefore,
are not only marked *off against* counterpositions; they are also
marked *by* them. In this regard, positions and counterpositions are
like neighbors; they will not stay completely on one side of the
fences that demarcate adjoining (and in that sense, contrary) positions; like it or not, they will interfere with each other, quietly or
obstreperously. Precisely because they are limited, they connote
one another. *Positions implicitly involve other positions.*[34]

[2] The description just given has already suggested that positions
and the counterpositions adjoining them involve, broadly speaking,
two realities, which, though distinguishable, are never completely
separate. The first concerns "things": the *content* that any position
embodies and conveys; the second concerns persons and communities: the *communication* that goes on in the process of the adoption
of a position, and the *relational* (or "responsive") *identity* that is established as a result (cf. §95, 1, esp. [*gg*]; 7). In regard to the former (the things posited), we must observe that most (if not, indeed,
all) positions, or clusters of positions, even the most nuanced, exclude opposites, at least implicitly; they also pass up other, supplementary positions that might be adopted but in fact are not. Thus
the avowal—even the nuanced avowal—of one position (or set of
positions) implies the disavowal, or at least the moving into the
background, of other positions that might conceivably also be pertinent to the situation. In regard to the latter (the persons doing
the positing), we have to observe that every position, no matter how

unassumingly adopted, involves some kind of self-affirmation or self-assertion on the part of those adopting the position: in the act of positing whatever it is we posit, we cannot help positing and affirming ourselves as well; that is, at least to some degree, we affirm ourselves over against others, which in practice frequently means: *ourselves rather than others*. We are liable to become especially aware of the latter whenever we find our positions challenged; even if we are not engaged in self-promotion when adopting our positions, any challenge offered to *what* we posit makes *us* feel self-conscious; our individual ego or our communal pride is on the line, at least to some extent, and with it, our relational identity. Thus, in adopting whatever position we adopt, we enter the lists, one way or another; willy-nilly, we set the scene for a contest, whether in the world of objectivity or in the interpersonal world, and usually in both.

[a] What has just been described obviously unmasks as illusory any kind of easy appeal to "the power of positive thinking."[35] *All* positions have implicit counterpositions lurking around them, niggling at them; we cannot will them away by being brisk and optimistic. The presence of these counterppositions casts at least a shadow of suspicion and doubt on the power and the clarity that (so we like to think) animates (or at least should animate) the positions we adopt and cherish. Could it be (so we can hear ourselves say) that our every position is forced—at least a bit? That our every statement is a veiled overstatement—at least a bit of one? That our every move is an endeavor—at least to some degree—to move others out of the way?

[b] In making these points, we also discover just how inescapable finitude is; no matter how positive we mean to be, some negativity is tied in with all our positions; even when we are at our most expansive, we have to be definite; we have to draw the line somewhere. But this implies something else as well: no position we adopt is ever uncomplicated or clean or neutral; brave and straightforward as they may appear to be, all our positions have a penumbra of wider meanings and connotations and broader commitments and (perhaps) hidden or unexamined agendas attached to them; our positions implicitly commit us, willy-nilly, to *involvements* of one kind or another.[36] Like the counterpositions, these involvements are largely implicit; consequently, they are not readily identifiable, and hence, frequently a source of irresolution and misunderstanding, both in the world

of objectivity and in the (inter)personal world.

[3] Positions that explicitly and thematically concern *the reality and the nature of God* are not exempt from the dynamics of affirmation just delineated. In fact, in their case, implicit counterpositions and involvements in the area of faith-positions are capable of creating huge problems. First of all (and here we are beginning to move from mere social theory to theological argument), at the level of *content*, all affirmative positions on God are doomed to be irretrievably inadequate; unless they are properly qualified, they are liable to be positively misleading. Thus, whatever position anybody may adopt in order to convey who or what God *is*, no matter how true or arguable or attractive, the law of analogy reminds us that there remains an infinite qualitative distance between the content of any position regarding God and the transcendent being of the living God itself (§102, 5; 7); this realization surely helps dwarf any differences there may be between the contents of competing human positions about God (cf. §3, 1, a). Secondly, at the level of *human relationships*, the problem does not get any better. To the extent that a position of mine, or ours, that explicitly concerns God should serve to promote *me*, or *us*, at the *expense* of others (even if they should be manifest heretics, agnostics, unbelievers, or militantly irreligious persons), it becomes self-defeating and implausible to the point of becoming comical. For, it may be asked, why should others rely on me, or us, rather than on someone else to represent the transcendent God? Why, for that matter, should others not simply rely on themselves and their own God-given attunement to God? Is the living God not the God of all at the expense of none (Mt 5, 38-48)? Thus the credibility of God *precisely as the living God* is diminished, not enhanced, to the extent that positions on God adopted by Christians involve, or are perceived to involve, self-assertions that threaten to displace or exclude others, no matter how implicitly or unintentionally.

[a] The question arises, of course, why we should allow ourselves to be bothered by counterpositions and involvements, or even be aware of them in the first place. Why do we not simply accept our limited positions as limited, contentedly? Accept them, that is, as our particular experience of finitude? The fact is, however, that our inner experience as human persons suggests powerful evidence that goes against such simple acceptance, and reflection can bring this evidence to explicit aware-

ness. That evidence is: even if we never entirely comprehend, in detail, exactly to what extent and how our positions are limited, we *know* they are. But reflection upon this very fact brings home to us that we are implicitly calibrating our limited positions, not only against other positions, but also, and fundamentally, against a horizon of infinity. Even the most particular position we adopt places us against that horizon. "The human soul becomes, to an extent, all things," Aquinas says (§2, 1; §102, 10). Every position we adopt, and every affirmation we venture, turns out to be undergirded, on our part, by *a fundamental, implicit, intuitive affinity with the widest possible reality.* Finite though we are, we are not the prisoners of finitude. That is, philosophically as well as theologically speaking, we cannot help acknowledging, natively, implicit in whatever positions we adopt, and *a fortiori* in religious positions, a reference to all of reality, and even, in a radical sense, to God (cf. §8, 8; and once again, §102, 10); no wonder sectarianism strikes us as incompatible with true humanity. We will come back to this point later (§109, 8, [*v*]; cf. §112, 1; 2, a); for the moment, let us pursue our argument.

[4] Implicit counterpositions and involvements conspire, quietly but effectively, to render *all* positions, including the Christian positions that explicitly concern God, incomplete and *ambiguous.* That is, positions concerning the Christian faith do not give a completely compelling account of themselves; they are not self-authenticating. If they are to be understood at all, they are to be understood interpretatively, which means that it takes sympathetic participation based on familiarity to understand them right (§63). In that sense, *all positions are weak,* since whatever is dependent on interpretation is susceptible to misinterpretation and misconstrual. Christian faith-positions are no exception, nor should they be considered to be; Christian positions are dependent on the way they are "accepted"; they have to be understood and interpreted right—that is, by way of generally recognized *discernments* [*q*].

We know this from experience. When someone insists on draw-

[*q*] To quote a characteristic instance of this conviction from the Tradition, note how Jan van Ruusbroec qualifies his very specific definition of the Catholic faith-position with references to *freedom* and *discernment:* "with a free will and desire [*met vrien wille ende moede*] we shall commit ourselves to believe, with discernment [*met onderscede*], all that Holy Church holds and believes" (*Van den gheesteliken tabernakel,* §XLI; RW II, p. 76; cf. §71, 4).

ing a caricature of the history of our country or of Christianity's understanding of God, we will typically suggest that "you have to be part of the tradition to get it right." The Christian position in regard to God, we may explain, must be taken (or "accepted") "in the right spirit," or "in the context of faith, hope and love," or (to put it more intellectually) analogically, symbolically, sacramentally.

[a] A caution. Lest what has been explained so far in this section be wholly misunderstood, let us hasten to point out that the Church of Christ and the truth of its positive teachings can be sufficiently identified in place and time by faithful, open-minded discernment guided by divine grace, even though it remains true that the nature of Christianity cannot be grasped in a definitive way (cf. §76, 2). In other words, our analysis of the nature of positions does not in the least imply that the credal, ethical, and liturgical positions of the Christian faith, and of the Catholic Church in particular, "weak" as they are, are ultimately doomed to remain relative and uncertain, and hence, that any acceptance of these positions in faith can never be strong and unqualified and unconditional. What *is* implied is that the ability of the Christian and catholic positions to guide those who embrace them to the truth, to the true life, and ultimately to the saving God lies, *not in the positions in and of themselves, in their naked particularity and weakness,* but in the positions insofar as they invite being embraced (and indeed demand to be embraced) as bearing reference to the living God, "who can neither be deceived nor deceive" (DH 3008; cf. DV 5; DH 4205; cf. also DH 307, 3010).

On the part of all individual Christian believers, this vital reference to God is given in the inner testimony of the Holy Spirit, graciously as well as most deeply enabling those who believe to accept and interpret and experience the positions they espouse as divinely inspired and as leading to God. Karl Rahner has expressed this by explaining that only those whose authentic, transcendental consciousness has been transformed by God's self-communication have the ability to interpret the historic symbols of Revelation; only they can understand divine Revelation as it has taken shape in concrete, "categorical" forms (§95, 11, d).

However, the Christian positions' reference to God is also available in habitual form, in the reliable objectivity of the Church and the great Tradition (cf. §95, 8-9), interpreted and accepted as the embodiment of the God-given assurance that the

Christian community can never be substantially in error about the truth, the way of life, and the worship which humanity needs to attain salvation (cf. DH 2780. It is to be noted that it is precisely as the community of faith, not as a socio-political or cultural establishment, that the Christian community professes to enjoy this assurance. On that basis (and not by way of self-assertion or self-promotion) Christians can even urge and implore others to rely on them for the truth about God, because they profess what the Church teaches about God.

[5] Now this is where the theme of *dominance* enters, and quite decisively. What a prevailing cultural climate (say, the culture of the Christian West) can do for a particular position (say, the Christian position on the nature of God), is to support it, by publicly giving it, at the very minimum, the benefit of the doubt. Thus cultural climates can support faith. They can do so by *making a correctly discerned acceptance and understanding of certain positions habitually and unthematically available,* and hence, habitually and unthematically dominant over other positions. They do so partly in a vague, atmospheric way, but partly also rather more concretely, by means of specific institutions generated by the climate and in turn supporting the climate. Thus, in the Christian West (even in its post-Christian phase), Christian faith-positions are supported and rendered credible (at least residually and in the eyes of many), not only by publicly recognized forms of Christian literature, art, and architecture, but also by socio-political institutions aptly called *establishments.* Some constitutional monarchies still support established churches; other governments, by concordats and other public accommodations, extend official guarantees to certain churches (while exacting, in not a few countries, tacit commitments to loyalty to the state in exchange for such guarantees); elsewhere again, favorable arrangements (like tax-exemptions) publicly identify churches and church-affiliated agencies as credible and trustworthy.

Such a cultural climate, reinforced by institutional forms of establishment, functions, as George Lindbeck has so thoughtfully suggested in *The Nature of Doctrine,* like a language or an idiom. We acquire them by being immersed in them; eventually, by dint of familiarity, we learn to use them effectively; and in the process, we also succeed in both adopting and conveying an accepted understanding (say, the Christian position on the nature of God). We do so even if we are not expressly aware of the fact that we are, in fact, implicitly *interpreting* a very particular position, and what is more, interpreting it by and large correctly—correctly, that is, within the reassuring framework of a publicly supported cultural climate. Like traditions, cultural climates and their institutional establishments provide particular positions and those who hold them with much-appreciated security.

But establishments, like cultural climates and features of language, wax and wane. What happens when a prevailing climate, on which Christians have relied for the security of their positions, no longer prevails? When new cultural developments end up prevailing over it instead? In such cases, the Christian community is going to find itself challenged to give a less habitual, more reasoned and more responsive account of its faith once again. When that happens, Christians may discover, painfully, the extent to which the former, habitual availability of the "right" acceptance of the Christian faith has caused them to forget, as a community, that the Christian positions have, in fact, never been entirely self-authenticating, let alone self-evident. And thus, they will discover that what once was—what must have been—a live, discerning tradition has imperceptibly degenerated, for lack of sufficient challenge, into mere conventionality and custom (cf. §51, 2; §74), both of which are notoriously forgetful and prone to complacency, prejudice, and hidden ideology [r].[37]

Christians may legitimately consider a stable, dominant Christian culture a desirable state of affairs—say, a restored Christian Europe vigorously breathing by using both of its lungs, the Western and the Eastern Christian traditions, as Pope John Paul II has suggested more than once, or a Catholic Latin America that has put its colonial past and the socio-political consequences of it behind itself, as Gustavo Gutiérrez has argued in his *Theology of Liberation.* In fact, many Christians are apt to positively strive for such an arrangement. The Church has a civilizing bent; it seeks to influence and transform culture (cf. §14, 1); it did so, with the perseverance of true meekness (cf. §109, 12, b), long before it became, in the course of the late fourth century, an increasingly authoritative socio-political power in establishing what was to be the normative cultural climate

---

[r] A good example of the latter is the traditionalist position, happily abandoned by the Second Vatican Council, in its Declaration of Religious Freedom *Dignitatis Humanæ,* that in the ideal situation, any State will favor and promote the Catholic Church, while putting other Churches and ecclesiastical communities, and especially other, non-Christian religious communities, at a disadvantage, under the axiom, "Error has no rights."

for more than a millennium. But despite its past successes in the transformation of Western culture, the fact remains that, *like any other particular community that professes one particular set of positions* (whether more dominant or less dominant), the Christian Church is not exempt from critical questioning; it is answerable to public challenge.

Christian positions, therefore, are appropriately *tested*; demands that Christians publicly verify their claims are inherently just, even if they come from quarters prejudiced against Christianity or indeed hostile to it. For only in the testing will the Jewish-Christian position be able to show its full depth and breadth; and if proven true in the testing, it will generate a deeper sense of Christian identity as well as a wider openness. This applies with special urgency to Christian positions that arouse suspicions of authoritarian totalitarianism. First among these is the Christian position that claims that the Christian Church has immediate access, in Christ risen, to the transcendent God (cf. §34, 2-3); unfortunately, Christian individuals and communities have all too often turned this central *religious* claim to a God-given assurance of indefectibility and in cases even infallibility in the profession of the Christian faith into essentially *secular* claims to divinely warranted, unquestionable possession of absolute truth (cf. §§63-64) [s].

Thus it is not surprising that centuries of establishment should have charged Western Christianity's encounter with the prevailing secular culture of the modern era with serious conflict (cf. §§29-30). But more recently, the conflict has turned out to be productive again: it has helped unmask sizable portions of the Christian establishment as the creature of mere custom—conventional, dated, prejudiced, dying, or dead. In this situation, embarrassing as it may be, the Christian community must learn not to pine for the restoration of the Christian position as culturally dominant. Rather, it has an opportunity to take the cues offered by both the ecumenical movement and the Second Vatican Council, and to attempt, boldly as well as sensitively, a new arrangement of the themes and empha-

---

[s] This has mainly taken the shape of a thoughtless, essentially *secular* interpretation of the Church as a triumphant empire directly and palpably endorsed by God, and of church establishments as integral to salvation history. Eusebius' *Ecclesiastical History* is the earliest example of this dubious idea (cf. §76, 4, [j]); the Spanish *Conquista* is one of the worst instances of the idea in action (cf. §62, 1, b, [g]). Finally, in this context, we must recall the systemic affinity between Roman Catholic integralism and totalitarianism (cf. §19, 1).

ses of the Christian identity-experience.[38]

[6] So far in this section, we have argued our case mainly on socio-philosophical grounds. It is time to point out that our contentions remain true when viewed as a matter of positive theological principle. Not only is the Church *sent* to meet the modern world; it is meant to encounter the various positions it finds in it, and encounter them in a neighborly fashion (cf. §64, 7). Consequently, it should embrace a posture of weakness as integral to its theological authenticity. In this context, it should recall that the blessings of establishment had a dark side, too: they deprived the Church of an element of the authentic Jewish-Christian Tradition that simply *must* rank higher than the institutional security of a former day, namely, the charism of prophetic witness, as Newman well saw (§106, 1, c). This recovery of witness is liable to involve some measure of loss of institutional security, for the characteristic feature of witness is that it positively *seeks* encounter with the real world, and hence, testing. Here as everywhere, the precarious will turn out the more precious; according as the great Tradition agrees to be under pressure to account for itself, it will find itself more authentically alive.

[7] In this light, we can better appreciate the significance of an element of renewal introduced by the Second Vatican Council. Its foremost achievement was the historic redefinition of the Church's nature and of its mission in a world that is and remains worthy of deep, searching appreciation and love, quite apart from the question whether its normative culture is, or is no longer, Christian. In thus redefining its position in relation to the world, the Catholic Church also had to define new relationships to political power structures. In one of its more vibrant documents, there is an historic passage, in which commitment to real partnership in the real world goes hand in hand with readiness to face the prospect of disestablishment and dissociation from the prevailing powers, and even to seek it:

The apostles, their successors, and those who collaborate with them have been sent to announce Christ, the Savior of the world, to people. Hence, in the exercise of the apostolate, they rely on the power of God, who quite often reveals *the power of the gospel in the weakness of the witnesses.* For whoever dedicate themselves to the service of God's Word should use *ways and means proper to the gospel,* and these differ in many respects from the means of the earthly city.

There are, indeed, close links between earthly affairs and those elements of the human condition that transcend this world, and the Church itself employs things of the temporal order to the extent required by its proper mission. Still, *it does not put its hope in privileges* offered to it by civil authority; in fact, *it will give up the exercise of certain legitimately acquired rights when it becomes clear that their use raises doubts about the sincerity of its witness or new conditions of life call for a different arrangement.* But always and every-where it has a right to preach the faith with true freedom, to teach its social doctrine, and to carry out its task among people without hindrance and to pass moral judgments, even on matters touching the political order, whenever fundamental personal rights or the salvation of souls require it. In so doing, it may use all means, and only those means, that accord with the gospel and with the general welfare according to the diversity of times and circumstances.

(GS 76; italics added)

Here, then, we have, after centuries of dependence (and indeed overdependence) on various forms of establishment, the recovery of the great Tradition. Jesus' disciples are to be in the world, yet not of it (Jn 17, 14-16). Accordingly, the Christian community must meet the culture with an offer of participation in every acceptable aspect of its public life; but since the offer is inspired by a commit-ment to evangelical freedom, it must include a pledge of authentic witness freely and boldly undertaken, in the teeth of the culture if necessary.

[8] Now that we have accounted for the solid ecclesial recovery of Christian witness, there remains one issue with which the present chapter, devoted to the Christian (and post-Christian) struggle with the conception of the living God, must grapple. It must do so by asking and answering an overwhelming, uncompromisingly theo-logical question: Does witness to the living God *work?* Does it do any justice to God at all, and if it does, how? How can Christians, or any human beings for that matter, bear reliable witness to the living God worshiped, obeyed, and professed by Israel and by the Jewish and Christian traditions—the Holy One who Alone is God as well as the Faithful One, utterly transcendent as well as most intimately present?

[§109] WITNESS: AFFIRMATION, REMOVAL, AND SELF-ABANDON

[1] Long ago in this systematic theology, the idea was launched that the Christian faith subsists in three integral "moments" or el-ements: worship, life, and teaching (§44, 3; cf. §38; §§42-43). This

conception was elaborated at length, to specify various ways in which the three elements mutually support, and thus verify, each other *internally*—that is, *within* the dynamic framework of the Christian faith as a positive religion (§§47-52). In the course of the treatment, it was explained more than once that the three elements are hierarchically ordered, with worship accorded pride of place, as the original, generative *locus* of the Christian community's encounter with God in ecstatic immediacy (§34).

Accordingly, the most authentic verification of the Christian faith occurs in the witness that is immediately generated by worship. That witness is twofold. It consists, first, in the holiness of life that bears out the community's commitment to the imitation of the Christ whom it acknowledges in its worship. Secondly, it consists in the faithful acceptance of the normative shape of its worship—the christological narrative—as the rule of faith (§§46-48).

Finally, it was argued that the three elements in the Christian faith also provide the Christian community with the dynamic structure that enables it to be a community of spiritual growth and development, in the form of three hierarchically ordered types of Christian faith and identity experience: mystic, charismatic, and pistic (§§53-54).

[2] In the same context, it was also explained that the claims involved in Christian worship demand an *external* verification as well —that is, a verification that occurs in the Christian community's encounter with the world it lives in. Towards that verification, what the community has to offer is, again, a witness of *life* and of *teaching* that is perceptibly backed up by *worship*—that is, a virtuous conduct of life in accordance with shared community standards, and a faithful profession, across differences of time and place, of the rule of faith as the authoritative, unifying statement of the Christian identity across differences of time and place. In the actual practice of the community's encounter with the world, that twofold witness naturally gets cross-examined by the culture. This occurs, proximately, at the level of *teaching*; here the Christian community has the opportunity to present itself to the world most articulately, both with a statement of its beliefs and with an invitation to dialogue.

More cogently, however, as well as more characteristically, the cross-examination and the witness occur at the level of *living*. As Ruusbroec, living in the midst of the not-so-Christian commonwealth of the later Middle Ages, could put it to his readers, who, he could assume, were motivated Christians:

we must make our home between the love of God and of our fellow-Christian.[39]

Put in more general terms, the Christian community must squarely mediate between the living God whom it worships in the Name of Jesus, and humanity and the world as it encounters them in the actuality of daily living; it must be like the sacrament, or the sign and the instrument, both of intimate union with God and of the unity of all humankind (cf. LG 1). In that capacity, it must adopt a life-style that the culture has reasons both to admire and to find morally and religiously persuasive (cf. §46, 4; cf. §50, 2).

The explorations of the present chapter have placed us in a position to deepen these themes of witness and verification as they deserve, in answer to the question raised at the end of the previous section: How do Christians witness to the living God?

[3] Most readily and perceptibly, as well as most *affirmatively*, the Christian community witnesses to the living God by way of the *pistic* type of faith, or (to adopt the terminology developed in the previous section) the pistic position (cf. §54, 3).[40] In this position, Christians profess themselves to be wholly *dependent*, by virtue of both creation and revelation, on the manifestation of God's creative and saving power in the world. This profession, enshrined in traditions of substantive and authoritative *teaching*, firmly identifies Christians and unites them in the *clearly delimited*, dependable, "visible" community of the Church. Thus the pistic form of faith is, firmly and spontaneously, *cosmological*; it is at home in the world of Aquinas' first three ways; it is not afraid to profess the living God at work in the sturdy world of *things* [*t*]. Impressed by objectivity, pistics emphasize *faith*; they revere the divine transcendence primarily by acknowledging God's omnipotence in and behind everything; everything is naturally weak and changeable, but God powerfully moves and encompasses all that is—the world of matter as well as the lives of human persons and communities. No wonder, in the pistic imagination, the cosmos is naturally (if seldom thematically) experienced as sacramental, and the divine work of creation through the Word culminates in the *Incarnation* of the Word and in the

---

[*t*] On "things," cf. §95, 1, [*gg*].

Church's sacraments, especially the Eucharist. There, God's gracious and mysterious presence attains a pinnacle of reliable objectivity to the point of becoming palpable. In Christ, God fully assumes and takes on and embraces humanity, including the world of matter it is part of (cf. §90, 6); *through* Christ, the Way to God the Father, pistics go to God.

Yet the pistic witness, while most affirmative, has deep inadequacies. Specifically in relation to God, a serious weakness of the pistic witness is that it tends to experience *human knowledge and power* as direct threats to God's omnipotence. Pistics delight in seeing God immediately and forcefully at work, both in the Church and in the cosmos; they are happy (and indeed, eager, often in a childlike fashion) to depend on God; but they tend to overlook that their position involves elements of an implicit disavowal of God's transcendence, as well as elements of human and Christian immaturity: they fail to appreciate their own God-given responsibility and power. The well-known anti-intellectualism of pistics and their oft-heard professions of humble faith are frequently predicated on the secret fear that the human maturity implied in knowledge and power will cause loss of faith. That fear is grounded. The pistic faith-experience is laced with the kind of insecurity that breeds overstatement; hence, pistics are prone to unbelief in the face of intimidation by atmospheric worldliness, raw power, or fast but vulgar argument. In the cultural experience of the West, much simple faith has been damaged by the pressure of purely rational technological power and theologically shallow, quasi-scientific argument.

[4] Without saying so, Aquinas appreciates the pistic position; he is not afraid to draw arguments for the existence of the living God from cosmology. He can do so because he is not yet caught up in the fixed, purely rational world of geometrically "objective" truth of a later era; cosmology, for him, is still a *position*—that is, a *relative* point of vantage that affords a particular vision of the world in relation to God. This means that he still knows how to supply, to the cosmological position on God, the counterposition that is critical to its theological integrity. So, both to protect the pistic position against erroneous involvements and to safeguard the transcendence of the living God, he puts the pistic eagerness to be affirmative in its proper place. Pistics do indeed witness to God, but they have to learn how to be content with a measure of ambiguity and even ignorance. For the cosmic, visible realities and forces that loom so large as the shaping forces of their religious world picture

are not to be identified without any further ado with the presence
and activity of the living God (§107, 1):

When we proceed towards God on the road of removal, we first deny everything corporeal of God.

This can also be put in the language of the *Letter to Diognetus* (§79,
1):

... the wielding of physical force is no attribute of God.

[5] The Christian community witnesses to the living God also, and
rather more cogently and persuasively, by way of the *charismatic*
position, which is Aquinas' fourth way in actuality (cf. §54, 4).[41]
That position is strongly characterized by *interiority* and *spirituality*—that is, both by religious self-awareness and by the restlessness
it tends to breed. Charismatics are motivated. No wonder they
tend to raise the hard questions about the true nature of Christianity; as a result, they will be marked by dissatisfaction with the pistic
position (cf. §71, 6; §72, 4, a). Charismatics experience the need
for freely chosen *discipleship*, in *openness* to humanity and the world,
and after the example of *Jesus' ministry*; no wonder they tend to insist that "real" Christianity consists in experience and discipleship,
with Christ, the Reliable Witness, and indeed, the Truth. Sincerely
seeking growth in faith and commitment, they will try to respond
freely and consciously, in the actuality of each situation, to the ever-
changing demands of the authentically human and Christian *conduct of life*, against the horizon of the needs of Church and world.
In this way, charismatics tend to think and live by the experience of
analogy: human life, and *a fortiori* Christian life, is a matter of active
participation in the hidden life and activity of God, who works in and
through all human persons and events. This moves them to foster
all that is true and good and noteworthy in humanity. Christians,
so charismatics tend to feel, should embody and exemplify the universal *hope* held out by Christ risen (cf. §42, 1); for God will extend
the blessings of the divine presence to those whose lives of responsible service promote the cause of humanity's true fulfillment. For
the world and the human community must be embraced and stirred
and inwardly and outwardly liberated from the oppression and the
suffering and the inauthenticity that still disfigure them, both outside the churches and inside it. In this way, the charismatic form
of faith is, ardently and spontaneously, *anthropological*; putting their
special gifts and services at the service of the Gospel, charismatics

are eager to turn potential for growth into actual maturity, to support one another and minister to one another, and to "keep up the good work" in the infinitely varied universe of human experience and attainment, across most lines of division, including ecclesiastical ones. Sensitive to personalness, community, and shared experience, charismatics will acknowledge the divine transcendence primarily by emphasizing the hidden mystery of God's participative presence with and in the travail of humanity. No wonder the charismatic imagination naturally experiences the world as a human responsibility; the divine presence in the world, for them, culminates in service freely and conscientiously undertaken, in the wisdom of the great minds and souls of all times and places, in the inspiration that comes from the Word of God, in the wisdom available to humanity in its great monuments, and especially in the ministry of Jesus: prophetic, brave, healing, non-conformist, non-discriminatory.

Yet the charismatic witness, too, has deep inadequacies. For all its depth of godliness, its experience of Christian faith and identity is often too self-regarding to be convincing as a vehicle of the presence of *God*. Wary of boundaries and authority, charismatics are tempted to prize freedom rather than fidelity and patient, undiscriminating love, experienced meaning rather than quiet truth, a felt sense of commitment rather than firm goodness, good intentions rather than realism, preferred themes and agendas rather than the integrity of the Christian identity, and special alliances cutting across church boundaries rather than unity. In the charismatic position, what always lurks around the corner is the self-righteousness that blinds people of good will both to their own foibles and to the true needs of others; for all their genuine devotion to community, charismatics frequently cause factionalism, and hence, scandal to their pistic brothers and sisters. As a result, for the charismatic, typically, the way to deeper participation in God lies in the direction of growth in selfless service, in patience with others, and in purity of intention. This will also ready the charismatic for even higher gifts. For, while truly feeling and relishing the human aspiration to transcendence, charismatics tend to be distrustful of the actual encounter with God in naked faith: being doers, they are often reluctant to abandon themselves to contemplation.

[6] Aquinas is familiar with the charismatic position; he is not afraid to draw arguments for the existence of the living God from anthropology: the typically human experience of analogy is a road to the transcendent God (cf. §102, 5-6). He can do so because he

is not yet caught up in the fixed, anthropocentric claims characteristic of a later era; the human experience of being the measure of all things (cf. §102, 4, b; 5) has not yet hardened into claims to human autonomy (§17, 1, a) [*u*]. For Aquinas, theological anthropology is a *position*—that is, a point of vantage that affords a particular, partial vision of humanity and the world it inhabits, in relation to God. This means that he still knows how to supply, to the anthropological position on God, the counterposition that is critical to its theological integrity. So, once again, both to protect the charismatic position against erroneous involvements and to safeguard the transcendence of God, Aquinas puts the charismatic eagerness to be self-assertive in its proper place. Taking a further step towards the living God on the road of removal, he implies that charismatics do indeed witness to God, but they have to learn, not only eager service, but also *patient endurance*, against the day when human truth and goodness—their own and that of their weaker brothers and sisters—turn out to be disappointingly limited. For the human intelligence and goodness that loom so large in their experience of humanity and the world are not to be simply identified with the transcendent attributes of God (§107, 1):

... we go on to deny everything spiritual as it is found in creatures, such as goodness and wisdom.

This can also be put more positively, in the prosaic, pertinent language of the fourth and final point of Ignatius of Loyola's "Contemplation to Obtain Love":

To see how all good things and gifts descend from above: for instance, my limited power from the highest and infinite [power] above, and in the same way justice, goodness, kindness, mercy, and so on, just as the rays come down from the sun, the waters from the spring, etc.[42]

[*u*] Here lies the weakness of the anthropological arguments for God's existence (cf. §104). Kant just about reduces any possible awareness of God to the immanent experience of moral conscience and the self-important, wholly autonomous moral life connected with it. David Jenkins' characterization of Schleiermacher's fundamental intuition: "God is out though godly attitudes may be in" (*Guide to the Debate About God*, p. 30; cf. §35, 3, a) may not be adequate; it is far from mistaken. It is true, of course, that John Henry Newman (§105) and, much later, Maurice Blondel and the tradition he helped inaugurate, have succeeded in reconnecting human inwardness with divine transcendence (§87; cf. also §95, 9-11), by more deeply appreciating the dynamism that is the soul of "immanence." But for all that, self-preoccupation and self-righteousness remain the standard temptations of the charismatic position.

[7] Having removed from the human witness to the living God the names derived from world of both cosmic matter and finite spirit, the mind has run out of matter for *particular* pronouncements. All it has left now is the language of naked ontological affirmation. So Aquinas continues (§107, 1):

At that point, all that is left in our minds is that God *is*, and nothing else; thus God *is*, so to speak, in some kind of perplexing fashion.

With this move, we have entered upon the third, least inadequate, most properly *theological* form of human and Christian witness to the living God: the *mystical* position (cf. §54, 5).[43] It is characterized by the ecstatic realism of *worship*, and corresponds to Aquinas' fifth way. Inwardly moved by the *attraction* of transcendence, the human spirit lifts itself up, gently but firmly, out of its known and experienced world and its known and experienced spiritual self. Rising above all the details, articulations, and specifications inherent in finite reality, and seeking to open itself to the gift of *union*, mystics direct their inner selves to God, in loving, reverent attention to God's simple, unadorned "being-there" (cf. §67, 3, a; 4, a). Now, far from displacing anything created, God enhances it (§79, 4), and puts it in its appropriate place. Hence, far from being an act in which everything cosmic and human is discarded, the mystics' "leaving everything behind" to focus on God involves, in fact, the *integration* of everything (cf. also §61, 3, a, [d]).

[a] Thus, first of all, mysticism takes in the universal *cosmic* dynamism and orients it to towards transcendence. Even the dynamism of creatures that do not enjoy intelligence, so Aquinas observes in the fifth way, shows a sense of direction that prompts them to seek higher ends. This must be rooted in their nature, and hence, God-given; somehow, all things must be natively seeking to return to the source. This dynamic desire in every creature to return to its origin manifests, to reason illuminated by faith, the depth of God's creative immanence; it also moves every creature to come to a fuller actuality. And this, in turn, culminates in that most natural of all things: the loving glorification of the transcendent God, on whom all creatures depend in the first place (cf. §80, 2). We are in the world of the theological cosmology of the Creation Psalms. We are, especially, in the world of the Song of the Three Young Men in the Fiery Furnace, which, after recognizing the transcendent praises of God that resound in the heavenly sanctuary, works its way from the firma-

ment down to the earth, calling on all creatures in due order to bless God, until it finally comes home to the three young men and the community of the just (Dan 3, 52-90 LXX).

[b] Thus, secondly, we come to the *anthropological* sphere. Its native dynamism is both cosmic and properly spiritual; consequently, human persons and communities are immanently prompted and invited to present themselves, not only to God as the Power on which they ultimately depend, but also to God as the Form to which they bear a proper resemblance by virtue of intelligence and spiritual desire. Thus humanity is naturally prompted to move, by way of a conscious and freely chosen self-offering, in the direction of full self-actualization in the love and worship of God (cf. §80, 2-3), by virtue of praise and thanksgiving.

[8] Thus, in the mystical position, humanity, in seeking union with God, is actualizing the dynamics of both dependence and participation (cf. §102, 9). On behalf of both the cosmos and humanity, the mystic actualizes what all of creation most deeply *is*: the worshipful desire to gather itself up as well as transcend itself, so as to find union with God in an encounter of ecstatic immediacy [*v*].

Here also lies the paradox of the mystical position. Immanence naturally inspires the search for transcendence; being is natively oriented to ecstasy. In the act of turning *away* from self-containment and *towards* transcendence, therefore, all creatures, each according to their proper place in the universe, actualize and identify their most authentic selves to the highest attainable degree. The essence of the mystical vision and experience is, therefore, that the free, patient, self-abandoning focus on the transcendent, unknowable God involves the recovery, in actuality, of the true, implicit identity of humanity and the world. Becoming de-centered turns

---

[*v*] Aquinas' naked affirmation that God simply *is*, therefore, is not the result of a mere act of the will; in other words, it is not the overcoming, by dint of affirmative endeavor, of an intellectual impasse caused by the finitude of human understanding. Aquinas is merely bringing to the surface something that is already there, even though it is implicit. It is a *given*—that is, something not self-achieved, and hence, something to be *accepted*. That "given" is implicit *in* all our particular affirmations, as the condition for their very possibility: our native, unstated, darkly intuitive attunement to all reality and hence, to God (§108, 3, a; cf. §112, 1; 2, a). On the threshold of the mystical life occurs the recovery of the ontological fact that God is creatively and enablingly present in the human mind, as the root of its ability to affirm anything at all, whether about God or humanity and the world (cf. §89, 1-2).

out to be the finding of the true Center; becoming selfless in this fashion turns out to be the finding of the self, in God; the encounter, in actuality, with the living God prompts true, experienced, minimally self-conscious, genuinely *responsive* identity (cf. §35, 1; 4; cf. esp. §121, 1, f).

Not surprisingly, mystics live by the actuality of the living God —that is, by the Holy Spirit, who is the actuality, both of the divine intensity and intimacy, and of the divine majesty and abundance (§34, 5). This means mystics live by *aspiring love.* In the very act of seeking God above all, mystics implicitly reach out to integrate and conciliate humanity and the world; the love of God and the love of all God's beloved are inseparable. Living, as they do, by the attractiveness of *holiness,* they encompass and transcend both the narrow fidelity of the pistic and the self-regarding devotion to active service of the charismatic. While firmly professing their dependence on the faith of the visible Church (and in that sense remaining pistics), they will not be identified by its limits; while firmly and unselfconsciously exercising their particular God-given gifts in the service of others (and in that sense remaining charismatics), they do not derive their sense of identity from the merit of their actions or from association with any cause, no matter how good or true. Thus the mystics' characteristic sense of identity is neither heteronomous nor autonomous: it is derived neither extrinsically, from the boundaries of the community and the definitions of the faith, nor intrinsically, from their own experience of active participation in the service of God. Instead, their sense of identity is properly theonomous, for it is transcendent in origin; it comes to them from their life *in* Christ, the Life. Identified with Christ's worshipful self-abandon to God, by way of the eternal Spirit, as a holy sacrifice without blemish (cf. Heb 9, 14; cf. §49, 1, a, [c]), mystics share in Christ's universal, reconciling mediatorship, and hence, experience how the love of God brings about the kind of inner focus that attunes them lovingly to all of humanity and the world.

Jan van Ruusbroec explains how total self-abandon to God is the source of personal integration in both loving contemplation and loving activity:

Now you must understand that God ceaselessly enters us with intermediary as well as without intermediary, and calls on us to enjoy and to be active, and that the one be not hampered by the other, but constantly reinforced [by it]. This is why the person of interior life possesses his life in these two modes: repose and activity. And in both of them he is entire and undivided, for he is all in God when he is reposing in enjoyment, and he is all in himself when is lovingly active. And he is reminded and called upon by God every moment to refresh both repose and activity. And righteousness of spirit will every moment expend what God calls upon it to expend. And this is why, at every divine illumination, the spirit turns inward, both in activity and in enjoyment; and thus it is both renewed in all virtues, and ever more deeply steeped in the repose of enjoyment. For God gives himself and his gifts in one single act of giving, and the spirit gives itself and all its activity in every act of turning inward. ... This is how a person is righteous: he moves toward God with interior love in everlasting activity, and enters into God disposed for enjoyment in everlasting repose, and remains in God, and yet goes out to all creatures in virtues and in righteousness, in a love that encompasses all. And this is the high point of the interior life.[44]

What else do we hear in this passage but the quiet, authoritative voice of mystical experience [w]?

[9] Spiritual growth and development, it was explained long ago (§54, 5, d), is not simply progressive or cumulative, but dialectical: the more someone advances, the greater the risk of loss of faith. Thus, precisely because the mystic type of faith is the most adequate to the living God, it involves the most significant hazards. This can be understood as follows.

The basic, decisive *entry* into the mystical life—the life of contemplative union with God—consists in the experiential discovery of that point in ourselves at which we are *naturally* (or, as Ruusbroec puts it, "essentially") united with God. There we find God as the unmediated Presence, more deep-seated in us than the deepest accessible reaches of our persons; there we simply *are* our original selves inasmuch as there we find ourselves natively anchored in God; consequently, that is where we are holy regardless of our actual holiness or sinfulness (§89, 1-2; §90, 3). It is precisely at this "fine point of the soul" that our *capacity* for *actual* union with God by grace resides, too. By virtue of this latter union, we come to participate in the inner life of the Blessed Trinity (which is why Ruus-

---

[w] For an analogous, typically nineteenth-century illustration of the mystical position as an experience of integrative and conciliatory sense of identity, cf. Saint Thérèse of Lisieux' account of the way in which she found her self-centered fantasies of martyrdom swept away, which enabled her to discover her specific vocation in the widest possible community: a call to self-abandoning, all-embracing love, deep inside the heart of Mother Church, empowering the activities of all the other members. Cf. *Histoire d'une Âme*, pp. 220ff. (ET *Story of a Soul*, pp. 193ff.).

broec calls it "superessential"); what is characteristic of mystics is
that they are granted *experiential* access to this union.

[a] Now it is precisely at the point of deepest identity, right on
the threshold of this life of felt actual union with God, that mystics may lose touch with reality and fall into inauthenticity. The
experience of fundamental natural identity with God—and of
the indestructible, immanent holiness that is its immediate con-
comitant—takes the shape of a boundless sense of identity, personal integration, and spiritual freedom. This sense of self is so
delightful and so tempting that it may cause the person to overlook the fact that, while the fundamental union with God is itself
natural, the *experience* of this union is strictly a gift— that is, a
matter of supernatural *grace* [x].

[b] This is precisely what the author of *The Cloud of Unknowing*
has in mind when he explains that only the actual gift of contemplative union with God can give us access to the sense of our
natural capacity for it (§36, 2). The mystical life starts with the
gift of the sense of inner union with the Source of life. The
experience obviously awakens the desire to maintain it, but what
the person must learn is that the experience can be maintained
only by holding on, not to the union itself, but to the Source.
Yet the Source is beyond grasp, so the holding on to the Source
can never be an accomplishment, but only a favor graciously
granted, and granted only to the purely receptive. Thus, in the
end, everything turns out to be pure gift. *Tout est grâce.*[45] That
is, it takes the gift of supernatural (cf. §82, 2-4) grace to make
the natural divine Presence in us a matter of actual experience,
and this in turn lays bare the fact that even our created being
and its potential for actual union with God is, in the final analysis, a gift from God. We are God's entirely free, gracious gift to
ourselves from the very start.

Mystics are true to the grace given to them to the extent that
they realize this directly and experientially. And to the extent

---

[x] This is the immediate consequence of the asymmetry in the relationship
between Creator and creature (cf. §82, 3, b). The finite creature's nature limits
neither God's transcendent sovereignty, nor God's access to the creature, which
remains as immediate and intimate as it is unconditioned and free. Yet by virtue
of its nature, the finite creature's *actual* access to God is as limited as its *capacity*
for it is real; that is, only the gift of supernatural grace can awaken the creature's
natural access to God.

they grow in union with God, they will come to the realization that, in the end, even the faintest self-assertion or self-maintenance on the part of any creature will open the door to total loss of contact with the life-giving Reality of God. Thus the life of union ceaselessly faces the mystic with the choice between the total self-abandon essential to loving union with the God who is Life itself and the urge towards self-maintenance that brings on the imminent fall into spiritual death. This is where union, in the Spirit, with Christ, the perfect lover and worshiper of the Father, becomes crucial. Thus Ruusbroec can explain: "And as often as such persons are allowed to die to themselves, by means of love, [so as to be drawn] into God's superessential freedom (whether in abundance or in dearth), so often their innermost richness is renewed and grows, as well as the fiery blaze of their love. For if Christ were not to burn up that richness instantaneously, such persons would turn complacent and conceited on account of great holiness, and they would fall into the kind of spiritual pride that is to be dreaded above all things" [y].[46]

[c] The thesis about the indispensability of grace for the experience of the mystical union with God also sheds light on the doctrinal traditions regarding the spiritual nature of the human soul, its immortality, and its immediate dependence on God's creative act (cf. DH 902; CF 405). In a general way, these doctrines had been part and parcel of patristic traditions of long standing. They came to be more precisely defined in the West, as a result of the fact that Western scholasticism adopted Aristotle's anthropology as the fundamental, normative philosophical account of human nature. In this anthropological conception, each human person is a composite of body and soul, in such a way that the soul does indeed immediately account for the body's physiological and sentient life in all its facets, yet is truly spiritual in its own right as well; by virtue of the spiritual and immortal soul, human persons are the only cosmic creatures that enjoy an immanent spiritual capacity for conscious and freely chosen immediacy to God: "there may and will be nothing at all between God and the human soul."[47] By virtue of that capacity, humanity is also im-

---

[y] This is why the teachers of the spiritual life insist that moral carelessness puts mystics at greater risk than it does sinners; that risk is known as *egkataleipsis* or "abandonment" (cf. §54, 5, d).

manently capable of relating to all that is (cf. §2, 1) [z].

In the catholic tradition, these doctrines are *not* designed to provide philosophical equivalents of the Christian doctrine of the salvation and elevation of humanity by divine grace, let alone to replace them by a notion of purely natural beatitude. For in and of themselves, the soul's spiritual nature, its immediate dependence on God's creative activity, and its natural preparedness for "afterlife" are only the natural, created preconditions for a free and conscious encounter with the living God; without this actual encounter, which is inconceivable apart from the gift of grace, the soul, for all its immortality, remains as pale and pointless as a promise made but never fulfilled. In thinking of grace as the fulfillment of the human soul's natural condition, the Christian community embraced and reinterpreted a conviction as widespread in first-century Hellenistic Judaism as in the Greco-Roman world, namely that natural immortality is of itself void, tedious, and unattractive; true immortality comes to the soul only if it does justice to its spiritual nature by seeking to live a valuable life.[48] Building on this, Saint Ambrose, in a homily on the

---

[z] In scholasticism, this thoroughly traditional piece of Christian anthropology took the shape of the thesis that the human soul combines a true engagement with matter with true transcendence over matter: while the soul truly "informs the body" (*anima est forma corporis*: cf. Aquinas, *S. Th.* I, 76, 3-4), it is in essence a spiritual substance (DH 902, 1440; CF 405, 410; cf. GS 14; DH 4314). Accordingly, the soul is not exhausted by its engagement with the body (that is, indirectly, with the cosmos taken as a whole: cf. §115, 8, [cc]); being transcendent, it informs the body (in neo-scholastic terminology) only "virtually" (*anima virtualiter est forma corporis*). The classic Jewish-Christian conception of the soul, as well as its correlative, the classic Jewish-Christian conception of God's transcendence as the guarantee of God's intimate presence, has often been misrepresented, in the modern era, in narrowly Cartesian terms: as God became merely remote, the soul became a wholly autonomous, unrelated spiritual entity operating an animal body. This is a far cry from the patristic conception of the soul as the *locus* of the human person's immediate and inalienable relatedness to God, which enabled theologians to think even of faith as a natural endowment. Thus Clement of Alexandria can write that "faith is some sort of immanent good; without seeking for God it acknowledges his existence and gives praise to him as existent" (*Strom.* VII, X, 55; *GCS* 17, p. 40). Evagrius Ponticus, who quotes Clement's oft-quoted statement (cf., e.g., *Philok* II, p. 18 [21]), can elaborate on it by adding that faith "naturally exists in [people], even in those who have not yet come to believe in God"; no wonder he can also characterize, in passing, the human mind as *pephykota proseuchesthai*: "naturally made for worship" (*Praktikos* 81, 49; *SC* 171, pp. 671, 612). Happily, this classic, *relational* conception of the human soul has been attractively retrieved by a capable modern patristics scholar, Piet Smulders, in creative dialogue with Pierre Teilhard de Chardin (cf. *Het Visioen van Teilhard de Chardin*, pp. 93-130; ET *The Design of Teilhard de Chardin*, pp. 60-85).

Christian faith in the resurrection delivered in the course of the funeral observances for his brother Satyrus, can convey the common Christian conviction by saying: "Immortality adds up to a burden rather than an advantage, if grace does not blow life into it"—a conviction shared by Augustine, who, as Brian Daley has explained, is convinced that "natural immortality is of itself of rather limited value, since the soul still experiences a kind of death if it is abandoned by God because of its sin."[49]

[d] These insights also help shed light on humanity's age-old (and, it would seem, almost universal) attempts to cultivate mysticism as a natural attainment—attempts very much alive today. The great Tradition acknowledges that mysticism has the deepest possible natural roots; it also holds that the pursuit of actual mystical experience as a natural attainment misinterprets what is originally an experience of privilege, and turns it into the mere assertion of a self-centered claim. This implies a denial of the dual proposition that *both* the sense of God's natural indwelling *and* the deeply-felt inner experience of identity, enlightenment, and freedom that is its flower are gracious divine gifts.

For this reason, the Tradition is suspicious of attempts to teach mysticism in the interest of the full actualization of the self [*aa*]; it also holds that the pursuit of mystical experience as a road to self-enrichment is an attempt to turn into a natural given what can only be God's self-gift. For while mysticism fits the natural self like a glove, deliberate *claims* to mysticism involve the kind of autonomous cultivation of God's immanence in the self that amounts to a denial of the divine transcendence and hence, to a lapse from every form of faith (§25, 4, d). Seen in this light, natural mysticism is a form of forgery: the cult of God, to which the human self is and remains most deeply attuned, is reduced to the cultivation of the human self as a free-standing repository of divinity; the human self made in the image and likeness of God is passed off as the original.

[e] The self-illuminated mystics' abandonment of God also accounts for the characteristic pride and disdain with which they

---

[*aa*] However, experience teaches that this alleged self-actualization is frequently nothing but a disguised form of overdependence on a guru. This suggests, of course, that the guru's ego can be a far more important concern than the enhancement of the disciple's self.

tend to relate to the world and humanity, and especially to the articulate faith of pistic and charismatic Christians. Ruusbroec describes this with his usual accuracy. Comparing the self-made mystic to the eagle (the king of the birds, but an unclean animal according to Deut 14, 12), he writes: "Whoever is capable, in turning inward, of emptying himself of all images and forms, and of all thought, and can lift up his desire in bare emptiness, he is king in nature, above all people. For he flies at the highest level that nature is capable of. And he makes his nest and takes his rest in his own being. And he gazes into the mere truth, which never ceases to illuminate his being and all beings. And his vision is single and devoid of thought. And that is why he contemplates the truth without reflection and without giving way to it. And this is so enjoyable to nature that he disdains and regards as ignoble: thought, and discernment, and every exercise of reason that impedes his pure vision or introduces images to it— just as the eagle kills his young if they shy away from the radiance of the sun. ... But when he comes down he is proud and arrogant, impatient and immoderate of speech. And all people who do not recognize his significance—he thinks of them as little and falling short of their best. And thus he is honored and respected by people whose flight is still within nature, and who would like to be good people. Nevertheless, he is deceived. For he wants to know and not believe; to have and not hope; to possess and not love. And so, however high the eagle flies, he does not fly above himself. Nor does anyone do so, within the light of nature. But grace and charity do carry a person above himself, into God. And that is where he makes his nest. For Godself is his dwelling and his rest. And therefore he is more enlightened and savors God more than any people may attain in bare nature. As for all works of reason, which give way to faith and to the First Truth, every good person loves them as a noble fruit he wishes to have, to adorn him and guide him, like the Saints in Holy Church. And in his ascent he transcends himself and all temptations. And his descent is so full of grace, by way of words and works and good example, that all his enemies must give way to him or flee from him. And he is so gentle and so meek that all good people who come near him are glad."[50]

[f] Not infrequently, the sense of spiritual self-sufficiency will induce self-made mystics to claim for themselves an inner freedom that somehow places them above the obligations and moral

norms proposed by the visible Church; they will also offer descriptions of the inner freedom experienced by "the mystics" as if they were ethical norms that anybody is welcome to follow. This in turn may lead to both encratism and laxism: on the one hand, self-professed mystics may practice striking forms of personal asceticism, which, however, mainly seems to serve to set them apart from the imperfect and the unenlightened; on the other hand they may condone forms of obvious immorality, even to the point where they themselves will engage in startling forms of lack of discipline and self-indulgence. No wonder natural mystics will characterize the pistic and charismatic forms of faith, as well as the visible Church that commends them, as irrelevant in the long run and thus basically *passé* (cf. §54, 5, d) [*bb*].

[g] At the risk of doing an injustice to a subject both too complex and too far-flung for fast treatment, let us simply observe, in the present context, that the main Tradition's aversion to what can be broadly called "the gnostic myth" corresponds with the points just made about its rejection of purely natural mysticism. The great Tradition has disavowed any drift toward an elitist, "acosmistic" Christianity, of which the second-century *Gospel of Thomas* is a prototypical example. In gnosticism, an altogether spiritual, barely incarnate Christ recalls his true elect, by the shortcut of esoteric teaching, to the pure self-knowledge that is their original divine birthright, and out of their exile in the dubious world of matter and flesh and virtue slowly acquired and confusing involvements with crude others.[51] In the footsteps of the unequivocally human Jesus of the Synoptics and the Fourth Gospel, normative Christianity is roundly committed, under the enabling presence of a God whose love of the whole world is manifest in a Christ who is dead and truly risen, to the laborious

---

[*bb*] Note how, in *The Book of Privy Counseling*, the author of *The Cloud of Unknowing* emphatically commends, as the necessary path to imageless contemplation, the meditation on one's sins, on the passion of Christ, and on the joys of the saints and angels, under the rubric of Jesus' word: "I am the door" (*The Cloud of Unknowing and the Book of Privy Counselling*, pp. 157/27-160/23; ed. Johnston, pp. 173-80). On this subject, cf. also §67, 4, a, and [*h*] and [*i*]; §90, 2. All this explains the vehemence of Ruusbroec's protest against the claims advanced by the Brethren of the Free Spirit and other, related spiritualist movements (cf. Norman Cohn, *The Pursuit of the Millennium*, pp. 148-97); it is part of Ruusbroec's insistence that vacancy of the mind is theologically legitimate only if the person keeps the faith-relationship to the living God alive, as he explains in *Vanden blinkenden steen* ("The Sparkling Stone").

transformation of real, sinful, mortal human persons living in a real world, yet inspired by the hope of a future fulfillment which, by God's design, will include all that is, and hence, to which all must now be boldly and publicly called. Consequently, normative Christianity has rejected dualism; it has been committed to an anthropology that acknowledges humanity's rootedness in the cosmos by divine design (cf. §115); it has not impatiently insisted on being anything but *transitional* (§79, 1); and, far from running away from positive religion—that is, the current, often all-too-palpable form of the Church—it has considered it the concrete shape of grace, and hence, accorded it theological superiority over natural religion (§26, 2).

[10] Without saying so, Aquinas is familiar with the mystical position; he is not afraid of nature, nor of God's natural indwelling in nature; he draws arguments for the existence of the living God from natural theology; the experience of natural design is a road to the transcendent God (cf. §102, 5-6). But he can do so only because he knows that grace is the reality we live in, and that "the gift of grace exceeds every power of created nature" (§26, 2, a). This also means that he knows how to supply, to the mystical position on God, the counterposition that is critical to its theological integrity. So once again, to avert erroneous involvements, and to safeguard the transcendence of the living God, Aquinas puts the naturally-mystical position on God in its proper place. Proceeding towards God on the road of removal, he goes to the end. Much as the mystical experience may give persons access to the point where they are experientially aware, in their deepest immanence, of proceeding from God's creative hand, the living God transcends even the deepest divine presence in creation. That is, the living God utterly transcends creation. Thus, in the end, Aquinas removes from the human witness to God any identification of creatureliness with the living God (§107, 1):

Last of all, however, we remove from God even this very being according as it occurs in creatures. At that point, God is left to dwell in a kind of darkness of ignorance; yet after the manner of this ignorance—at least as long as we are on our present way—we are best united with God, as Dionysius says. This is a dark cloud of sorts, in which God is said to dwell.

[11] A passage from *The Sparkling Stone*, from which we have quoted before (§90, 2), provides the experiential equivalent of this profoundly paradoxical insight. Ruusbroec here describes the mystical

experience in wholly negative terms—that is, as the failure of all sufficiency. Unsettlingly, the immediacy of contemplative union is an *ontwerden*—an "un-becoming." What Ruusbroec means is so perplexing that he seems to feel that he can best explain it by contrast, so he conveys it by setting it side by side with something more accessible and affirmative: the continuing experience of the life of faithful, active pursuit of virtue. In comparison with that "outflowing" life, Ruusbroec says, the mystical experience is the event of spiritual dying:

"But, [you say,] one more thing I would like to know, namely how we can become God's hidden children [*sonen*: "sons"] and possess a contemplative life." I have thought of this, as follows.

As explained before, we must always both live and be watchful in [the practice of] all virtues, and die and pass away in God beyond all virtues. For we are to die to sins and be born of God into a virtuous life, and we are to deny ourselves and die in God into an everlasting life. And hence, the following order applies.

If we are born of God's Spirit, we are children of grace, and our whole lives are adorned by virtues, and thus we overcome all that is contrary to God; for whatever is born of God overcomes the world, says Saint John [1 Jn 5, 4]. And in regard to this birth all good people are children of God. And God's Spirit enkindles and moves each person individually to such virtues and such good works as each is prepared for and habitually inclined to. And thus they please God all together, each in an individual way, according to the measure of their love and the generosity of their exercises. At the same time, they do not have the sense that they are established, nor that they are in possession of God, nor that they are assured of life eternal, for they may still turn away and fall into sin. And this is why I call them servants or friends rather than children.

But when we rise above ourselves, and in our ascent to God are made so single that bare love can get hold of us, on the high plane where, above and beyond every exercise of virtue, love cultivates love (that is, in our origin, out of which we are born spiritually), there *we will unbecome and in God die to ourselves and to all that is ours.* And in this dying we become God's hidden children, and we find a new life in us, and this is an everlasting life. And it is of these children that Saint Paul says, "You are dead and your life is hidden with Christ in God" [Col 3, 3].

Now pay attention and note that the order is as follows. In our *approach* to God we are to carry ourselves and all our works in front of ourselves as an everlasting offering to God; and in the *presence* of God we will abandon ourselves and all our works, and, dying in love, we will pass beyond all creatureliness into the superessential abundance of God; there we will possess God in an everlasting death of ourselves to ourselves.

And this is why the Spirit of God says, in the Book of Revelation, that "those dead are blessed that die in the Lord" [Rev 14, 13]. He rightly calls them "blessed dead," for they remain eternally dead and sunk beneath themselves, [steeped] in the enjoyment of God's Oneness, and they are always dying anew in love, as that same Oneness draws them into itself, transforming them.[52]

[12] Language taken as live speech is antecedent to language taken as stable system; language is a form of activity before it is ever an instrument of cognition; it is the medium of interpersonal communication before it is ever the tool of objectivity; it is rhetorical before it is ever logical.[53] These four propositions add up to the thesis that no language, not even the most abstract, philosophical or scientific idiom, ever completely loses touch with the basic fact that language is first and foremost a form of *communicative behavior.* Not surprisingly, therefore, the *remotio* commended by Aquinas (cf. §67, 2) is more than a rule for God-talk or a mere noetic exercise; at every level of faith, it is a warrant for *conduct* as well—that is, it leads to self-involving engagement in encounter with others. And the ultimate, highest form of that self-involvement is the commitment, not to affirmations and assertions and other forms of active self-engagement, but to the kind of weakness that distinguishes witness from mere affirmation and action—the linguistic weakness whose outer boundary is eloquent silence.

That silence marks the end of all exclusive reliance on fixed positions affirmatively expressed and upheld (§108). All positions are hazardous enough, on account of the rival positions they necessarily connote and elicit; yet positions specifying matters of religion are especially dangerous, for the overstatements of zealous, but undiscerning and partisan believers may end up eclipsing the living God, who is the God of all to the exclusion of none. For this reason, those who can never get themselves to abandon affirmative positions on the living God are liable to bear witness, not so much to the God for whom they mean to stand up, as to their own finitude, which they attempt to prop up by self-reliance, self-assertion, and self-maintenance. Thus, though there will always be a positive need, both for religious establishments and for confident affirmations and bold proclamations of faith in God, these forms of faith will become suspect if they lose their connection with weakness and suffering voluntarily undertaken.

Thus we have stumbled on the tradition that commends, as the way *par excellence* for chosen witnesses to testify to the living God, not the explicit, forceful, assertive upholding of faith-positions, but the silent, willing, patient abandonment of all *explicit* affirmations of them. For this suspense of express profession of faith (which to the outsider may look like the abandoning of every affirmative position rather than the living-out of them in their fullness) bears witness to God in a way no explicitly affirmed position, no matter how authentic or authoritative, ever will. In the end, those witnesses truly count who would rather stand and be silent than insist on establishments and affirmations, the upholding of which might turn them into heroes (cf. §49, 1, e, [*f*]) and to that extent obstruct the way to the living God. Such witnesses testify to the reality of the living God by weakness suffered and even voluntarily undertaken, and to the extent they do so maturely and without morbid self-preoccupation, they also become the associates and representatives of all the losing causes and concerns in the world (cf. §93, 9) and of all the human beings in the world who have no alternative but to suffer—that is, all those concerns and persons whose only champion is the living God. Aware that there is more to life than the flexing of the powers of flesh and blood and the having and wielding of things, such witnesses will accept poverty and physical suffering; always conscious of the limits of the share of truth and goodness that is theirs by God's gracious gift, they will not be devastated when others more forceful consider them deceived and deluded, unethical and irresponsible. And in this way, they will anticipate the extremity where witness to the living God has nothing to offer but reverent, yet helpless silence; that is, where they will find themselves faced with the powers of unbelief, with no resource other than their thirst for the living God to carry them through that ultimate weakness which is the self-abandon of death [*cc*].

In the final analysis, therefore, all faith in God does—or rather, all it can really be expected to do—is glorify God and sustain and

---

[*cc*] Cf. Karl Rahner (*Foundations of Christian Faith*, p. 35; cf. *Grundkurs*, pp. 45-46): "This real transcendence ... in its purity ... can be approached asymptotically at most, if at all, in mystical experience and perhaps in the experience of final loneliness in the face of death." — In this connection, it may be illuminating to ponder the meanings of two Greek verbs that are etymologically cognate with the noun *mystērion*—"mystery." There is, first of all, the root verb, *myō*, which means "to close the eyes and the mouth," in an attitude of religious awe; the verb intimates that the true Light is invisible and that the true Truth is best revealed in silence. The other, related verb, *myeō*, means "to initiate into the mystery"; it conveys that explicit instruction is needed by way of propaedeutic, to open the person initiated to the luminous darkness and the eloquent silence of mystery.

exalt those who believe; consequently, its definitive verification consists in martyrdom (cf. §49, 1, e); the powerless confidence that is implicit in the martyr's total self-abandon—that is, the self-abandon in regard to both body and soul—best conveys the conviction that the living God is really greater than anything that can be thought of (cf. §101, 9) or expressed in positions.

[a] Witness by virtue of weakness is part and parcel of Israel's faith tradition. From Egypt on, Israel glorifies God by lifting up to God, not only all that is glorious in its own history and in the world, but also all that it acknowledges as unfinished, painful, and even downright repugnant and sinful in itself and the predicament it finds itself in. Not surprisingly, praise and lament, in their mutual relationships, are the two basic forms of prayer in the Book of Psalms. Prophetic writings like the Songs of the Servant in Second Isaiah (Is 42, 1-7; 49, 1-6; 50, 4-9; 52, 13 - 53, 12) enhance this tradition during the Exile, by making meekness and even suffering the mark of God's special favor. And when, in late Judaism, Israel's condition becomes one of a dispersal and a powerlessness that are apparently irreversible, suffering, not power, becomes the hallmark of the pious—the *hasîdîm*: it is the poor—the *'anāwîm*—that truly know the living God and are known by the living God. A late psalm can even envision the moment when the songs of praise on the lips of the pious will be the equivalent of the double-edged sword in warriors' hands (Ps 149, 6-9): not power, but the prayer and the witness of the defenseless poor will conquer the world and all the powers that be.[54] No wonder that the Letter to the Hebrews can present martyrdom as the single most telling feature of Israel's faith-tradition: the faith of the cloud of witnesses (Heb 12, 1) is proved true precisely by the fact that they did *not* live to see the fulfillment of the promises, but persevered in hope (Heb 11).

Most traditions in the New Testament bear out analogous understandings. A few examples out of many must suffice to make the point. There is Paul's insistence, notably in the Second Letter to the Corinthians, that the precariousness of his way of life and even of his reputation in the Christian communities, and especially an unspecified personal affliction—his "thorn in the flesh" (2 Cor 12, 7)—mark him as one that truly lives for God; for it is precisely in his weakness that God's strength can reveal itself to full advantage. There is the commendation of undeserved punishment willingly suffered as a mark of God's approval and an invitation to the imitation of Christ in the *prima Petri* (1 Pet 2, 18-24; 3, 14-17). Very explicitly, the fourth Gospel casts Jesus himself, and his disciples after him, as witnesses to God precisely inasmuch they are rejected by those who by their violence show they do not know God.

[b] The understanding of witness as divine power manifested and verified by weakness is the thread that runs through an attractive account, popular in tone and presentation, but historically and theologically quite sophisticated, of the Christian Church's first three centuries: Michael Walsh's *The Triumph of the Meek: Why Early Christianity Succeeded.* The book ends with the Edict of Milan of A. D. 313, which gave the Christians respectability. But, the author adds, "one may doubt whether respectability was what all Christians wanted. After the upheavals of the previous three hundred years, it is little wonder that, in the century which followed the Edict of Milan, many chose to seek a new sort of martyrdom, that of the religious life" (cf. §79, 5, a).[55]

[13] Finally, it is hardly surprising that, from the beginning of the Christian tradition on, the decisive warrant for witness to the living God in weakness and martyrdom has been christological. Thus the account, in the Acts of the Apostles, of the witness and the execution of the first Christian martyr, Stephen (Acts 6, 8 - 7, 60), has characteristic features in common with the Lukan account of Jesus' passion and execution (Lk 22, 54 - 23, 49). Thus, too, the Epistle to the Hebrews can appeal to Jesus as the culmination of Israel's tradition of authentic, long-suffering witness to God, so as to propose him, "the pioneer of faith and its accomplisher to the end" (Heb 12, 2), to the disheartened Christian community as the archexample of devotion to God, learned in the school of compassion and patient endurance (Heb 2, 10-18; 4, 14-15; 5, 7-10). And Paul, in commending unselfish, other-regarding affection and unity in the Christian community at Philippi, can appeal to the painfully self-effacing testimony of the single most authentic witness to the living God:

> Let this mentality prevail among you
> which we also find in Christ Jesus:
> He shared the condition of God,
> yet did not consider equality with God
> a matter of grasping, of seeking advantage.

Instead, he made himself empty—of no account:
he took on the condition of a slave.
Born in human likeness and found in human form,
he lowered himself:
he became obedient to the point of death—death on a cross.
That is why God exalted him above all,
and bestowed on him the name above all names.
Thus, at the name of Jesus, every knee should bend,
in heaven, on earth, and under the earth;
and every tongue should confess,
to the glory of God the Father:
"Jesus Christ is Lord!"

(Phil 2, 5-9)[56]

[§110] "WHAT IS WEAK OF GOD IS STRONGER" (1 COR 1, 25)[57]

[1] In St. Ignatius of Antioch's Letter to the Ephesians, we find the following striking profession of faith:

For by [divine] dispensation, our God, Jesus the Christ, was conceived by Mary, of the seed of David indeed, but also of the Holy Spirit, and he was born, and he was baptized in order that the water might be purified by what he underwent. And what escaped the notice of the ruler of this age was Mary's virginity and her giving birth, as well as the Lord's death: three resounding mysteries [mystēria kraugēs], such as [hatina] were wrought in the stillness of God.[58]

The point is delicately made, yet unmistakable: God has wrought telling things, but the powers that be, which run much of the world as we know it, have been too crude and unsubtle to notice them, let alone appreciate them, for God's things were wrought in the way that is characteristic of God—that is, without a show of power.

[2] Ignatius' famous text raises the final question in our theological inquiry "beyond the power of being." So far, we have argued that testimony borne in weakness and even death is the preferable, because more persuasive, form of witness to the living God. Its persuasiveness derives from the nature of faith itself: in the end, naked faith is not a position of cosmic power or human self-assertion, but of silent, deferential, and indeed, worshipful acknowledgment of the transcendent God—an acknowledgement that also reveals the full depth of the human attunement to the transcendent (cf. §9, 1-2).

Yet there is a further question. Is this form of witness merely a

matter of tactful and fitting deference to the transcendent in testify-
ing, or is there a *substantive* appropriateness to it? That is, does witness borne in weakness represent and reveal something about Godself—something about God only weakness can represent and reveal?
Ignatius seems to imply it does. He suggests it takes a certain affinity with God to notice and appreciate God's work, and since God's
work is "wrought in God's stillness," weakness has an inner affinity
with the living God inasmuch as God relates to the world and humanity—an affinity that power does not have, or at least not to the
same extent.

[3] For a bold statement, both about God's weakness vis-à-vis creation and about weakness in interpersonal relationships viewed as
the worldly analog of that weakness, we must turn to Origen's homilies on Ezekiel, which have come down to us in Jerome's Latin
translation. In the sixth homily, Origen offers what is essentially a
Christian midrash on Ezekiel's stirring parable about Jerusalem, the
helpless, newborn foundling tenderly and mercifully taken up and
embraced and espoused by God, and gone astray to become an
adulteress nevertheless (Ez 16). In the course of his comments,
Origen asks the question, What does this say about God? He explains:

Let me borrow an example from human life; after that (if the Holy Spirit
grants it to me) I will move on to Jesus Christ and God the Father. When
I talk to a person and implore him or her to have mercy on me on some
account, if this is a person without mercy, he or she will not be pained in
any way [*nil patitur*] by what I say; but if this person is tenderly disposed,
with no ingrained hardness of heart, then he or she will listen to me and
have mercy on me, and his or her innermost being will turn tender at my
plea.

You are to understand something comparable with regard to the Savior.
He came down to earth out of pity for the human race; he was pained at
our pains [*passiones perpessus est nostras*] before he ever suffered the cross
[*crucem pateretur*] and, in his kindness, took on our flesh; for if he had not
been pained [*si non fuisset passus*], he would not have come to share human life. First he was pained, then he came down and showed himself
[*primum passus est, deinde descendit et visus est*]. What is this pain [*passio*] he
was pained by [*passus est*] on our behalf? The pain [*passio*] of love!

The Father himself, too, and the God of the universe, "long-suffering
and abounding in mercy" [Ps 103, 8], and compassionate, is he not in
some sense pained [*quodammodo patitur*]? Or do you not know that, when
he governs human affairs, he is pained by human pain [*passionem patitur
humanam*]? For "the Lord your God bore your ways, like a man bears his

son" [Deut 1, 31]. Thus God bears [*supportat*] our ways, just as God's Son takes upon himself our pains [*portat passiones nostras*]. The Father himself is not incapable of being pained [*Ipse Pater non est impassibilis*]. If he welcomes prayers, is merciful, and identifies with our pain, he is pained by something akin to love [*patitur aliquid caritatis*], and he involves himself in what he cannot be involved in by virtue of the majesty of his nature: for our sake he endures human pains [*humanas sustinet passiones*].[59]

In bluntly refusing to call either God's eternal Son or God the Father impassible, Origen is but restating in Christian terms (and in the teeth of the Stoic and Neo-Platonist theological conceptions of his day [dd]), the central article of Israel's faith.   Israel knows the living God as self-revealing—that is, as intimately *present*. But Israel also knows that the Most High God is under neither inner compulsion nor obligation from outside to be present in this fashion; any divine presence is a matter of purely prevenient, free graciousness and mercy. This makes God's sovereign transcendence all the more mysterious, adorable, and incomprehensible (§34, 2). Yet the sense of YHWH's actual presence also makes it impossible for Israel to think of God's incomprehensibility in terms of a fundamentally neutral, remote, faceless, expressionless, impassive immutability (cf. §98, 4, c and [dd]). Whatever transcendent immutability Israel will think of as characteristically God's, it will be the immutability of *faithfulness*—of the kind that is pained by Israel's inconstancy, yet in the end undeterred by it. That is, Israel does know God as all-powerful, but far from conceiving of the divine all-powerfulness in terms of the absolute, overriding dominance of a superpower, it thinks of it in ways that rule out both the violence of power and the apathy of weakness. That is, Israel's conception of God weds the intensity of passion to the thoughtfulness of kindness: God is the God of *exigent love freely, faithfully, and patiently shown*:

YHWH, YHWH,

[dd] Both types of philosophies had reasons of their own to regard the connection between transcendent divinity and *apatheia* as axiomatic. Note that Origen, in the final sentence of the quotation, recognizes this philosophical axiom; this, however, makes his refusal to endorse divine impassibility all the more striking. In one famous passage (*Ad Eph.* 7, 2; *AF* I, pp.), Ignatius of Antioch attributes impassibility, not to the pre-existent divine *Logos*, but to Jesus Christ, on account of his unity with God in the Resurrection: "First [he was] passible, then impassible." If we combine what Origen and Ignatius wrote, we can anticipate the later tradition, which will limit the possibility of God to Jesus' days in the flesh. That is, it will attribute impassibility both to the Risen Christ and to the Eternal Word.

God merciful and gracious,
long-suffering, and abounding in steadfast love and loyalty,
keeping steadfast love for thousands,
forgiving iniquity and transgression and sin,
but who will by no means clear the guilty.

(Ex 34, 6-7)

No wonder Israel will insist that never-ending care for humanity and the world is a true feature of God; it will revel in the realization that God's own Wisdom is delighted to dwell with the children of Adam (Prov 8, 31); it will be able to marvel at God's sustained concern for humanity (Ps 8, 5); YHWH is the God of steadfast love freely and lavishly shown. No wonder, either, that Israel will count on God to be so faithful, and so deeply affected by humanity and the world, that it can set aside most of its worries about anthropomorphism and its dangers, and, in praising God and lamenting before God, treat God as thoroughly affected by emotion and even passion [ee].

That the New Testament is completely dependent on this tradition is clear on every page. Let one quotation stand in for many:

God's love was made manifest among us by this:
God sent his Son, the Only-begotten, out into the world,
so that we might come to life through him.
Love consists in this:
not that we have come to love God,
but that God did love us
and sent his own Son as a means to atone for our sins.

(1 Jn 4, 9-10)

[4] In our own day, there are decisive reasons of an historic and cultural nature that make it dubious to regard power, and especially omnipotence, as unproblematic theological concepts. Over the past century and a half, we have seen Objective Reality as Spinoza conceived it (§107, 5, c, [n]) explode on us with a vengeance, in the form of an unprecedented rise in the deployment of military, political, economic, and cultural dominance based on the human power of scientific knowledge and technological manipulation and management of the world and humanity. We have also lived through what may well have been the most murderous period in human his-

---

[ee] The opening seven chapters of the second volume of Abraham J. Heschel's *The Prophets* remain a classic treatment of this theme.

tory. Unfortunately, it is hard to believe that this has been a matter of mere coincidence. Even more unfortunately, for all the desire for peace in the world, there are reasons to believe that the pursuit and cultivation of Reality in terms of power, dominance, and violence is not about to end.

To take one example out of many, the developing nations are unlikely to abdicate the quest for scientific-technological advantage and the capacity for domination associated with it, simply because the nations that have been in the vanguard of these developments and have hugely profited from them are now realizing their potential for destruction and preaching moderation. But the resolute poor have little to lose, so they do not have much of an investment in moderation; even less do they welcome the homilies of the rich, who stand to lose rather a lot. In this predicament, the rich tend to get irresolute. This means, they are liable to jump to a nervous, ill-focused defense of what they have acquired—a defense that will turn out all the more aggressive according as the rich feel more embarrassed and guilty for having acquired them. Thus there are many signs that the inequalities created by the power of wealth will come back to haunt the wealthy, as the poor ready themselves for their opportunity by hook or by crook. And to compound the picture, in the whole area of power and opportunity, the line between justified demands for justice and unjustified readiness to commit violence is notoriously hard to draw.

In light of these and other possible observations, uncritical appeals to divine omnipotence must be considered theologically suspect today. But in making this statement, we are to remember that facile calls for "Christian" patience, compassion, and forgiveness directed by Christians to the disadvantaged and the marginal, and to those unjustly suffering are equally suspect. This very ambivalent predicament forces upon the Christian world, not only the task of developing a liberation theology truly in line with the demands for justice enshrined in the great Tradition, but also the hard task of a critical rereading of those creedal statements and biblical narratives that suggest that power is the prime divine attribute, and that, therefore, the service of faith and justice may warrant violence and destruction, and even that God in person occasionally commands them [*ff*].

No wonder that recent decades have seen numerous efforts—the-

---

[*ff*] We shall have to return to this perplexing subject: §128,7,[*l*].

ological, philosophical, literary, and otherwise—to develop conceptions in which the categories of power and omnipotence are no longer allowed to retain their once-obvious theological status. Some instances must be mentioned.

[a] After the shock of the Holocaust, some Jewish scholars have taken a fresh interest in the broader question of Israel's conception of God as the "Lord of History." In post-biblical, rabbinical Judaism, and especially after the destruction of the Temple (A. D. 70) and the failure of the revolt led by Bar Cochba (A. D. 135), the Jewish conviction of God's nearness to historic Israel took a new, prophetic turn—even though it was not always warranted by the biblical text. Since the faithful remainder of Israel was now a suffering nation, the conviction arose that God must be more, not less, closely involved with it. But this in turn meant that God must be in a real sense *suffering* as well. To make this claim, some rabbis seized upon texts which have God save Israel by dint of birthpangs (cf. Is 42, 14-15), or which present God as afflicted in the very afflictions of God's people (Is 63, 9); others would express their assurance that God shared in Israel's affliction by claiming that a close enough reading of the biblical text warranted the theological opinion that the Lord, present in the Shekina, had previously joined Israel in person on its exile into Egypt (cf. 1 Sam 2, 27), Elam (cf. Jer 49, 38), and Edom (cf. Is 63, 1), and would eventually join Israel in person again in its return from exile (cf. Deut 30, 3).[60]

Slender as the strictly exegetical merit of these rabbinical interpretations may be, they are important in that they reveal beyond the slightest doubt the depth as well as the theological consistency of Israel's continuing faith-tradition. As the experience of total defeat made God's closeness to Israel (and hence, God's Lordship over history) more and more questionable, God's transcendent glory began to look more and more like mere impenetrability and remoteness. But rabbinical Judaism resisted the temptation of choosing *between* the two—that is, it refused to let the experience of the forbidding riddle of God's ways push it into a denial of God's intimate presence. For Israel's faith-tradition prohibits the playing off of the divine transcendence against the divine presence, the glory against the tenderness, the awe against the intimacy, so as to uphold the former and deny the latter. In insisting that God was now sharing the very suffering of Israel, the rabbis also pointedly refused to teach that faithfulness to Israel made it incumbent upon God to abandon the divine mercy and crush the powers that be with an enormous show of power. Instead, they patiently taught that the great disaster of God's apparent absence, while a most severe test of faith, was the decisive sign of the divine favor in the midst of a world estranged from God. That is, God was the same God as the God that had looked down on Israel in Egypt: God was once again the God of the poor and the downtrodden [gg].

[b] Again (cf. §95, 10, [vv]), a recent work of Iris Murdoch takes its cue from this Jewish theme. In her earlier novel *The Unicorn*, she had already offered a penetrating critique of the identification of God with omnipotence, and suggested that not the appeal to God or gods, but rather, the appreciation of transcendent Goodness would succeed in breaking the vicious circle of violence, and foster what is so badly needed: the absorption of violence by suffering willingly undertaken [hh].

In her recent *The Message to the Planet*, Murdoch has reverted even more insistently to this pressing theme. Here, the eccentric Marcus Vallar—a genius vaguely aware of his Sephardic Jewish descent—moves beyond his early mathematical and artistic accomplishments (a hint that both Newtonian cosmology and Romantic humanism are now *passé*—cf. §96, 4, c, [d]), and, moved by forces or instincts that defy description, becomes the half-compassionate, half-reluctant instrument for the raising to life of an apparently dead, or at least dying, Irish poet. From then on,

---

[gg] Note that a modern Jewish author, Zvi Kolitz, in his short story *Yossel Rakover's Appeal to God*, shows the same depth of theological insight in his interpretation of the religious significance of the Holocaust. Cf. Cf. F. J. van Beeck, *Loving the Torah More than God?*, pp. 13-28.

[hh] Cf. *The Unicorn*, p. 116: "Até [Gk. *Atè* 'fate'] is the name of the almost automatic transfer of suffering from one being to another. Power is a form of Até. The victims of power, and any power has its victims, are themselves infected. They have then to pass it on, to use power on others. This is evil, and the crude image of the all-powerful God is a sacrilege. Good is not exactly powerless. For to be powerless, to be a complete victim, may be another source of power. But Good is non-powerful. And it is in the good that Até is finally quenched, when it encounters a pure being who only suffers and does not attempt to pass the suffering on." It is not farfetched to suppose that the allusions to christological themes are intentional. Incidentally, in Albert Camus' *La Peste* (ET *The Plague*) the theme of evil willingly undertaken is embodied in the figure of Tarrou, who has decided that, since the real plague—the desire to fight and kill for life and justice—has affected all people, the only way to peace and sanctity is to be consistently on the victims' side, so as to at least limit the damage. Here, too, the christological overtones are obviously deliberate.

he begins to move beyond all affirmativeness, and to aim for a "simple purity of vision" in his striving to become "empty yet attentive."[61] Feeble and mildly crazed, and confined to a lunatic asylum for the rich, he becomes the silent, cryptic messenger of a higher world: seekers find enlightenment and even a renewed faith in God by being associated with him, and large numbers of sweet, innocent New Age devotees, apparently drawn by magnetic forces of empathy, begin to show up simply to watch him and draw inspiration from his person as he presents himself outside his residence for daily contemplation opportunities.

The secret of this wholly effortless missionary success is Vallar's inner quest: those close to him sense that he is spiritually identifying with the Holocaust—that is, reliving and absorbing, by voluntarily empathy, the violence that the helpless Jews that died in the Nazi gas chambers had gotten forced upon them. "He said once that only a god could suffer purely and that if some ultimate knowledge were attained it must be turned at once automatically into a special sort of death ... and that this would cause some sort of cosmic shock which would save the world from destruction."[62] When Vallar is eventually found dead, in the kitchen, in front of an open oven, with the gas on, the medical diagnosis is cardiac insufficiency, but it is clear that he must have died from sheer, serene compassion. The quest for pure suffering has opened the door to the pure suffering that is Transcendence itself.

[c] Ever since J. K. Mozley, in *The Impassibility of God* (1926), first raised, in this war-torn century, the subject of God's impassibility with both urgency and sophistication, systematic theology has made decisive (if often clumsy and exaggerated) moves to take its distance both from the Cartesian-Newtonian heritage and from its indebtedness to Kantian and Romantic humanism, so as to retrieve the idea that the forthright affirmation of God's transcendence does not commit the Christian to the idea that God is supremely impassive. It would seem to be no coincidence that some of the more creative recent attempts at reintegrating compassion into the modern conception of God's transcendence have come from women theologians. Thus we have Dorothee Sölle's *Leiden* (ET *Suffering*), Rosemary Haughton's ardent *The Passionate God*, Monika Hellwig's *Jesus, the Compassion of God*, Catherine M. LaCugna's polished essay "The Relational God," and Elizabeth A. Johnson's two pertinent (if by no means undebat-

able: cf. §99, 3, a, [gg]) final chapters in *She Who Is*.[63] But women are far from being the only ones to have been touched by the theme. Thus Paul Schlüngel has given us a profound little essay on God as suffering Father ("Der leidende Vater"); and more recently, Michael J. Dodds has shown, in his careful article "Thomas Aquinas, Human Suffering, and the Unchanging God of Love," that Aquinas' view of God as compassionate is a great deal more nuanced than Thomists (and for that matter, anti-Thomists) had long thought. Louis Dupré, in a critique of the objectivist prejudices inherent in modern theodicy ("Evil—A Religious Mystery"), has made related points. In a similar fashion, John R. Stacer has drawn upon some of the resources of process thought in his "Divine Reverence for Us: God's Being Present, Cherishing, and Persuading." Other systematic attempts have been based on the traditional orthodox Protestant distrust of purely philosophical approaches to theology; in this area, we have Jürgen Moltmann's reflections on "God's *pathos*" in *Der gekreuzigte Gott* (ET *The Crucified God*).[64] Eberhard Jüngel deserves special mention on account of his creative retrieval of themes taken from both natural theology and the work of Karl Barth, not only in *Gottes Sein ist im Werden* (ET *The Doctrine of the Trinity*),[65] but also in his masterpiece *Gott als Geheimnis der Welt* (ET *God as the Mystery of the World*)[66]—important works which Leo J. O'Donovan has provided with a perceptive and sensitive commentary ("The Mystery of God as a History of Love"). Competent monographs on the subject, like Jung Young Lee's *God Suffers for Us*, and, more recently, Paul S. Fiddes' cautious *The Creative Suffering of God*, and especially Joseph M. Hallman's *The Descent of God: Divine Suffering in History and Theology*, suggest that this immemorial Jewish-Christian theme may continue to give rise to fresh reflection for some time to come.

[d] In the Anglo-Saxon world, these reflections on Israel's faith and on modern Christian theological reflection invite a comparison with modern process thought. Modern Western conceptions of God and God's relationship to the world (cf. §96, 4, b) tend to operate on a twofold assumption: (1) God's transcendence, which is axiomatic, is to be understood in terms of remoteness, and hence, (2) awareness of the divine transcendence is inversely proportioned to any notion of divine presence or immanence. Consequently, it is usually only at the expense of the full affirmation of the divine transcendence that modern thought succeeds

in attributing to God some degree of closeness to the world and humanity, not to mention the kind of participation in cosmic and human experience that the Jewish-Christian tradition professes. It is the indubitable merit of the pioneers of process thought to have insisted on God as immanent and as participating in worldly processes, even to the point of suffering. Nevertheless, such process thought as the present author is aware of gives the impression of being too ready to sacrifice the divine transcendence to the divine immanence; thus the nagging suspicion persists that process thought still shares some of the modern West's apparently ineradicable tendency to play off the one against the other.[67]

[5] In the light of the reflections developed in this section, we can now revisit, cautiously, Aquinas' classical definition of God as "Being Itself" (§102, 6). In this effort, if we wish to take seriously Aquinas' warning that, in the end, God is left to dwell in a kind of darkness of ignorance (cf. §107, 1; §109, 10), we must accept the likelihood that we will find ourselves using the language of bold negation, not to mention paradox.

God, as transcendent Being Itself, is not the victim of the transcendent ontological status of the divine. God, therefore, is not the One who is condemned to assert the divine Being with the infinite inertia of the all-powerful, all-displacing super-thing, or to posit the divine Presence with the infinite self-assertiveness of the supremely self-justifying super-person [*ii*]. God *is*, without being condemned, by dint of being God, to "being *It.*"

For God is beyond every form of seeking position or advantage. Contrary to Kant's portrayal of God (§107, 2), God is not self-en-

---

[*ii*] In this area, incidentally, lies the crucial difference between the Christian interpretation of Jesus' death and Kant's. For Kant, who is committed to the axiom that what matters is religion rather than God, and that religion is reducible to ethics, Jesus' death is the supreme instance of the victory of goodness over evil, in the form of *the self-assertion of the morally good person*, prepared to suffer the worst in order to spread the good by teaching and example (cf. *Die Religion innerhalb der Grenzen der bloßen Vernunft*, B 75, A 69; ed. Weischedel, vol. 4, p. 714). Kant overlooks the fact that the New Testament consistently pictures the suffering and dying of the sinless Jesus as the *defeat* of justice, and Jesus himself not as morally victorious, but as the Man of God who is rejected by all. In that rejection, Jesus does not assert himself over against those who reject him; rather, he keeps himself essentially related: on the one hand, he willingly accepts defeat at the hands of those who inflict injustice on him, and on the other, he commits both himself and his cause to God, the just Judge. He dies, not on his own behalf, as a witness to his own integrity, but for others, as the witness to the omnipotent clemency of God.

grossed, but transcendently free, and

Freedom entails self-dispossession, which in the creaturely realm is always limited and only partially realized. But in God there is absolute capacity for self-dispossession (*kenōsis*).[68]

Thus God's being "Being Itself" encompasses God's transcendent freedom not to "be" in the strong, self-affirmative, self-assertive sense of that word; God's Being is beyond all forms of being "it." For this reason, we might even go to the edges of both language and articulate thought once again, and say that God's omnipotence encompasses the power to be wholly self-effacing—that is, the ability not to *be* in any effective sense. In relation to creation, God has the absolute ability to "un-be"; it is integral to the divine countenance that it may be hidden. But in that case, we should draw the consequences of what we have said, and add that the more adequate witness to the hidden God is borne by the person who would rather be misunderstood than force the point—that is, the person who (in Emmanuel Lévinas' words) "fears murder more than death."[69]

This observation, of course, brings us back to "the faithful and true witness" (Rev 3, 14)—the guiltless one who chose to be led to his death rather than call on the Father for more than twelve legions of angels to defeat those who had come to arrest him (Mt 26, 53), and who was restrained and even silent before his human judges. No wonder Origen could comment on the text "He had compassion for them" (Mt 14, 14):

Being a lover of humanity, the impassible One suffered, from the act of taking pity.[70]

No wonder, either, that a contemporary philosopher can write:

The ability to "not-be" is the vestige that Transcendence has left of itself in passing. In that sense, the entire course of Jesus' life is one testimony to God. No wonder they called him God later on, "one in being" with the Father.[71]

In this passage, the phrase "in passing" indubitably alludes to God's passing before Moses (Ex 33, 19; cf. §97, 8). But in the intention of its author, it also conveys the proposition that *narrative*— that "central literary experience," which is "most likely to remain a part of our lives from childhood to old age,"[72] and which patiently passes from silence into silence in the act of being told—has for that very reason a deeper affinity with the living God than any powerful affirmations that are designed to stand and be proclaimed forever. There is nothing wrong with the Christian community's firm rules of faith, creeds, and established doctrinal positions, but if the living Church is forever in tension between the "Already" and the "Not Yet" (that is, if Christianity is genuine according as it is in dynamic transition from the order of graced nature to the order of grace fulfilled: cf. §76, 1), the continuing journey is a more eloquent, because gentler, witness to the living God than the proud doctrinal milestones and signposts that mark the road traveled. For much as wayfarers may know with precision where they have been and how they have come to where they are now, they do not know just by what way they will reach the destination that inspired them to become wayfarers in the first place. Theologically speaking, therefore, the living Tradition is greater than its greatest moments, teachers, and establishments. It is so because it represents the ongoing test of faith rather than its temporary triumphs; for that reason it is also more patient than its past accomplishments and establishments would lead one to believe. Hence, it is also more appealing and less amenable to outright definition— that is, more like the living God who is its Guide as well as its Goal.

[§111] APATHEIA, MERCY, AND LOVE

[1] Yet for all this, one vexing theological question remains. In fairness to the patristic tradition, we must observe that Origen's denial of God's impassibility (§110, 3) is the exception, not the rule. So is the rather un-philosophical, but profoundly Christian statement by a fourth-century bishop of some importance in the South of France, Phoebadius of Agen: "But if God is immune from passion, God is obviously immune from compassion."[73] One glance at the standard patristic Greek lexicon will show that in meditating on the divine transcendence, the Apostolic Fathers, the early apologists, and the Church Fathers from the third century onward were invariably eager to borrow from ancient philosophy, not only from Stoicism, but also from Neo-Platonism, the term *apatheia*—"freedom from *pathē*" ("passions") and hence, "passionlessness"—and apply it to God [*jj*]. In light of our contention that God is the God of

---

[*jj*] Cf. *PGL*, s.v. *apatheia* and *apathēs*. The *Thesaurus Linguæ Latinæ* shows that *impassibilitas* and *impassibilis* in the Latin Church Fathers and ecclesiastical writers have a comparable semantic range, from the turn of the third century on. Cf. also G. Bardy's important article *Apatheia* in *DictSp*.

mercy who shares in our hardships, this demands an interpretation.

[a] A caution. Genuine interpretation operates prudently. Being alive and vocal gives us a powerful advantage over the silent dead (at least for the time being), and one of the more insolent forms this advantage takes is a certain readiness, on our part, to decry the (allegedly) obvious errors of past masters, without our having to worry about their coming back to offer explanations that might embarrass us. Hermeneutically speaking, therefore, it is unwise and superficial for contemporary theologians to hint that the massive patristic affirmation of *apatheia* as a divine attribute is simply an example of the Church making common cause with Greek philosophy as well as protecting its own sociopolitical privilege by projecting status and stoic impassiveness onto Christ and the Father by way of divine attributes. For the patristic tradition's indubitable respect for Greek philosophy was exceeded only by its eclectic use of it.[74] If anything, its sheer consistency on the subject of divine impassibility was theological. We are well advised, therefore, to be careful in treating the subject—more careful, in fact, than some of the otherwise commendable theologians mentioned in the previous section (§110, 4, c) have been.[75]

[2] The Greek noun *pathos*, especially in its plural form *pathē* ("passions"), generally denotes all those affections in which an experiencing subject is unavoidably, and not always voluntarily, implicated and involved with the object of the affection. This gives the (negative) noun *apatheia* ("passionlessness") a broad, fairly imprecise range of meanings, not only in the Christian idiom, but also in the general usage: "impassibility, incapability of suffering, incapacity for change, insensibility, freedom from emotion, freedom from self-interest, freedom from sin." Specifically in reference to human persons (and hence, eventually, in the idiom of Christian asceticism and mysticism), it conveys the (originally Stoic) ideal of "mastery over the passions, detachment, tranquillity, imperturbability, insensitivity to suffering"; it also denotes the Christian ideal of "contemplative peace." Behind this range of meanings, it has been rightly pointed out, it is indeed possible to discern the broad tendency, so characteristic of pre-Christian and non-Christian Greek thought, to place permanent, reliable truth and goodness in a purely spiritual realm, wholly above the instability of matter—including the flesh and the passions inherent in it, to the point where any association,

whether involuntary or voluntary, with matter was considered a sign of imperfection and even sin. Not surprisingly, the suggestion of distance from the world of matter and passion also gave the word *apatheia* strong connotations of remoteness, impassiveness, and indifference. Needless to say, many of these connotations are incompatible with Jewish-Christian conceptions, both about the living God and about both the inconstancy and the native goodness of the world of matter. No wonder, eventually, that these connotations generated serious problems for Christian theology when it became important to give a coherent account of the Incarnation of the *Logos*, and especially of the suffering of Jesus Christ, the *Logos* Incarnate [*kk*].

[3] But this is not the end of the discussion, for the concept of *apatheia* has one enormous strength as well. This can be approximated as follows. We human beings know from experience that we (like everything else with which we share this world) require all kinds of stimuli, catalysts, and incentives to induce us to act— that is, to bring out into the open what we have in us by way of either potential or predisposition or habit or nature. This occurs at all levels. A protruding tree-root on our path makes us stub our toe and stumble, thus causing us to exhibit the precariousness of our balance; the smell of food makes my mouth water and occasions me to buy something not very good to eat, thus bringing out once again my compulsive eating habits; the fetching phrase in a Broadway show that brings tears to my eyes shows that sentiment is alive and well underneath my appearance of clerical propriety; a cab that barely misses me as I cross the street occasions me to show off my potential for violence, as, in a fury of self-assertion, I aim an angry outburst at a hapless police officer; the sunset stirs me to such a sense of inner peace that my companion asks me if I'm all right; the sight of an invalid touches me so deeply that I find myself reaching out and offering help and realizing: this is some of the best I have to give. *Our real capacity for spontaneous self-disclosure is tempered by at least some degree of dependence on the influence of outside agents.* In the language of Aquinas' first way (§102, 2): much as we may be poised for spontaneity, whether for good or for ill, we also have to be "moved" into action. (Incidentally, the above examples make the

---

[*kk*] For a telling example of a fourth-century Christian theologian grappling with these issues, cf. R. P. C. Hanson's account of the thought of Eusebius of Emesa, *The Search for the Christian Doctrine of God*, pp. 387-98.

same point: they are given to jog the memory, to "move" readers to come up, "spontaneously," with similar experiences of their own.) No matter how much we are inclined, for better, for worse, to take initiatives, both in regard to ourselves and to our world, not even the most spontaneous and creative among us ever completely lose their dependence on change (*motus*: §102, 4, b, [*m*]) thrust upon them from the outside.

[4] *Apatheia*, when applied to God, conveys that God is wholly different in this regard. God is not waiting, whether impotently or impassively, for inducements to action in order to manifest the divine nature. God is transcendently free to be self-manifesting and self-communicating. So if God does create, this is neither God's predictable, conditioned response to the provocation of chaos, nor an enigmatic production, by an inscrutable God, of a collection of distant objects; it is the free self-expression of the divine goodness in meaningful and purposeful realities that are not God. And if God, having created, does show mercy, this is not a concession extorted from a feeble deity unable to face the misery of humanity and the world; nor is it an indulgence nonchalantly thrown at humanity and the world by a cryptic deity that remains impervious. For if and whenever God does self-manifest and self-communicate, God freely initiates, and freely allows those who receive the gift of the divine self-communication a glimpse of what is—must be—at the heart of God: transcendently free self-giving.

Here, in other words, under the canopy of a term borrowed from Greek philosophy, we are face to face with Israel's faith (cf. §97, 8):

> And I will favor whom I favor,
> and befriend whom I befriend.
>
> (Ex 33, 19)

Far from denying God's tenderness and care, therefore, *apatheia* serves precisely to give Christian theology the latitude to profess it, and profess it as God's very own in regard to the world and humanity. In this way *apatheia* helps convey the asymmetry at the heart of the Jewish-Christian conception of the mysterious relationship between a truly transcendent God and creation (cf. §23, 4, b). That most accomplished student of the doctrinal tangles of the fourth century, Bishop Richard Hanson, explains how Basil the Great, in a treatise otherwise replete with allusions to Neo-Platonic philosophy, can state his *theological,* Christian understanding of the Triune God's transcendence by teaching that "God's self-giving in the Incarnation is the highest sign we could have of Christ's glory and pre-eminence." And Hanson (who, incidentally, does little to conceal his conviction that some great patristic theology suffers from an unacceptable tendency to present the Incarnate *Logos* as somehow unaffected by the harsh impact of human weakness, and of the pains of the Passion in particular[76]) goes on to comment that, in Basil's thought,

It is not so much the superb ordering of the world that commends [God's] superior might, "as that God the infinite should be involved without impairment (*apathōs*) by the flesh with death, so that he should graciously give us freedom from suffering by his own suffering."[77]

What better way to say that *apatheia* safeguards God's transcendent freedom to be God-in-self-manifestation—that is, to communicate the divine Self to the world in wholly self-initiated love and mercy, regardless of humanity's or the cosmos' readiness or response?

[a] This has an immediate theological consequence, for this understanding of *apatheia* is capable of clarifying in what sense the immutable God can be said to be *mutable.* In Christian theology, this issue reaches its critical mass with the doctrine of the Incarnation, in which the divine *Logos* is professed as having "become flesh," which involves the affirmation that "God was made man." Ever since Athanasius (who, despite serious inadequacies in his christology, had a fundamental and quite revolutionary clarity of conviction on this particular issue) and from his successors the Cappadocians, Christian theology has had to learn again and again the unconventional truth that the Son is *not* a divine being of subordinate rank. The *Logos*, in other words, is *not* the kind of divine being that can afford to undertake contact with humanity and the world because it lacks the fullness of God the Father's divinity. Rather, the *Logos* is Incarnate precisely as the "one *who represents the way in which God himself chooses to have such contact.*"[78] In our own day, Karl Rahner has devoted some profound reflections to this issue, culminating in the statement: "If we face squarely and uncompromisingly the fact of the Incarnation which our faith in the fundamental dogma of Christianity testifies to, then we have to say plainly: God can become something. He who is not subject to change in himself can *himself* be subject to change *in something else.*"[79] That is, certain discernible events of divine mercy and compassion in the world of space and time are rooted in God's everlasting mercy and compassion, and bear

witness to the actual, self-involving presence, in the world, of the transcendent God who is Everlasting Mercy and Love.

[5] The use of *apatheia* in the human realm—that is, in the ascetical and mystical theology of the Greek Fathers, including the desert monks—is at least as revealing as its use to denote an attribute of God. The Fathers depict the necessity of habitually rising above the self-regarding impulse of the moment as an essential precondition of contemplative union with God. Only those, therefore, who have acknowledged the twofold passion of self-maintaining craving (Gk. *epithymia*, Lat. *concupiscentia*) and self-assertive temper (Gk. *thymos*, Lat. *ira*) in themselves (cf. §126, 5, a) and have risen above it by the practice of self-denial, can attain to the inner peace and humility that will enable them to contemplate and find God, the source of the true freedom of the spirit.

> [a] In the idiom of the fathers, it is true, the praise of *apatheia* usually serves to commend the *negative* aspects of the pursuit of this freedom; what is chiefly stressed is the practice of renunciation, which leads to detachment from the passions and thus to inner tranquillity. Still, one of the great ascetical and mystical masters of the period, the fourth-century monk Evagrius Ponticus, never ceases to emphasize the profoundly positive elements of *apatheia* [*ll*]. Thus he can suggest, in the treatise in which he details the first, ascetical phase of the life of dedication to God, entitled *Praktikos* (also known as *The Monk*), that *agapē* is an essential ingredient of asceticism: "A fairly spare regimen that is not too singular, combined with *agapē*, will speedily lead the monk into the haven of *apatheia*."[80] And even though he can, in the second saying of the treatise, overstate his case for the need for *apatheia*, by taking a characteristic shortcut and writing that "the Kingdom of Heaven is *apatheia* of soul along with true understanding of reality,"[81] he does show that he recognizes a hierarchy of purposes: while *apatheia* is "the flower of the life of ascetical practice,"[82] its goal is *agapē*—the love that is of God.[83] No wonder Evagrius writes more than once that "the progeny of

---

[*ll*] On Evagrius' understanding of *apatheia*, cf. A. Guillaumont's introduction to the *Praktikos* in *SC* 170 ("Étude historique et doctrinale"), pp. 98-112. John Eudes Bamberger's introduction to the English translation of Evagrius' principal works (*The Praktikos* and *Chapters on Prayer*), which is partly dependent on Guillaumont's, offers a treatment of the same subject (pp. lxxxi-lxxxviii).

apatheia is *agapē*."[84] And he offers a most appealing picture of
the coherence between asceticism, charity, and the contemplative
love of God when he writes that, while it is "the function ... of
continence to look without passion [*apathōs*] at everything that
sets off irrational fantasies in us," it is the function "of love [*a-
gapē*] to put itself at the service of every image of God almost as
it would put itself at the service of [Christ] the First Image as
well, even if the demons should seek to defile them" (cf. §89,
5).[85] The treatise ends on a touching note of spiritual realism
and sobriety: "It is true, it is not possible to love all the brothers
equally, but all can live together without passion [*apathōs*], free
from resentment and hatred."[86]

Thus, in the end, the measure of *apatheia* in the human realm
turns out to be, not any Stoic ideal of impassiveness, but the patient pursuit of love [*mm*], just as the attribution of *apatheia*
to God had served to affirm the divine mercy and love.

[6]   This realization also gives access to that most characteristic
product of the liturgical spirituality of the Greek Fathers: the *icon.*
Icons embody *apatheia.* That is, they portray a serenity and a composure that makes one wonder, initially, if the piety that holds them
dear has not lost touch with the doctrine of the Incarnation, fallen
victim to monophysitism, or at least lost touch with present human
suffering. But icons do not give away their theological secret until
we notice that they do not contain shadows; the images in the icons
are not illuminated by a source of light outside them. The light
comes wholly from inside. "They need no lamplight or sunlight,
for the Lord God will be their light" (Rev 22, 5). Thus, far from
being untouchable and remote, Christ the Lord, and Mary most
holy, and the Saints and Sages as well, are suffused with a holy fire
that enlightens and cleanses—the awe-inspiring glow of God's radiance, which is also the kindly, appealing light of God's love. For
apatheia weds majesty to appeal, awe to intimacy (cf. §34, 7); en-

---

[*mm*] Gregory Nazianzen, who had ordained Evagrius to the diaconate in 379-80
A.D., and whom Evagrius repeatedly claims as his chief teacher and mentor, had
suggested the same, by means of two successive rhetorical questions in the eulogy
devoted to his late, very ascetical sister Gorgonia, delivered in 371 A.D. (*Or.* VIII,
XII, [3-4]; *PG* 35, 801C): "... who evidenced a more dispassionate mind on painful
occasions [*noun ... apathesteron en tois pathesi*]? Yet who [evidenced] a more compassionate soul to those who struggle [*sympathesteran psychēn tois kamnousi*]?" (I
owe this reference to "Gorgonia's Silence: Gregory Nazianzen's Interpretation of
his Sister's *Askēsis*," an unpublished paper by Dr. Robin A. Darling Young.)

countering *apatheia* in an icon is an invitation to pure worship—that is, to union with God in the Spirit.

No wonder Symeon the New Theologian can write about the effects of repentance and purification in terms that evoke the icon. Those who, in their quest for God, have let themselves be cleansed by the fear of eternal punishment and have found compunction (cf. §113, 3, d), humility, and inner peace, will, in a cathartic experience, be delivered from passion and find a deep freedom and a heart transformed. In themselves, that is, they will experience God's glory:

They become like persons aglow, somehow, with a fire in their innermost being. Enkindled by it and incapable of enduring the burst of the blaze, they become, as it were, beside themselves; and not in control of themselves any longer at all, inundated by a flood of tears and exhausted by it, they stir the flame of desire even more vehemently. They go on to shed tears more copiously and, cleansed by their abundance, they light up all the more radiantly. And when they are utterly consumed and have become like light, then the saying comes true: «God seeking union with gods as well as making himself known to them»; and this occurs, presumably, to the extent that God is at last united with those who have held on to him, and unveiled to those who have come to know him [*nn*].[87]

No wonder, either, that the Second Council of Nicaea (A. D. 787) canonized the veneration of icons; they are part of the Christian community's loving worship of the living God (DH 600-01; CF 1251-52).

[7] Finally, both the eternal *apatheia* of the God of Love and the *apatheia* that keeps human persons clinging to this God in faith are movingly professed in a celebrated text by Saint Teresa of Avila. Not surprisingly, the tell-tale words are neither "power" nor "dispassionateness," but "patience" and "having God":

Nada te turbe,	Let nothing disturb you,
nada te espante,	Let nothing alarm you,
Todo se pasa,	Everything passes,
Dios no se muda.	God does not change.
La paciencia	Patience will
Todo lo alcanza.	obtain everything.
Quien a Dios tiene	Those who have God

[*nn*] For the importance of the divinization theme so prominently sounded in Symeon's quotation from Gregory Nazianzen's oration *On the Theophany* (PG 36, 319C; *SC* 358, pp. 116-17), cf. §23, 2, a-d.

Nada le falta;	Are short of nothing;
Solo Dios basta.[88]	God alone is enough.

Amen.

Notes

Chapter 9

1. The original (*Oeuvres complètes* [ed. Chevalier], pp. 553-54):

†

L'AN DE GRÂCE 1654

Lundi 23 novembre jour de saint Clément pape et martyr
et autres au Martyrologe.

Veille de saint Chrysogone martyr et autres.

Depuis environ dix heures et demi du soir jusques environ minuit et demi.

FEU

Dieu d'Abraham, Dieu d'Isaac, Dieu de Jacob, non des Philosophes et des
savants.

Certitude, certitude, sentiment, joie, paix.

Dieu de Jésus-Christ.

Deum meum et deum vestrum.

Ton Dieu sera mon Dieu.

Oubli du monde et de tout hormis Dieu.

Il ne se troûve que par les voies enseignées dans l'Évangile.

Grandeur de l'âme humaine.

Père juste, le monde ne t'a point connu, mais je t'ai connu.

Joie, joie, pleurs de joie.

Je m'en suis séparé ⸺

Deliquerunt me fontem aquae vivae.

Mon Dieu me quitterez-vous? ⸺

Que je n'en sois séparé éternellement.

Cette est la vie éternelle, qu'ils te connaissent seul vrai Dieu et celui que tu
as envoyé J.-C.

Jésus-Christ ⸺

Jésus-Christ ⸺

Je m'en suis séparé, je l'ai fui, renoncé, crucifié.

Que je n'en sois jamais séparé! ⸺

Il ne se conserve que par les voies enseignées dans l'Évangile.

Renonciation totale et douce.

Soumission totale à Jésus-Christ et à mon directeur.
Éternellement en joie pour un jour d'exercice sur la terre.
Non obliviscar sermones tuos. Amen.

(The Latin quotations are taken from the Vulgate: Jn 20, 17; Jer 2, 13; Ps 119
[Vg 118], 16); the French text also quotes Ex 3, 15; Ruth 1, 16; Jn 17, 25; Jn
17, 3.)

2. Theo de Boer, *De God van de filosofen en de God van Pascal*, p. 9.

3. "[...] anima hominis fit omnia quodammodo secundum sensum et intellectum, in quo cognitionem habentia ad Dei similitudinem quodammodo appropinquant, in quo omnia præexistunt [...]" (*S. Th.*, I, 80, 1, *in c.*).

4. *Pensées* 200 [347] (*Oeuvres complètes* [ed. Lafuma], p. 142): "L'homme n'est qu'un roseau, le plus faible de la nature, mais c'est un roseau pensant. Il ne faut pas que l'univers entier s'arme pour l'écraser; une vapeur, une goutte d'eau suffit pour le tuer. Mais quand l'univers l'écraserait, l'homme serait encore plus noble que ce qui le tue, puisqu'il sait qu'il meurt et l'avantage que l'univers a sur lui. L'univers n'en sait rien.

    Toute notre dignité consiste donc en la pensée. C'est de là qu'il nous faut relever et non de l'espace et de la durée, que nous ne saurions remplir."

5. T. S. Eliot, "Choruses from *The Rock*," I; *Collected Poems 1909-1962*, p. [161].

6. Cf. Erich Przywara's famous book by that title.

7. *Canaanite Myth and Hebrew Epic*, pp. 60-75, esp. 71.

8. *ANET*, pp. 60-61.

9. "'Ehje 'ašer 'ehje," p. 498: "... ich gestehe, daß man bei der Beurteilung des ganzen Textbestandes nicht durchaus ohne ein Moment der 'Intuition' auskommen kann."

10. For an enlightening interpretation of the *Šᵉmaʿ*, cf. S. Dean McBride, Jr., "The Yoke of the Kingdom: *An Exposition of Deuteronomy 6: 4-5*."

11. Text (*Akdamuth*) in *Ha-Siddur Ha-Shelem—Daily Prayer Book* (ed. Birnbaum), p. 647 (Gimel-Daleth-He). Hugh Miller kindly drew my attention to this passage.

12. Some suggestive reflections on this in H. de Lubac, *Le mystère du surnaturel*, pp. 155-77 (ET *The Mystery of the Supernatural*, pp. 154-80).

13. Cf. Claus Westermann, *God's Angels Need No Wings*, p. 125-26. Aquinas explains why this latter move is a mistake on principle. Not being material, spiritual substances are not properly members of a species; hence, each must be considered a species in its own right (*S. Th.* I, 50, 4, *in c.*).

14. Cf. Athanasius, *Contra Gentes*, 44: tas ... theias theioterōs kineisthai ("the divine [powers] move in a more divine fashion").

15. Cf. R. P. C. Hanson, *The Search for the Christian Doctrine of God*, pp. 357-62.

16. Chaps. 39-40 (ed. Srawley, pp. 154-64; ET, pp. 321-25).

17. On this subject, cf. the first chapter of a now largely dated best seller, Harvey Cox's *The Secular City*.

18. Cf. Norbert Lohfink, *Lobgesänge der Armen*, p. 103, n. 1.

19. Cf., among an avalanche of literature, William C. Schutz, *The Interpersonal Underworld*, and W. G. Bennis and H. A. Shepard, "A Theory of Group Development."

20. Cf. Jon D. Levenson, *Creation and the Persistence of Evil*.

21. Cf. Norbert Lohfink's commentary on 1QH 2, 20-30, esp. 22-25 (lines 06-13 in Lohfink's arrangement), in *Lobgesänge der Armen*, pp. 49, 53.

22. A wholly monadic conception of divine transcendence was one of the "fixed points" of the theology of Arius' teacher, Lucian of Antioch; cf. R. P. C. Hanson, *The Search for the Christian Doctrine of God*, pp. 31-32.

23. "[Deus] praedicandus est re et essentia a mundo distinctus ... et super omnia quae praeter ipsum sunt et concipi possunt, ineffabiliter excelsus."

24. Cf. *Confessiones* I, II, 2; *S. Th.* I, 8, 1, *ad 2*.
25. Cf. Karl Rahner, "Die ignatianische Mystik der Weltfreudigkeit" (ET "The Ignatian Mysticism of Joy in the World").
26. Hugo Rahner, "Die Grabschrift des Loyola."
27. Quotations from the essay "Aimer la Thora plus que Dieu" (*Difficile liberté*, pp. 189-93), p. 193: "Dans quelle vigoureuse dialectique s'établit l'égalité entre Dieu et l'homme au sein même de leur disproportion. ... Humanisme intégral et austère, lié à une difficile adoration! Et inversement, adoration coïncidant avec l'exaltation de l'homme!" Cf. F. J. van Beeck, *Loving the Torah More than God?*, p. 40; cf. also the discussion in that book, pp. 51-52.
28. Cf. F. J. van Beeck, *Loving the Torah More than God?*, pp. 41-53.
29. On religious projection, cf. Han M. M. Fortmann's monumental *Als ziende de onzienlijke*.
30. "Aimer la Thora plus que Dieu," in *Difficile Liberté*, p. 190: "Réaction la plus saine .... un dieu, un peu primaire, distribuait des prix, infligeait des sanctions ou pardonnait des fautes et, dans sa bonté, traitait les hommes en éternels enfants." Cf. also F. J. van Beeck, *Loving the Torah More than God?*, p. 37.
31. Cf. "The Metaphysical Poets," in *Selected Essays 1917-1932*, pp. 241-50.

Chapter 10

1. Cf. Aristotle, *Categories*, 5, 2ª (*AristBWks*, p. 9): "Substance (*ousia*), in the truest and most primary sense of the word, is that which is neither predicable of a subject nor present in a subject; for instance, the individual man or horse."
2. On this subject, cf. Karl Rahner, *Grundkurs*, pp. 28-53 (ET *Foundations of Faith*, pp. 17-43).
3. Cf. R. W. Southern, *Saint Anselm and His Biographer*, pp. 51-57.
4. Eadmer's *Life of St Anselm*, I, xix; cf. Southern's edition, pp. 29-31 (translation revised).
5. *The Life of St Anselm*, p. 29, note 3.
6. Schmitt I, pp. 100/12-104/7 (cf. Charlesworth's edition, pp. 114-121): "[c. I] Fateor, domine, et gratias ago, quia creasti in me hanc imaginem tuam, ut tui memor te cogitem, te amem. Sed sic est abolita attritione vitiorum, sic est obfuscata fumo peccatorum, ut non possit facere ad quod facta est, nisi tu renoves et reformes eam. Non tento, domine, penetrare altitudinem tuam, quia nullatenus comparo illi intellectum meum; sed desidero aliquatenus intelligere veritatem tuam, quam credit et amat cor meum. Neque enim quæro intelligere ut credam, sed credo ut intelligam. Nam et hoc credo: quia »nisi credidero, non intelligam«. ... [c. II] Ergo, domine, qui das fidei intellectum, da mihi, ut quantum scis expedire intelligam, quia es sicut credimus, et hoc es quod credimus. Et quidem credimus te esse aliquid quo nihil maius cogitari possit. An ergo non est aliqua talis natura, quia »dixit insipiens in corde suo: non est deus«? Sed certe ipse idem insipiens, cum audit hoc ipsum quod dico: 'aliquid quo maius nihil cogitari potest', intelligit quod audit; et quod intelligit in intellectu eius est, etiam si non intelligat illud esse. Aliud enim est rem esse in intellectu, aliud intelligere rem esse. Nam cum pictor præcogitat quæ facturus est, habet quidem in intellectu, sed nondum

intelligit esse quod nondum fecit. Cum vero iam pinxit, et habet in intellectu et intelligit esse quod iam fecit. Convincitur ergo etiam insipiens esse vel in intellectu aliquid quo nihil maius cogitari potest, quia hoc cum audit intelligit, et quidquid intelligitur in intellectu est. Et certe id quo maius cogitari nequit, non potest esse in solo intellectu. Si enim vel in soqlo intellectu est, potest cogitari esse et in re, quod maius est. Si ergo id quo maius cogitari non potest, est in solo intellectu: id ipsum quo maius cogitari non potest, est quo maius cogitari potest. Sed certe hoc esse non potest. Existit ergo procul dubio aliquid quo maius cogitari non valet, et in intellectu et in re. ... [*c.* III] Quod utique sic vere est, ut nec cogitari possit non esse. Nam potest cogitari esse aliquid, quod non possit cogitari non esse; quod maius est quam quod non esse cogitari potest. ... Sic ergo vere est aliquid quo maius cogitari non potest, ut nec cogitari possit non esse. Et hoc es tu, domine deus noster. Sic ergo vere es, domine deus meus, ut nec cogitari possis non esse. Et merito. Si enim aliqua mens posset cogitare aliquid melius te, ascenderet creatura super creatorem, et iudicaret de creatore; quod valde est absurdum. Et quidem quidquid est aliud præter te solum, potest cogitari non esse. Solus igitur verissime omnium, et ideo maxime omnium habes esse: quia quidquid aliud est non sic vere, et idcirco minus habet esse. Cur itaque »dixit insipiens in corde suo: non est deus«, cum iam in promptu sit rationali menti te maxime omnium esse? Cur, nisi quia stultus et insipiens? ... [*c.* IV] Verum quomodo dixit in corde quod cogitare non potuit; aut quomodo cogitare non potuit quod dixit in corde, cum idem sit dicere in corde et cogitare? Quod si vere, immo quia vere et cogitavit quia dixit in corde, et non dixit in corde quia cogitare non potuit: non uno tantum modo dicitur aliquid in corde vel cogitatur. Aliter enim cogitatur res cum vox eam significans cogitatur, aliter cum id ipsum quod res est intelligitur. Illo itaque modo potest cogitari deus non esse, isto vero minime. Nullus quippe intelligens id quod deus est, potest cogitare quia deus non est, licet hæc verba dicat in corde, aut sine ulla aut cum aliqua extranea significatione. Deus enim est id quo maius cogitari non potest. Quod qui bene intelligit, utique intelligit id ipsum sic esse, ut nec cogitatione queat non esse. Qui ergo intelligit sic esse deum, nequit eum non esse cogitare. Gratias tibi, bone domine, gratias tibi, quia quod prius credidi te donante, iam sic intelligo te illuminante, ut si te esse nolim credere, non possim non intelligere."

7. R. W. Southern, *Saint Anselm and his Biographer,* p. 55, note 1.

8. Cf. the quotations from Augustine in the apparatus in Schmitt I, p. 100.

9. For text and commentary, cf. *SC* 182, pp. 528-35; for further commentary, cf. Adalbert de Vogüé's detailed discussion in *SC* 185, pp. 383-588. For the actual arrangement of the psalms in the divine office according to the Benedictine tradition, cf. the table in *SC* 181, p. 103, by the same author.

10. *Confessiones,* VII, iv, 6 (*CSEL* 33, p. 145): ... et ideo te, quidquid esses, esse incorruptibilem confitebar. neque enim ulla anima umquam potuit poteritue cogitare aliquid, quod sit te melius, qui summum et optimum bonum es. cum autem uerissime atque certissime incorruptibile corruptibili praeponatur, sicut ego iam praeponebam, poteram iam cogitatione aliquid attingere quod esset melius deo meo, nisi tu esses incorruptibilis.

11. Cf. Augustine's etymological explanation (*Confessions* X, 11; *CSEL* 33, p. 240): Quod in animo colligitur, id est *cogitur, cogitari* proprie iam dicatur ("What

is collected—that is, gathered—in the soul, that is what we say we think of").
The cultivation of *cogitatio* understood as inner awareness shaped by integrated experience is one of the principal themes of the *Confessions*.

12. Text in Schmitt I, pp. 125-29; Anselm's reply on pp. 130-39. In Charlesworth's edition, pp. 156-67, 168-91.

13. *S.c.G.* I, 10-11; *S. Th.* I, 2, 1.

14. Cf. *S. Th.* I, 2, 1, *ad 1.*

15. Cf. *S. Th.* I, 2, 1, *in c.*

16. Cf. *S. Th.* I, 2, 1, *in c.*

17. Cf. *S. c. G.* I, 11, *Prædicta autem*; *S. Th.* I, 2, 1, *ad 2.*

18. Cf. *S. Th.* I, 2, 1, *in c.*

19. Schmitt I, pp. 111/8-112/20 (cf. Charlesworth, pp. 134-37): [*c.* 14] An invenisti, anima mea, quod quærebas? Quærebas Deum, et invenisti eum esse quiddam summum omnium, quo nihil melius cogitari potest; ... Si vero invenisti: quid est, quod non sentis quod invenisti? Cur non te sentit, domine deus, anima mea, si invenit te? ... Domine deus meus, formator et reformator meus, dic desideranti animæ meæ, quid aliud es, quam quod vidit, ut pure videat, quod desiderat. Intendit se ut plus videat, et nihil videt ultra hoc quod vidit nisi tenebras; immo non videt tenebras, quæ nullæ sunt in te, sed videt se non plus posse videre propter tenebras suas. Cur hoc, domine, cur hoc? Tenebratur oculus eius infirmitate sua, aut reverberatur fulgore tuo? Sed certe et tenebratur in se, et reverberatur a te. ... Quid puritatis, quid simplicitatis, quid certitudinis et splendoris ibi est! Certe plus quam a creatura valeat intelligi. [*c.* 15] Ergo Domine, non solum es quo maius cogitari nequit, sed es quiddam maius quam cogitari possit. Quoniam namque valet cogitari esse aliquid huiusmodi: si tu non es hoc ipsum, potest cogitari aliquid maius te; quod fieri nequit. [*c.* 16] Vere, Domine, hæc est lux inaccessibilis, in qua habitas.

20. *Meditationes*, III, 45, 11-14 (Ed. Rodis-Lewis, p. 45): "Dei nomine intelligo substantiam quandam infinitam, independentem, summe intelligentem, summe potentem, & a quâ tum ego ipse, tum aliud omne, si quid aliud extat, quodcumque extat, est creatum." For the whole context, cf. 45, 9-22 (Ed. Rodis-Lewis, pp. 45-46).

21. *Meditationes* V, 66, 16-19 (Ed. Rodis-Lewis, p. 65).

22. *Meditationes* V, 67, 2-5 (Ed. Rodis-Lewis, p. 66): "... ex eo quòd non possim cogitare Deum nisi existentem, sequitur existentiam a Deo esse inseparabilem, ac proinde illum reverà existere."

23. Cf. *Meditationes*, III, 51, 15 - 52, 20 (Ed. Rodis-Lewis, p. 51-52).

24. Still, *Summa contra Gentiles*, book 1, chapter 13 is a close second.

25. The *Leonina* edition introduces the article with the following references: I *Sent.*, d. III, *div. prim. part. textus*; *S. c. G.* I, 13, 15, 16, 44; II, 15; III 64; *Q. D. de Ver.* 5, 2; *Q. D. de Pot.*, 3, 5; *Comp. Theol.*, c. 3; *Phys.* VII, *lect.* 2; VIII, *lect.* 9 ff.; *Met.* XII, *lect.* 5, ff.; the Marietti edition lists some of the above, and adds I *Sent.*, d. 8, *q.* 1, *art.* 1; *Q. D. de Ver.* 1, 4, *ad 7*; *Q. D. de Pot.* 4, 7. All these passages are worth reviewing, among other things, because they illustrate the variety of philosophical and theological topics upon which Aquinas has drawn for the comprehensive argument of the *Summa theologiæ.*

26. The reference is to Aristotle's *Metaphysics* II, 1, 993^{b}25-30 (*AristBWks*, pp. 712-13). Due to the defective Latin text he was using, Aquinas' quotation is an

inaccurate translation of the Greek; still, it is broadly consistent with what Aristotle means.

27. *S. Th.* I, 2, 3, *in c.*: "Deum esse, quinque viis probari potest.

Prima autem et manifestior via est, quae sumitur ex parte motus. Certum est enim, et sensu constat, aliqua moveri in hoc mundo. Omne autem quod movetur, ab alio movetur. Nihil enim movetur, nisi secundum quod est in potentia ad illud ad quod movetur: movet autem aliquid secundum quod est actu. Movere enim nihil aliud est quam educere aliquid de potentia in actum: de potentia autem non potest aliquid reduci in actum, nisi per aliquod ens in actu: sicut calidum in actu, ut ignis, facit lignum, quod est calidum in potentia, esse actu calidum, et per hoc movet et alterat ipsum. Non autem est possibile ut idem sit simul in actu et potentia secundum idem, ... Impossibile est ergo quod, secundum idem ..., aliquid sit movens et motum, vel quod moveat seipsum. Omne ergo quod movetur, oportet ab alio moveri. Si ergo id a quo movetur, moveatur, oportet et ipsum ab alio moveri; et illud ab alio. Hic autem non est procedere in infinitum: quia sic non esset aliquod primum movens; et per consequens nec aliquod aliud movens, quia moventia secunda non movent nisi per hoc quod sunt mota a primo movente, ... Ergo necesse est devenire ad aliquod primum movens, quod a nullo movetur: et hoc omnes intelligunt Deum.

Secunda via est ex ratione causae efficientis. Invenimus enim in istis sensibilibus esse ordinem causarum efficientium: nec tamen invenitur, nec est possibile quod aliquid sit causa efficiens sui ipsius; quia esset prius seipso, quod est impossibile. Non autem est possibile quod in causis efficientibus procedatur in infinitum. Quia in omnibus causis efficientibus ordinatis, primum est causa medii, et medium est causa ultimi, sive media sint plura, sive unum tantum: remota autem causa, removetur effectus: ergo, si non fuerit primum in causis efficientibus, non erit ultimum nec medium. Sed si procedatur in infinitum in causis efficientibus, non erit prima causa efficiens: et sic non erit nec effectus ultimus, nec causae efficientes mediae: quod patet esse falsum. Ergo est necesse ponere aliquam causam efficientem primam: quam omnes Deum nominant.

Tertia via est sumpta ex possibili et necessario: quae talis est. Invenimus enim in rebus quaedam quae sunt possibilia esse et non esse: cum quaedam inveniantur generari et corrumpi, et per consequens possibilia esse et non esse. Impossibile est autem omnia quae sunt talia, semper esse: quia quod possibile est non esse, quandoque non est. Si igitur omnia sunt possibilia non esse, aliquando nihil fuit in rebus. Sed si hoc est verum, etiam nunc nihil esset: quia quod non est, non incipit esse nisi per aliquid quod est; si igitur nihil fuit ens, impossibile fuit quod aliquid inciperet esse, et sic modo nihil esset: quod patet esse falsum. Non ergo omnia entia sunt possibilia: sed oportet aliquid esse necessarium in rebus. Omne autem necessarium vel habet causam suae necessitatis aliunde, vel non habet. Non est autem possibile quod procedatur in infinitum in necessariis quae habent causam suae necessitatis, sicut nec in causis efficientibus, ut probatum est. Ergo necesse est ponere aliquid quod sit per se necessarium, non habens causam necessitatis aliunde, sed quod est causa necessitatis aliis: quod omnes dicunt Deum.

Quarta via sumitur ex gradibus qui in rebus inveniuntur. Invenitur enim in rebus aliquid magis et minus bonum, et verum, et nobile: et sic de aliis huiusmodi. Sed *magis* et *minus* dicuntur de diversis secundum quod appropinquant diversimode ad aliquid quod maxime est: sicut magis calidum est, quod magis appropinquat maxime calido. Est igitur aliquid quod est verissimum, et optimum, et nobilissimum, et per consequens, maxime ens: nam quae sunt maxime vera, sunt maxime entia, ut dicitur II *Metaphysic.* Quod autem dicitur maxime tale in aliquo genere, est causa omnium quae sunt illius generis: ... Ergo est aliquid quod omnibus entibus est causa esse, et bonitatis, et cuiuslibet perfectionis: et hoc dicimus Deum.

    Quinta via sumitur ex gubernatione rerum. Videmus enim quod aliqua quae cognitione carent, scilicet corpora naturalia, operantur propter finem: quod apparet ex hoc quod semper aut frequentius eodem modo operantur, ut consequantur id quod est optimum; unde patet quod non a casu, sed ex intentione perveniunt ad finem. Ea autem quae non habent cognitionem, non tendunt in finem nisi directa ab aliquo cognoscente et intelligente, sicut sagitta a sagittante. Ergo est aliquid intelligens, a quo omnes res naturales ordinantur ad finem: et hoc dicimus Deum."

28. *Systematic Theology*, I, pp. 205 (last two sets of italics added for emphasis); cf. also pp. 208-10.

29. *S. Th.* I, 2, 2, 2: "... medium demonstrationis est quod quid est. Sed de Deo non possumus scire quid est, sed solum quid non est ... Ergo non possumus demonstrare Deum esse."

30. For this train of thought, cf. *S. Th.* I, 2, 2, *ad* 2.

31. Cf. his "Meditation on the Word 'God'," in *Foundations of Christian Faith*, pp. 44-51 (*Grundkurs*, pp. 54-61).

32. Cf. especially chapters 1 and 2 (pp. 11-89).

33. For a summary of Ramsey's theories, cf. my *Christ Proclaimed*, pp. 75-78; for multiple applications in christology, cf. that same book, *passim.*

34. For the following paragraphs, cf. *S. Th.* I, 13, 5-6.

35. On metaphors, and how they mediate between God (or, as the case may be, Christ), humanity, and human concerns, cf. my *Christ Proclaimed*, pp. 85-93, 111-14, 122-29, 137-43, 146-47.

36. *Pantōn chrēmatōn metron estin anthrōpos.* Not surprisingly, the experts are divided as to the original meaning of Protagoras' adage, as a quick look at, say, the first volume of Frederick Copleston's *History of Philosophy* will bear out.

37. Cf. for example, *S. Th.* I, 3, 7, *in c.*

38. Cf. Theo de Boer, *De God van de filosofen en de God van Pascal*, pp. 49-52, for a description of the modern tendency to think otherwise on this central issue.

39. *Expositio super secundam Decretalem* (*Opuscula theologica* I, ed. Marietti, nr. 11-98): "Non tamen est idem modus perfectionis humanae et divinae, quia non potest esse tanta similitudo inter Creatorem et creaturam, quin major inveniatur ibi dissimilitudo, propter hoc quod creatura in infinitum distat a Deo."

40. The proposition just formulated is the principal thesis of a fine essay by my former teacher Han Geurtsen, S.J.: "The innerlijke structuur van het godsbewijs" ("The inner structure of the arguments for the existence of God").

41. *S. Th.* I, 5, 2, *in c.*: "Primo autem in conceptione intellectus cadit ens; quia secundum hoc unumquodque cognoscibile est, in quantum est actu." Aquinas refers to Aristotle for this latter maxim; cf. the discussion in *Metaphysics* IX, 9, 1051^{a}21-34 (*AristBWks*, pp. 832-33).

42. "[...] anima hominis fit omnia quodammodo secundum sensum et intellectum, in quo cognitionem habentia ad Dei similitudinem quodammodo appropinquant, in quo omnia præexistunt [...]" (*S. Th.*, I, 80, 1, *in c.*).

43. *Q. D. de Ver.* 22, 2, *ad 1*: "Omnia cognoscentia cognoscunt implicite Deum in quolibet cognito."

44. *L'Être et les êtres*, p. 167: "... le monde est, pour nous, le point de départ normal et nécessaire de la démonstration de Dieu; mais en même temps l'aptitude foncière et congénitale de l'esprit à connaître et désirer Dieu est la cause initiale et suprême de tout le mouvement de la nature et de la pensée; en sorte que notre certitude de l'être se fonde ainsi sur l'Être même." Quoted in H. Geurtsen, "De innerlijke structuur van het godsbewijs," p. 282.

45. This sentence, and indeed this whole paragraph, serves to correct a sweeping statement made earlier in *God Encountered* (§80, 3): "Gone is any residual Platonism [Aquinas] might have held over from Augustine."

46. *De hom. opif.* VIII, 5-6 (*PG* 44, 145A-147A; ET *The Making of Man*, *NPNCF*, Second Series, vol. 5, pp. 393-94).

47. Cf. *Die geestelike brulocht*, pp. 289 (cf. *The Spiritual Espousals and Other Works*, p. 73). For a comparable passage, cf. *Vanden seven sloten*, pp. 171-75 (RW III, pp. 108-11).

48. *Die geestelike brulocht*, pp. 291; I am following the *varia lectio* explained in the footnote to line 73, which is also supported by Surius' Latin translation (b 72-73); Wiseman adopts it in *The Spiritual Espousals and Other Works* (p. 73).

49. William Cowper, "Light Shining Out of Darkness" ("God moves in a mysterious way").

Chapter 11

1. For a suggestive account, cf. the beginning of Hans-Georg Gadamer's essay "Die anthropologischen Grundlagen der Freiheit des Menschen," in: *Das Erbe Europas*, pp. 126ff.

2. Cf. Hans-Georg Gadamer, *Das Erbe Europas*, p. "... die kantische Aufklärung bestand gerade darin, den Primat der praktischen Vernunft and der Freiheitsbestimmung des Menschen als ein Vernunftpostulat anzunehmen *und allem Erklärungszwang zu entziehen*" (italics added).

3. *Grundlegung zur Metaphysik der Sitten*, BA 52 (*Werke*, ed. Weischedel, vol. 4, pp. p. 51): "... handle nur nach derjenigen Maxime, durch die du zugleich wollen kannst, daß sie ein allgemeines Gesetz werde." For the whole train of thought, cf. BA 49-52 (Weischedel ed. pp. 49-51; cf. ET *Foundations of the Metaphysics of Morals* [Beck], pp. 37-39, quotation p. 39).

4. Kant treats the two postulates in reverse order. Cf. *Kritik der praktischen Vernunft*, A 220-37 (*Werke*, ed. Weischedel, vol. 4, pp. 252-64).

5. Theo de Boer, *The God van de filosofen en de God van Pascal*, p. 86.

6. "Mengt aber und rührt, wie Ihr wollt, dies geht nie zusammen, ihr treibt ein leeres Spiel mit Materien, die sich einander nicht aneignen, ihr behaltet immer nur Metaphysik und Moral. Dieses Gemisch von Meinungen über das höchste Wesen oder die Welt und von Geboten für ein menschliches Leben (oder gar für zwei) nennt Ihr Religion! und den Instinkt, der jene Meinungen sucht, nebst den dunklen Ahndungen, welche die eigentliche letzte

Sanktion dieser Gebote sind, nennt ihr Religiosität! Aber wie kommt Ihr denn dazu, eine bloße Kompilation, eine Chrestomathie für Anfänger für ein eigenes Werk zu halten, für ein Individuum eignen Ursprungs und eigner Kraft?" (*Über die Religion*, p. 45; cf. ET *On Religion*, pp. 30-31).

7. Cf. *Über die Religion*, pp. 41-89 (cf. ET *On Religion*, pp. 26ff.).

8. Cf. *Über die Religion*, ed. Otto, pp. 41-99 [38-133]; ET pp. 28-101.

9. Cf. George A. Lindbeck, *The Nature of Doctrine*, pp. 31-32.

10. For a comprehensive treatment, cf. Louis Dupré, *The Other Dimension*.

11. Cf. chapter 5, section 1: "Belief in One God" (ed. Lash, pp. 95-109).

12. For instances, cf. A. Boekraad, "Newman's Godsbewijs uit het geweten."

13. *Grammar of Assent* (ed. Lash), p. 97.

14. *Grammar of Assent* (ed. Lash), pp. 98-99.

15. *Grammar of Assent* (ed. Lash), p. 99.

16. *Grammar of Assent* (ed. Lash), p. 101.

17. *Grammar of Assent* (ed. Lash), p. 101.

18. *University Sermons*, pp. 18-19 (italics added).

19. *Confessions*, III, VII, 13.

20. Cf. *Grammar of Assent* (ed. Lash), pp. 49-91.

21. Cf. *Parochial and Plain Sermons*, vol. 1, pp. 282-94.

22. *In I Sent.*, 8, 1, 1, *ad 4* (italics in the translation added for emphasis). For the Latin text, cf. §67, 2, endnote 11.

23. *Kritik der reinen Vernunft*, B 641, A 613 (ed. Weischedel, vol. 2, p. 543): "Die unbedingte Notwendigkeit, die wir, als den letzten Träger aller Dinge, so unentbehrlich bedürfen, ist der wahre Abgrund für die menschliche Vernunft. Selbst die Ewigkeit, so schauderhaft erhaben ..., macht lange den schwindelichten Eindruck nicht auf das Gemüt; denn sie *mißt* nur die Dauer der Dinge, aber *trägt* sie nicht. Man kann sich des Gedanken nicht erwehren, man kann ihn aber auch nicht ertragen: daß ein Wesen, welches wir uns auch als das höchste unter allen möglichen vorstellen, gleichsam zu sich selbst sage: Ich bin von Ewigkeit zu Ewigkeit, außer mir ist nichts, ohne das, was bloß durch meinen Willen etwas ist; *aber woher bin ich denn?* Hier sinkt alles unter uns, und die größte Vollkommenheit, wie die kleinste, schwebt ohne Haltung bloß vor der spekulativen Vernunft, der es nichts kostet, die eine so wie die andere ohne die mindeste Hindernis verschwinden zu lassen." The passage is also quoted by Theo de Boer, *De God van de filosofen en de God van Pascal*, p. 72.

24. Cf. for example, *S. Th.* I, 10, 2-3; I, 45, 5.

25. Cf., for example, *S. Th.* I, 44, 4, and I, 105, 2, *ad 2*; *S. c. G.* 3, 64, *Adhuc. Sicut supra*; *Q. D. de Pot.* 3, 15, *ad 12*; 3, 17, 1, and *ad 1*; 5, 3, *sed contra 3*.

26. Cf. Kant's text (note 18): "... vor der spekulativen Vernunft, *der es nichts kostet*, die eine so wie die andere ohne die mindeste Hindernis verschwinden zu lassen."

27. For comparable commentary on the passage from Kant's *Critique*, cf. Theo de Boer, *The God van de filosofen en de God van Pascal*, p. 73.

28. On the former, cf. Pierre Hadot, *Exercices spirituels et philosophie antique*.

29. On the proposition that "the thing in itself" is an "unknown x," cf. *Kritik der reinen Vernunft*, B 294-316, A 103-30, 236-60 (ed. Weischedel, vol. 2, pp. 165-82, 267-85).

30. Cf. *Kritik der reinen Vernunft*, B 391-96, A 334-39 (ed. Weischedel, vol. 2, pp. 335-39).
31. Cf. Avery Dulles, "John Paul II and the New Evangelization."
32. Cf., again, John Coulson's *Religion and Imagination*, pp. 63-72.
33. On "positions," and on the related themes of "horizons" and "stances," cf. F. J. van Beeck, *Christ Proclaimed*, pp. 185-88; also, Stephen Happel and James J. Walter, *Conversion and Discipleship*, pp. 205-22.
34. Cf. Karl H. Neufeld, "Läßt sich Glaubenswahrheit absichern?" for some consequences of this.
35. Cf. §20, 5, a, and note 27.
36. On the most important kind of involvement, namely *self*-involvement, Donald D. Evans' sensitive monograph *The Logic of Self-Involvement* remains an indispensable resource.
37. On these themes, and despite the fact that the treatment too strongly suggests the atmosphere of the 'sixties and 'seventies, cf. W. H. van de Pol's classic *Het einde van het conventionele christendom* (ET *The End of Conventional Christianity*). For a treatment of conventional Christianity as it applies to Catholic Latin America, cf. Gustavo Gutiérrez, *A Theology of Liberation* as well as its extensive bibliography.
38. On this theme, cf. F. J. van Beeck, *Catholic Identity After Vatican II*.
39. *Van den gheesteliken tabernakel* ("The Spiritual Tabernacle"), §LIV (*RW* II, p. 125): "... wi moten woenen tusscen die minne Goods ende ons evenkerstens."
40. Cf. also F. J. van Beeck, *Catholic Identity After Vatican II*, pp. 24-34.
41. Cf. also F. J. van Beeck, *Catholic Identity After Vatican II*, pp. 34-41.
42. *Spiritual Exercises*, [237] (italics added for emphasis).
43. Cf. also F. J. van Beeck, *Catholic Identity After Vatican II*, pp. 51-78.
44. *Die gheestelike brulocht*, pp. 532-37 (cf. *The Spiritual Espousals and Other Works*, pp. 134-35).
45. Sainte Thérèse, *J'entre dans la vie*, p. 41 (June 5, 1897); cf. ET *Her Last Conversations*, p. 57.
46. *Van den gheesteliken tabernakel*, §CVIII (*RW* II, pp. 231-32; singulars in the original translated as plurals). "Richness" represents *vetheid* ("fatness") in the original; Ruusbroec is offering an allegorical interpretation of the sacrifice of the ram of ordination and the three unleavened cakes in Lev 8, 22-28; the burning of the fat on the entrails and around the kidneys means complete self-denial as the precondition for union with God.
47. Thus, with appropriate forcefulness, Julian of Norwich, quoted by Joan M. Nuth, *Wisdom's Daughter*, p. 102.
48. Cf. Pheme Perkins, *Resurrection*, pp. 47-63.
49. "Immortalitas enim oneri potius quam usui est, nisi aspiret gratia" (*De excessu fratris* II, 47; *PL* 16, 1327; ET *FC* 22, p. 216); Brian E. Daley, *The Hope of the Early Church*, p. 142.
50. *Van den gheesteliken tabernakel*, §CXXXVIII; RW II, pp. 336-37. Cf. also the allegorical explanation of the owl, pp. 342-43.
51. Cf. John P. Meier, *A Marginal Jew*, vol. I, pp. 123-39, esp. pp. 125-27.
52. *Vanden blinkenden steen, etc.*, pp. 142-45 (italics added; ET cf. *The Spiritual Espousals and Other Works*, pp. 169-70).
53. Cf. F. J. van Beeck, *Christ Proclaimed*, pp. 93-98.

54. Cf. N. Lohfink, *Lobgesänge der Armen*, pp. 124-25. Lohfink points out that this interpretation is supported by the Talmud.
55. *The Triumph of the Meek*, p. 248.
56. On this passage, cf. Martin Hengel's poignant treatment of crucifixion as the *servile supplicium*—the punishment associated with the condition of a slave (*doulos*): *Crucifixion*, pp. 51-63, esp. 62-63. For my translation of verse 6, cf. N. T. Wright, "*harpagmos* and the Meaning of Philippians 2, 5-11." Wright suggests, convincingly in my view, that C. F. Moule's interpretation of *harpagmos* as *nomen actionis* ("a matter of grasping"), though grammatically and syntactically incompatible with R. W. Hoover's later, more likely construal ("he did not view his equality with God as something to be used for his own advantage"), is *sachlich* completely compatible with it.
57. For this section and the next, I am indebted to stimulating conversations with Professors Robert Wilken and Richard A. Norris.
58. *Ad Eph.* 18, 2 - 19, 1 (*AF* I, pp. 190-93).
59. *Hom. in Ezech.* I, 6 (*SC* 352, pp. 228-31): "Exemplum ab hominibus accipiam, deinde si Spiritus sanctus dederit, ad Iesum Christum et ad Deum Patrem transmigrabo. Quando ad hominem loquor et deprecor eum pro aliqua re ut misereatur mei, si sine misericordia est, nihil patitur ex his quae a me dicuntur; si vero molli est animo et nihil in eo rigidi cordis obduruit, audit me et miseretur mei, et molliuntur viscera eius ad meas preces. Tale mihi quiddam intellige super Salvatorem. Descendit in terras miserans humanum genus, passiones perpessus est nostras, antequam crucem pateretur et carnem nostram dignaretur assumere; si enim non fuisset passus, non venisset in conversatione humanae vitae. Primum passus est, deinde descendit et visus est. Quae est ista quam pro nobis passus est passio? Caritatis est passio. Pater quoque ipse et Deus universitatis, *longanimis et multum misericors* et miserator, nonne quodammodo patitur? An ignoras quia, quando humana dispensat, passionem patitur humanam? *Supportavit* enim *mores tuas Dominus Deus tuus, quomodo si quis supportet homo filium suum.* Igitur mores nostros supportat Deus, sicut portat passiones nostras Filius Dei. Ipse Pater non est impassibilis. Si rogetur, miseretur, et condolet, patitur aliquid caritatis, et fit in iis in quibus iuxta magnitudinem naturae suae non potest esse, et propter nos humanas sustinet passiones." I am indebted to my friend Professor Robert Wilken for this reference.
60. I am indebted to Dr. Yisrael Knohl, Lecturer at Hebrew University, Jerusalem, for drawing my attention to these passages, found, respectively, in the talmudic tractates known as *Širata'* and *Pisḥa'*, which are part of the *Mikhilta de Rabbi Ishmael*, a halakhic midrash.
61. *The Message to the Planet*, p. 353.
62. *The Message to the Planet*, p. 499.
63. Chapters 11-12, pp. 224-72.
64. Esp. pp. 255-67 (ET pp. 267-90).
65. Esp. pp. 97-103 (ET pp. 83-88).
66. Esp. pp. 430-53 (ET pp. 314-30).
67. For a sensitive if inconclusive discussion, cf. "Christian Theism and Whiteheadian Process Philosophy: Are They Compatible?" in W. Norris Clarke, *The Philosophical Approach to God.* Also, cf. William J. Hill's careful essay "The Historicity of God."

68. Catherine M. LaCugna, "The Relational God," p. 662.

69. Quoted by Theo de Boer, *De God van de filosofen en de God van Pascal,* p. 161.

70. *Comm. in Matt.,* X, 23 (*PG* 13, 900C): *hōs philanthrōpos, peponthen ho apathēs to splanchnisthēnai.* The translation accommodates the variant that reads *tōi splanchnisthēnai.*

71. Theo de Boer, *De God van de filosofen en de God van Pascal,* p. 161.

72. J. A. Appleyard, *Becoming a Reader,* p. 4.

73. *Porro autem si impassibilis Deus, utique et incompassibilis* (*Liber contra Arianos,* 19; *PL* 20, 27D). Quoted in R. P. C. Hanson, *The Search for the Christian Doctrine of God,* p. 517.

74. For the (crucial) fourth century in particular, cf. R. P. C. Hanson, *The Search for the Christian Doctrine of God,* pp. 856-69.

75. In retrospect, my own treatment of the issue, in *Christ Proclaimed,* esp. pp. 510-18, could have profited from this advice.

76. Cf., for example, *The Search for the Christian Doctrine of God,* pp. 447-57 (on Athanasius), pp. 492-502 (on Hilary of Poitiers), and pp. 732-34 (on the Cappadocians).

77. *The Search for the Christian Doctrine of God,* p. 866 (alignment, punctuation, and translation modified). The quotation is from Basil's *On the Holy Spirit,* VIII, 18.

78. R. P. C. Hanson, *The Search for the Christian Doctrine of God,* p. 447. The "serious inadequacies" concern, of course, Athanasius' virtual denial of Christ's spiritual soul.

79. *Foundations of Christian Faith,* p. 220 (*Grundkurs des Glaubens,* pp. 218-19).

80. *Praktikos,* 91: *tēn xēroteran kai mē anōmalon diaitan agapēi syzeuchtheisan thatton eisagein ton monachon eis ton tēs apatheias limena* (*SC* 171, pp. 692-694; cf. ET p. 39; cf. *Gnostikos,* 37; *SC* 356, pp. 158-59 and notes).

81. *Praktikos,* 2: *Basileia ouranōn estin apatheia psychēs meta gnōseōs tōn ontōn alēthous* (*SC* 171, p. 498; cf. ET p. 15).

82. *Praktikos,* 81: *apatheia ... estin anthos tēs praktikēs* (*SC* 171, p. 670; cf. ET p. 36).

83. *Praktikos,* 84: *Peras ... praktikēs agapē* (*SC* 171, p. 674; cf. ET p. 37).

84. *Praktikos,* Prologue: ... *apatheia, hēs eggonon hē agapē* (*SC* 171, p. 492; cf. ET p. 14) Cf. also 81 (*SC* 171, p. 670; cf. ET p. 36).

85. *Praktikos,* 89: *sōphrosynēs ... ergon to blepein apathōs ta pragmata ta kinounta en hēmin phantasias alogous; agapēs de to pasēi eikoni tou Theou toiautēn heautēn emparechein hoian kai tōi prōtotypōi schedon, kán miainein autas epicheirōsin hoi daimones* (*SC* 171, pp. 684-86; cf. ET p. 38).

86. *Praktikos* 100: *pantas men ep' isōs ou dynaton tous adelphous agapan, pasi de dynaton apathōs syntynchanein mnēsikakias onta kai misous eleutheron* (*SC* 171, p. 710; cf. ET p. 41).

87. *Chapters on Theology, Gnosis, and Practice,* III, 21 (*SC* 51[bis], pp. 132-33).

88. *Obras completas,* Vol. 2, p. 960.

Bibliography

[Anselm of Canterbury, Saint.] *St. Anselm's Proslogion, with A Reply on Behalf of the Fool by Gaunilo and The Author's Reply to Gaunilo*. Edited by M. J. Charlesworth. Notre Dame and London: University of Notre Dame Press, 1979.

Appleyard, J. A. *Becoming a Reader: The Experience of Fiction from Childhood to Adulthood*. Cambridge: Cambridge University Press, 1990.

Athanasius, [Saint]. *Contra Gentes* and *De Incarnatione*. Edited and translated by Robert W. Thomson. Oxford: Clarendon Press, 1971.

Augustine, Saint. *Confessions*. Translated with an Introduction and Notes by Henry Chadwick. Oxford: Oxford University Press, 1991.

Barth, Karl. *Fides quærens intellectum: Anselms Beweis der Existenz Gottes im Zusammenhang seines theologischen Programms*. München: C. Kaiser, 1931 (ET *Anselm: Fides Quaerens Intellectum: Anselm's Proof of the Existence of God in the Context of his Theological Scheme*. London: SCM, 1960).

Beeck, Frans Jozef van. *Catholic Identity after Vatican II: Three Types of Faith in the One Church*. Chicago: Loyola University Press, 1985.

―――. *Christ Proclaimed: Christology as Rhetoric*. New York, Ramsey, NJ, and Toronto: Paulist Press, 1979.

―――. *Loving the Torah More than God? Towards a Catholic Appreciation of Judaism*. Chicago: Loyola University Press, 1989.

Bennis, W. G., and Shepard, H. A. "A Theory of Group Development." *Human Relations* 9(1956): 415-37.

Berg, J. H. van den. *De dingen: Vier metabletische overpeinzingen*. Nijkerk: G. F. Callenbach, 1965 (ET *Things: Four Metabletic Reflections*. Pittsburgh: Duquesne University Press, 1970).

―――. *Leven in meervoud: Een metabletisch onderzoek*. Nijkerk: G. F. Callenbach, 1963 (ET *Divided Existence and Complex Society: An Historical Approach*. Pittsburgh: Duquesne University Press, 1974).

Berger, Peter. *A Rumor of Angels: Modern Society and the Rediscovery of the Supernatural*. Anchor Books. Garden City, NY: Doubleday, 1970.

Blondel, Maurice. *L'Être et les êtres: Essai d'ontologie concrète et intégrale*. Bibliothèque de philosophie contemporaine. Paris: Librairie Félix Alcan, 1935.

Boberski, Heiner. "Das 'Engelwerk': Die seltsamen Lehren und Praktiken eines 'katholischen' Geheimbundes." *Herder Korrespondenz* 44(1990): 384-89.

Boekraad, A. "Newman's Godsbewijs uit het geweten." *Bijdragen* 12(19-51): 205-23.

Boer, Theo de. *De God van de filosofen en de God van Pascal: Op het grensgebied van filosofie en theologie.* s-Gravenhage: Meinema, 1989.

Bomans, Godfried. *Capriolen: Een tweede bundel buitelingen.* Amsterdam and Brussels: Elsevier, 1953.

Bonaventure, Saint. *The Soul's Journey into God. The Tree of Life. The Life of St. Francis.* Translated by Ewert Cousins. Introduced by Ignatius Brady. The Classics of Western Spirituality. New York, Mahwah, and Toronto: Paulist Press, 1978.

Brown, Peter. *Augustine of Hippo: a Biography.* Berkeley, Los Angeles, and London: University of California Press, 1969.

Buckley, Michael J. *Motion and Motion's God: Thematic Variations in Aristotle, Cicero, Newton, and Hegel.* Princeton, NJ: Princeton University Press, 1971.

———. *At the Origins of Modern Atheism.* New Haven and London: Yale University Press, 1987.

Buren, Paul van. *The Edges of Language: An Essay in the Logic of a Religion.* New York: Macmillan, 1972.

Busch, Eberhard. *Karl Barth: His life from letters and autobiographical texts.* Philadelphia: Fortress Press, 1976.

Camus, Albert. *La Peste.* In *Théâtre, Récits, Nouvelles.* Edited by Roger Quilliot. *Bibliothèque de la Pléiade,* 61. [Paris]: Gallimard, 1962 (ET *The Plague.* New York: Alfred A. Knopf, 1971).

Clarke, W. Norris. *The Philosophical Approach to God.* Winston-Salem: Wake Forest University Press, 1979.

Clifford, Richard J. *Fair Spoken and Persuading: An Interpretation of Second Isaiah.* New York, Ramsey, and Toronto: Paulist Press, 1984.

———. "The Hebrew Scriptures and the Theology of Creation." *Theological Studies* 46(1985): 507-23.

The Cloud of Unknowing and the Book of Privy Counseling. Edited by William Johnston. Image Books. Garden City, NY: Doubleday, 1973.

The Cloud of Unknowing and the Book of Privy Counselling. Edited by Phyllis Hodgson. *Early English Text Society,* 218. Revised 1958. Reprinted 1981. London, New York, and Toronto: Oxford University Press, 1944 (for 1943).

Cohn, Norman. *The Pursuit of the Millennium: Revolutionary Millenarians and Mystical Anarchists of the Middle Ages.* Revised edition. New York: Oxford University Press, 1970.

Coulson, John. *Religion and Imagination: 'in aid of a grammar of assent'.*

Oxford: The Clarendon Press, 1981.

————. *Newman and the Common Tradition: A Study in the Language of Church and Society.* Oxford: The Clarendon Press, 1970.

Cox, Harvey. *The Secular City: Secularization and Urbanization in Theological Perspective.* Revised edition. New York: The Macmillan Company, 1966.

Cross, Frank Moore. *Canaanite Myth and Hebrew Epic: Essays in the History of the Religion of Israel.* Cambridge, Massachusetts and London, England: Harvard University Press, 1973.

Dahmen, Ulrich. See Lohfink, Norbert.

Daily Prayer Book. Ha-Siddur Ha-Shalem. Translated by Philip Birnbaum. New York: Hebrew Publishing Company, 1949.

Daley, Brian E. *The Hope of the Early Church: A Handbook of Patristic Eschatology.* Cambridge: Cambridge University Press, 1991.

Descartes, [René]. *Meditationes de Prima Philosophia: Méditations métaphysiques.* Introduced and annotated by Geneviève Rodis-Lewis. Bibliothèque des textes philosophiques. Paris: J. Vrin, 1970.

Dodds, Michael J. "Thomas Aquinas, Human Suffering, and the Unchanging God of Love." *Theological Studies* 52(1991): 330-44.

Dulles, Avery. "John Paul II and the New Evangelization." Lawrence J. McGinley Lecture, December 4-5, 1991. New York: Fordham University, 1992. (Cf. *America* 166(1992): 52-59. 69-72.)

Dupré, Louis. "Evil—A Religious Mystery: A Plea for a More Inclusive Model of Theodicy." *Faith and Philosophy* 7(1990): 261-80.

————. *The Other Dimension: A Search for the Meaning of Religious Attitudes.* Garden City, NY: Doubleday, 1972.

Eadmer. *The Life of St Anselm, Archbishop of Canterbury.* Edited by R. W. Southern. London: Thomas Nelson and Sons, 1962.

Eliot, T. S. *Collected Poems 1909-1962.* London: Faber and Faber, 1963.

————. *Selected Essays 1917-1932.* New York: Harcourt, Brace and Company, 1932.

Evagrius Ponticus. See Guillaumont, Antoine.

————. *The Praktikos* and *Chapters on Prayer.* Edited by John Eudes Bamberger. Spencer, MA: Cistercian Publications, 1970.

Evans, Donald D. *The Logic of Self-Involvement: A Philosophical Study of Everyday Language with Special Reference to the Christian Use of Language about God as Creator.* New York: Herder and Herder, 1969.

Fiddes, Paul S. *The Creative Suffering of God.* Oxford: Clarendon Press, 1988.

Folk Literature of the Yamana Indians: Martin Gusinde's Collection of Yamana Narratives. Edited by Johannes Wilbert. Latin American Studies Series, 40. Berkeley, Los Angeles, and London: University of California Press, 1977.

Fortmann, Han M. M. *Als ziende de onzienlijke: Een cultuurpsychologische studie over de religieuze waarneming en de zogenaamde religieuze projectie.* 4

vols. Hilversum: Paul Brand, 1968.

Gadamer, Hans-Georg. *Das Erbe Europas: Beiträge.* Bibliothek Suhrkamp, 1004. Frankfurt am Main, Suhrkamp, 1989.

Geurtsen, H. "De innerlijke structuur van het godsbewijs." *Tijdschrift voor Philosophie* 4(1944): 3-54, 207-82.

Gregory of Nyssa, [Saint]. *The Catechetical Oration.* Edited by James Herbert Srawley. Cambridge: University Press, 1956 (ET "An Address on Religious Instruction." In *Christology of the Later Fathers.* Edited by Edward Rochie Hardy, with Cyril C. Richardson. *The Library of Christian Classics.* Philadelphia: Westminster, 1954, pp. 268-325).

Guillaumont, Antoine. "Étude historique et doctrinale." In *Évagre le Pontique. Traité pratique ou Le moine.* Vol. 1. *SC* 170, pp. 21-125.

Gusinde, Martin. See *Folk Literature of the Yamana Indians.*

Gutiérrez, Gustavo. *A Theology of Liberation: History, Politics, and Salvation.* Revised edition. Maryknoll, NY: Orbis, 1988.

Hadot, Pierre. *Exercices spirituels et philosophie antique.* Second edition. Paris: Études augustiniennes, 1987.

Hallman, Joseph M. *The Descent of God: Divine Suffering in History and Theology.* Minneapolis: Fortress Press, 1991.

Hanson, Richard P. C. "The Achievement of Orthodoxy in the Fourth Century A.D." In *The Making of Orthodoxy: Essays in Honour of Henry Chadwick.* Edited by Rowan Williams. Cambridge: Cambridge University Press, 1989.

————. *The Search for the Christian Doctrine of God: The Arian Controversy 318-381.* Edinburgh: T. & T. Clark, 1988.

Happel, Stephen, and Walter, James J. *Conversion and Discipleship: A Christian Foundation for Ethics and Doctrine.* Philadelphia: Fortress Press, 1986.

Harrison, Verna E. F. "Male and Female in Cappadocian Theology." *Journal of Theological Studies,* N.S. 41(1990): 441-71.

Hart, Ray L. *Unfinished Man and the Imagination: Toward an Ontology and a Rhetoric of Revelation.* New York: Herder and Herder, 1968.

Haughton, Rosemary. *The Passionate God.* New York: Paulist Press, 1981.

Hawking, Stephen M. *A Brief History of Time: From the Big Bang to Black Holes.* Toronto, New York, London, Sidney, and Auckland: Bantam Books, 1988.

Heidegger, Martin. *Sein und Zeit.* Fifteenth edition. Tübingen: Max Niermeyer Verlag, 1979 (ET [seventh German edition] *Being and Time.* Translated by John Macquarrie and Edward Robinson. New York, Hagerstown, San Francisco, and London: Harper & Row, 1962).

Heisenberg, Werner. *The Physicist's Conception of Nature.* London: Hutchinson, 1958.

The Heliand: The Saxon Gospel. Translated and edited by G. Ronald Murphy. New York and Oxford: Oxford University Press, 1992.

Hellwig, Monika. *Jesus, the Compassion of God: New Perspectives on the Tradi-

tion of Christianity. Wilmington, DE: Michael Glazier, 1983.

Hengel, Martin. *Crucifixion in the ancient world and the folly of the message of the cross.* Philadelphia: Fortress, 1977.

Heschel, Abraham J. *The Prophets.* Two vols. Colophon Books. New York, Evanston, San Francisco, and London: Harper & Row, 1975.

Hick, John. See *The Many-Faced Argument.*

Hill, William J. "The Historicity of God." *Theological Studies* 45(1984): 320-33.

Ignatius of Loyola, Saint. *St. Ignatius' Own Story, As told to Luis Gonzáles de Cámara, With a sampling of his letters.* Translated by William J. Young. Reprint. Chicago: Loyola University Press, 1980.

[————.] *The Spiritual Exercises of Saint Ignatius.* Translated by Thomas Corbishley. London: Burns and Oates, 1963.

James, William. *The Varieties of Religious Experience.* Ninth edition. New York: Collier; London: Macmillan, 1974.

Jenkins, David. *Guide to the Debate About God.* London: Lutterworth Press, 1966.

John Paul II, Pope [Karol Wojtyla]. Encyclical *Redemptoris missio.* ET in *Origins* 20(1991): 541-68.

Johnson, Elizabeth A. "The Incomprehensibility of God and the Image of God Male and Female." *Theological Studies* 45(1984): 441-65.

————. *She Who Is: The Mystery of God in Feminist Theological Discourse.* New York: Crossroad, 1992.

Jüngel, Eberhard. *Gott als Geheimnis der Welt: Zur Begründung der Theologie des Gekreuzigten im Streit zwischen Theismus und Atheismus.* Third edition. Tübingen: J. C. B. Mohr (Paul Siebeck), 1978 (ET *God as the Mystery of the World: On the Foundation of the Theology of the Crucified One in the Dispute Between Theism and Atheism.* Grand Rapids, MI: William B. Eerdmans, 1983).

————. *Gottes Sein ist im Werden: Verantwortliche Rede vom Sein Gottes bei Karl Barth. Eine Paraphrase.* Third Edition, with an Appendix. Tübingen: J. C. B. Mohr (Paul Siebeck), 1976. (ET *The Doctrine of the Trinity: God's Being is in Becoming.* Grand Rapids, MI: William B. Eerdmans, 1976).

[Kant, Immanuel.] *Immanuel Kant's Critique of Pure Reason.* Translated by Norman Kemp Smith. New York: St. Martin's Press, 1965.

————. *Critique of Practical Reason.* Translated by Lewis White Beck. The Library of Liberal Arts. Indianapolis and New York: Bobbs Merrill, 1956.

————. *Foundations of the Metaphysics of Morals* and *What is Enlightenment?* Translated by Lewis White Beck. The Library of Liberal Arts. Indianapolis, New York, and Kansas City: The Bobbs-Merrill Company, 1959.

————. *Werke in sechs Bänden.* Edited by Wilhelm Weischedel. [Wiesbaden]: Insel-Verlag, 1956-64.

Kristensen, W. Brede. *The Meaning of Religion: Lectures in the Phenomenology of Religion.* Introduced by Hendrik Kraemer. The Hague: M. Nijhoff, 1960.

Küng, Hans. *Existiert Gott? Antwort auf die Gottesfrage der Neuzeit.* München: R. Piper, 1978 (ET *Does God Exist? An Answer for Today.* Garden City, NY: Doubleday, 1980).

————. *Menschwerdung Gottes: Eine Einführung in Hegels theologisches Denken als Prolegomena zu einer künftigen Christologie.* Ökumenische Forschungen II, vol. 1. Freiburg, Basel, and Wien: Herder, 1970 (ET *The Incarnation of God: An Introduction to Hegel's Theological Thought as Prolegomena to a Future Christology.* New York: Crossroad, 1987).

LaCugna, Catherine M. "The Relational God." *Theological Studies* 46(1985): 647-63.

Lash, Nicholas. *Easter in Ordinary: Reflections on Human Experience and the Knowledge of God.* Charlottesville: The University Press of Virginia, 1988.

Lee, Jung Young. *God Suffers for Us: A Systematic Inquiry into a Concept of Divine Impassibility.* The Hague: Martinus Nijhoff, 1974.

Levenson, Jon D. *Creation and the Persistence of Evil: The Jewish Drama of Divine Omnipotence.* San Francisco: Harper & Row, 1988.

Lévinas, Emmanuel. *Difficile liberté: Essais sur le judaïsme.* Second edition. Paris: Albin Michel, 1976.

Lienhard, Joseph T. "The 'Arian' Controversy: Some Categories Reconsidered." *Theological Studies* 48(1987): 415-37.

————. Review of R. P. C. Hanson's *The Search for the Christian Doctrine of God: The Arian Controversy. Theological Studies* 51(1990): 334-37.

Lindbeck, George A. *The Nature of Doctrine: Religion and Theology in a Postliberal Age.* Philadelphia: Westminster Press, 1984.

Lohfink, Norbert. *Lobgesänge der Armen: Studien zum Magnifikat, den Hodajot von Qumran und einigen späten Psalmen.* Mit einem Anhang: *Hodajot-Bibliographie 1948-1989* von Ulrich Dahmen. *Stuttgarter Bibelstudien,* 143. Stuttgart: Verlag Katholisches Bibelwerk, 1990.

————. *Le mystère du surnaturel. Theologie,* 64. [Paris]: Aubier, Éditions Montaigne, 1965 (ET *The Mystery of the Supernatural.* New York: Herder and Herder, 1967).

Macquarrie, John. *God-Talk: An Examination of the Language and Logic of Theology.* London, SCM Press, 1967.

The Many-Faced Argument: Recent Studies on the Ontological Argument for the Existence of God. Edited by John Hick and Arthur C. McGill. New York: Macmillan, 1967.

McBride, Jr., S. Dean. "The Yoke of the Kingdom: An Exposition of Deuteronomy 6: 4-5." *Interpretation* 27(1973): 273-306.

McGill, Arthur C. See *The Many-Faced Argument.*

Meier, John P. *A Marginal Jew: Rethinking the Historical Jesus.* Vol. I. *The Roots of the Problem and the Person.* The Anchor Bible Reference

Library. New York: Doubleday, 1991.

Metz, Johann Baptist. "Theologie gegen Mythologie: Kleine Apologie des biblischen Monotheismus." *Herder-Korrespondenz* 42 (1988): 187-93.

Moltmann, Jürgen. *Der Gekreuzigte Gott: Das Kreuz Christi als Grund und Kritik christlicher Theologie.* München: Chr. Kaiser Verlag, 1972. (ET *The Crucified God: The Cross of Christ as the Foundation and Criticism of Christian Theology.* New York, Evanston, San Francisco, and London: Harper & Row, 1974).

Mozley, J. K. *The Impassibility of God.* Cambridge: Cambridge University Press, 1926.

Murdoch, Iris. *The Message to the Planet.* London: Chatto & Windus, 1989.

———. *Metaphysics as a Guide to Morals.* London: Chatto & Windus, 1992.

———. *The Unicorn.* London: Chatto & Windus, 1963.

Murphy, G. Ronald. See also *The Heliand.*

———. *The Saxon Savior: The Transformation of the Gospel in the Ninth-Century Heliand.* New York and Oxford: Oxford University Press, 1989.

Neufeld, Karl H. "Läßt sich Glaubenswahrheit absichern? Die begrenzte Aufgabe des kirchlichen Lehramts." *Herder-Korrespondenz* 45(19-91): 183-88.

"New examination of 'Opus Angelorum'." *Osservatore Romano* (Weekly Edition in English), June 24, 1992, p. 12.

Newman, John Henry. *An Essay in Aid of a Grammar of Assent.* Edited by Nicholas Lash. Notre Dame and London: University of Notre Dame Press, 1979.

———. *Lectures on the Prophetical Office of the Church, viewed relatively to Romanism and popular Protestantism.* London: J. G. & F. Rivington; Oxford: J. H. Parker, 1837.

———. *Newman's University Sermons: Fifteen Sermons Preached before the University of Oxford 1826-1843.* Reprinted from the third edition, 1871. Edited by D. M. MacKinnon and J. D. Holmes. London: S.P.C.K., 1970.

———. *Parochial and Plain Sermons.* New edition. 8 vols. London: Rivingtons, 1882.

Niebuhr, H. Richard. *Radical Monotheism and Western Culture, with supplementary essays.* Harper Torchbooks, 1491. New York: Harper & Row, 1970.

Niebuhr, Richard R. *Schleiermacher on Christ and Religion.* London: SCM Press, 1964.

Nuth, Joan M. *Wisdom's Daughter: The Theology of Julian of Norwich.* New York: Crossroad, 1991.

Oden, Thomas C. *The Living God. Systematic Theology: Volume One.* San Francisco: Harper & Row, 1987.

O'Donovan, Leo J. "The Mystery of God as a History of Love: Eberhard Jüngel's Doctrine of God." *Theological Studies* 42(1981): 251-71.

Ollenburger, Ben C. *Zion, the City of the Great King: A Theological Symbol of the Jerusalem Cult. Journal for the Study of the Old Testament Supplement Series*, 41. Sheffield: The Academic Press, 1987.

Otto, Rudolph. *Das Heilige: Über das Irrationale in der Idee des Göttlichen und sein Verhältnis zum Rationalen.* 29th-30th edition. München: C. H. Beck, [1963] (ET *The Idea of the Holy: An inquiry into the non-rational factor in the idea of the divine and its relation to the rational.* Translated by John W. Harvey. Reprint. London, Oxford, and New York: Oxford University Press, 1970).

Paley, William. *Natural Theology: or, Evidences of the Existence and Attributes of the Deity, Collected from the Appearances of Nature.* Reprint. Houston, TX: St. Thomas Press, 1972.

Parke-Taylor, G. H. *Yahweh: The Divine Name in the Bible.* Waterloo, Ontario: Wilfrid Laurier University Press, 1975.

Pascal, Blaise. *Oeuvres complètes.* Edited by Jacques Chevalier. *Bibliotèque de la Pléiade*, 34. Paris: Gallimard, 1954.

———. *Oeuvres complètes.* Preface by Henri Gouhier. Introduced and annotated by Louis Lafuma. Paris: Éditions du Seuil, 1963.

Perkins, Pheme. *Resurrection: New Testament Witness and Contemporary Reflection.* Garden City, NY: Doubleday, 1984.

Pol, W. H. van de. *Het einde van het conventionele christendom.* Roermond en Maaseik: Romen & Zonen, 1966 (ET *The End of Conventional Christianity.* New York: Newman Press, 1968).

Przywara, Erich. *Deus semper maior: Theologie der Exerzitien.* 3 vols. Freiburg im Breisgau: Herder, 1938-40.

Quay, Paul M. "Angels and Demons: The Teaching of IV Lateran." *Theological Studies* 42(1981): 20-45.

Rahner, Hugo. "Die Grabschrift des Loyola." In *Ignatius von Loyola als Mensch und Theologe.* Freiburg, Basel, and Wien: Herder, 1964, pp. 422-40.

———. *Der spielende Mensch.* Augmented edition. Einsiedeln: Johannes-Verlag, 1952 (ET of the 1949 original: *Man at Play, or, Did You Ever Practise Eutrapelia?* London: Burns & Oates, 1965).

Rahner, Karl. "Christlicher Humanismus." In *SchrzTh*, 8, pp. 239-59 (ET "Christian Humanism." In *TheoInv*, 9, pp. 187-204).

———. "Experiment Mensch." In *SchrzTh*, 8, pp. 260-85 (ET "The Experiment with Man." In *TheoInv*, 9, pp. 205-24).

———. *Grundkurs des Glaubens: Einführung in den Begriff des Christentums.* Third edition. Freiburg, Basel, and Wien: Herder, 1976 (ET *Foundations of Christian Faith: An Introduction to the Idea of Christianity.* Translated by William V. Dych. New York: Seabury, 1978).

———. *Hörer des Wortes: Zur Grundlegung einer Religionsphilosophie.* Revised by J. B. Metz. München: Kösel, 1963 (ET *Hearers of the Word.* Translated by Michael Richards. New York: Herder and Herder, 1969. Partial translation in *A Rahner Reader.* Edited by Gerald

A. McCool. New York, Seabury, 1975).

————. "Die ignatianische Mystik der Weltfreudigkeit." In *SchrzTh*, 3, pp. 329-48 (ET "The Ignatian Mysticism of Joy in the World." In *TheoInv*, 3, pp. 277-93).

————. "Zum Problem der genetischen Manipulation." In *SchrzTh*, 8, pp. 286-321 (ET "The Problem of Genetic Manipulation." In *TheoInv*, 9, pp. 225-52).

————. "Selbstverwirklichung und Annahme des Kreuzes." In *SchrzTh*, 8, pp. 322-26 (ET "Self-Realisation and Taking up One's Cross." In *TheoInv*, 9, pp. 253-257).

Ramsey, Ian T. *Religious Language: An Empirical Placing of Theological Phrases*. Second edition. London: SCM Press, 1967.

Renckens, Henricus. *De Godsdienst van Israel*. Roermond and Maaseik: J. J. Romen & Zonen, 1963 (ET *The Religion of Israel*. New York: Sheed and Ward, 1966).

Robinson, John A. T. *Honest to God*. London: SCM Press, 1963.

Ruusbroec, Blessed Jan van. *Die geestelike brulocht*. [*The Spiritual Espousals*; Ioannis Rvsbrochii *De ornatv spiritualivm nvptiarvm*]. *Corpus Christianorum, Continuatio Mediaevalis*, 103. Tielt: Lannoo; Turnhout: Brepols, 1988.

————. *The Spiritual Espousals and Other Works*. Introduced and translated by James A. Wiseman. The Classics of Western Spirituality. New York, Mahwah, and Toronto: Paulist Press, 1985.

————. *Vanden blinkenden steen. Vanden vier becoringen. Vanden kerstene ghelove. Brieven.* [*The Sparkling Stone. The Four Temptations. The Christian Faith. Letters.* Ioannis Rvsbrochii *De calcvlo sev perfectione filiorvm Dei. De qvattvor svbtilibvs tentationibvs. De fide et ivdicio. Epistolae.*] *Corpus Christianorum, Continuatio Mediaevalis*, 110. Tielt, Lannoo; Turnhout: Brepols, 1991.

————. *Vanden seven sloten*. [*The Seven Enclosures*; Ioannis Rvsbrochii *De septem cvstodiis*]. *Corpus Christianorum, Continuatio Mediaevalis*, 102. Tielt: Lannoo; Turnhout: Brepols, 1989.

Schleiermacher, Friedrich. *Über die Religion: Reden an die Gebildeten unter ihren Verächtern*. Sixth edition. Edited by Rudolf Otto. Göttingen: Vandenhoeck & Ruprecht, 1967. (Also in: *Schriften aus der Berliner Zeit, 1796-1799*. Edited by Günter Meckenstock. [*Kritische Gesamtausgabe*, I, 2.] Berlin and New York: Walter de Gruyter, 1984, pp. 185-326. (ET *On Religion: Speeches to its Cultured Despisers*. Translated by John Oman. New York: Harper & Row, 1958).

Schlüngel, Paul H. "Der leidende Vater." *Orientierung* 41 (1977): 49-50.

Schutz, William C. *The Interpersonal Underworld* (*FIRO: A Three-Dimensional Theory of Interpersonal Behavior*). Palo Alto, CA: Science and Behavior Books, 1966.

Shepard, H. A. See Bennis, W. G.

Siddur. See Daily Prayer Book.

Smith, Mark S. *The Early History of God: Yahweh and the Other Deities in Ancient Israel.* San Francisco: Harper & Row, 1990.

———. "God Male and Female in the Old Testament: Yahweh and his 'asherah.'" *Theological Studies* 48(1987): 333-40.

Smulders, Pieter. *Het visioen van Teilhard de Chardin: Poging tot theologische waardering.* Brugge and Utrecht: Descleé De Brouwer, 1963 (ET *The Design of Teilhard de Chardin: An Essay in Theological Reflection.* Westminster, MD: The Newman Press, 1967).

Snow, C. P. *The Two Cultures and the Scientific Revolution.* New York: Cambridge University Press, 1959 (Expanded edition: *The Two Cultures: And a Second Look.* Cambridge: Cambridge University Press, 1963).

Söderblom, Nathan. *The Living God: Basal Forms of Personal Religion.* [London: Oxford University Press, Humphrey Milford, 1933.] Reprint. New York: AMS Press, 1979.

Sölle, Dorothee. *Leiden.* Stuttgart: Kreuz-Verlag, 1973 (ET *Suffering.* Philadelphia: Fortress Press, 1975).

Southern, R. W. See Eadmer.

———. *The Making of the Middle Ages.* London: Hutchinson University Library, 1967.

———. *Saint Anselm and His Biographer: A Study of Monastic Life and Thought, 1059-c. 1130.* Cambridge: Cambridge University Press, 1963.

Spinoza, Benedictus de. *Opera.* Edited by Carl Gebhardt. 4 vols. Heidelberg: Carl Winters Universitätsbuchhandlung, [1925] (ET *The Collected Works of Spinoza.* Edited and Translated by Edwin Curley. Vol. 1. Princeton, NJ: Princeton University Press, 1985).

Stacer, John R. "Divine Reverence for Us: God's Being Present, Cherishing, and Persuading." *Theological Studies* 44(1983): 438-55.

Teresa de Jesús, Saint. *Libro de la Vida.* In *Obras completas.* Edited by Efrén de la Madre de Dios and Otilio del Niño Jesús. Vol. 1. Madrid: Biblioteca de Autores Cristianos, 1951, pp. 595-877.

———. *Moradas del Castillo Interior.* In *Obras completas.* Edited by Efrén de la Madre de Dios. Vol. 2. Madrid: Biblioteca de Autores Cristianos, 1954, pp. 307-495 (ET In *The Complete Works of Saint Teresa of Jesus.* Translated by P. Silverio de Santa Teresa. Edited by E. Allison Peers. Vol. 2. New York: Sheed & Ward, 1946, pp. 199-351).

Thérèse de l'Enfant-Jésus et de la Sainte-Face, Sainte. *J'entre dans la vie: Derniers Entretiens.* Paris: Éditions du Cerf et Desclée De Brouwer, 1973 (ET St. Thérèse of Lisieux. *Her Last Conversations.* Translated by John Clarke. Washington, DC: ICS Publications, 1977).

———. *Histoire d'une Âme: Manuscrits autobiographiques.* Paris: Éditions du Cerf et Desclée De Brouwer, 1972. (ET *Story of a Soul: The Autobiography of St. Therese of Lisieux.* Translated by John Clarke. Washington, DC: ICS Publications, 1975).

Tigay, J. H. *You Shall Have No Other Gods: Israelite Religion in the Light of*

Hebrew Inscriptions. Harvard Semitic Studies, 31. Atlanta, GA: Scholars Press, 1986.

Tillich, Paul. *The Courage To Be.* The Fontana Library. London: Collins, 1962.

————. *Dynamics of Faith. Harper Torchbooks*, 42. New York: Harper & Row, 1958.

————. *Systematic Theology.* Three volumes in one. Chicago: The University of Chicago Press, 1967.

Vriezen, Th. C. "'Ehje 'ašer 'ehje." In *Festschrift Alfred Bertholet.* Edited by W. Baumgartner, O. Eissfeldt, K. Elliger, and Leonhard Rost. Tübingen: J. C. B. Mohr (Paul Siebeck), 1950, pp. 498-512.

Walsh, Michael. *The Triumph of the Meek: Why Early Christianity Succeeded.* San Francisco: Harper & Row, 1986.

Walter, James J. See Happel, Stephen.

Westermann, Claus. *Gottes Engel brauchen keine Flügel.* Stuttgart: Kreuz Verlag, 1978 (ET *God's Angels Need No Wings.* Philadelphia: Fortress Press, 1979).

Wright, N. T. "*harpagmos* and the Meaning of Philippians 2, 5-11." *The Journal of Theological Studies* 37(1986): 321-52.

Young, Frances M. *The Making of the Creeds.* London: SCM Press; Philadelphia: Trinity Press International, 1991.

Young, Robin A. Darling. "Gorgonia's Silence: Gregory Nazianzen's Interpretation of his Sister's *Askēsis.*" Unpublished paper.

Zakovitch, Yair. "A Study of Precise and Partial Derivations in Biblical Etymology." *Journal for the Study of the Old Testament* 15(1980): 31-50.

Subject Index

Name Index

Scripture Index

Frans Jozef van Beeck, S.J., Ph. D., is the author of nine books and about fifty essays and articles. In the area of theology, examples are "Towards an Ecumenical Understanding of the Sacraments" (1966); "Sacraments, Church Order, and Secular Responsibility" (1969); *Christ Proclaimed: Christology as Rhetoric* (1979); *Fifty Psalms: An Attempt at a New Translation* (with Huub Oosterhuis and others; 1969); *Grounded in Love: Sacramental Theology in an Ecumenical Perspective* (1981); "Professing the Uniqueness of Christ" (1985); *Catholic Identity after Vatican II: Three Types of Faith in the One Church* (1985); "The Worship of Christians in Pliny's Letter" (1988); *God Encountered: A Contemporary Catholic Systematic Theology*, Volume I, *Understanding the Christian Faith* (1989), and Volume II/1 *The Revelation of the Glory: Introduction and Fundamental Theology* (1993); *Loving the Torah More than God? Toward a Catholic Appreciation of Judaism* (1989); "Tradition and Interpretation" (1990); "Divine Revelation: Intervention or Self-Communication? (1991); "Professing Christianity Among the World's Religions" (1991); "Two Kind Jewish Men: A Sermon in Commemoration of the Shoa" (1992); "Christian Faith and Theology in Encounter with Non-Christians: Profession? Protestation? Self-maintenance? Abandon?" (1994). In the area of literature, there are pieces like *The Poems and Translations of Sir Edward Sherburne (1616-1702)* (1961); "Hopkins: *Cor ad Cor*" (1975); "A Note on *Ther* in Curses and Blessings in Chaucer" (1985); "The Choices of Two Anthologists: Understanding Hopkins' Catholic Idiom" (1989). He is working on the third and fourth parts of the second volume of *God Encountered.* Personal predilections include liturgy, spiritual direction, preaching, as well as music (he used to be a decent violinist) and some bird watching.